AN INTERNATIONAL BILL
OF THE RIGHTS OF MAN

BY H. LAUTERPACHT, M.A., LL.D.

WHEWELL PROFESSOR OF INTERNATIONAL LAW IN
THE UNIVERSITY OF CAMBRIDGE; OF GRAY'S INN,
BARRISTER-AT-LAW

THE LAWBOOK EXCHANGE, LTD.
Clark, New Jersey

ISBN 978-1-58477-923-0

Lawbook Exchange edition 2009, 2018

The quality of this reprint is equivalent to the quality of the original work.

THE LAWBOOK EXCHANGE, LTD.
33 Terminal Avenue
Clark, New Jersey 07066-1321

*Please see our website for a selection of our other publications
and fine facsimile reprints of classic works of legal history:*
www.lawbookexchange.com

Library of Congress Cataloging-in-Publication Data

Lauterpacht, Hersch, Sir, 1897-1960
 An international bill of the rights of man / by H. Lauterpacht.
    p. cm.
 Originally published: New York : Columbia University Press, 1945.
 Includes bibliographical references and index.
 ISBN-13: 978-1-58477-923-0 (cloth : alk. paper)
 ISBN-10: 1-58477-923-3 (cloth : alk. paper)
 1. Liberty. 2. Civil rights. 3. International law. I. Title.

JC571.L343 2009
341.4'8--dc22

                                                    2008052815

Printed in the United States of America on acid-free paper

AN INTERNATIONAL BILL
OF THE RIGHTS OF MAN

BY H. LAUTERPACHT, M.A., LL.D.

WHEWELL PROFESSOR OF INTERNATIONAL LAW IN
THE UNIVERSITY OF CAMBRIDGE; OF GRAY'S INN,
BARRISTER-AT-LAW

COLUMBIA UNIVERSITY PRESS

NEW YORK · MCMXLV

PREFACE

IN THE COURSE of the second World War "the enthronement of the rights of man" was repeatedly declared to constitute one of the major purposes of the war. The great contest, in which the spiritual heritage of civilization found itself in mortal danger, was imposed upon the world by a power whose very essence lay in the denial of the rights of man as against the omnipotence of the State. That fact added weight to the conviction that an international declaration and protection of the fundamental rights of man must be an integral part of any rational scheme of world order. However, the idea of an International Bill of the Rights of Man is more than a vital part of the structure of peace. It is expressive of an abiding problem of all law and government. So long as that problem remains unsolved, it will continue to be both topical and urgent long after declarations of war and peace aims have become a matter of mere historical interest and after the effective elimination of war has become a reality. But it is a problem which cannot be solved except within the framework and under the shelter of the positive law of an organized Society of States. At the end of the eighteenth century Emmanuel Kant proclaimed good government through the instrumentality of the State to be essential to the fulfilment of the destiny of mankind, which, in his view, is the development of the capacities of man to the highest possible perfection. He saw in an international political association of States an essential prerequisite of the performance of that highest function of the State. For reasons no less cogent, this is also a paramount condition of ensuring what may without embarrassment or apologies be called the natural rights of man.

The problem of the international protection of the fundamental rights of man is of greater difficulty and complexity than the question of international organization conceived as an instrument for securing peace through the prohibition of war and the parallel developments in the fields of compulsory judicial settlement and international legislation. Touching, as it does, intimately upon the relations of the State and the individual, a subject which even in the domestic sphere is still a disputed province of jurisprudence and of the science of government, it implies a more drastic interference with the sovereignty of the State than the renunciation of war and the acceptance of the principle of compulsory judicial settlement. For, when all has been said, such progress signifies no more than the recognition of rudimentary principles of order. The international protection of the rights of man goes substantially beyond that irreducible minimum.

It is not easy to formulate concrete proposals and schemes on a controversial subject of this complexity and implications without inviting outspoken and impatient criticism. Such criticism is desirable and effective even if it is often contradictory. The proposals put forward in this book have been described by various persons—occasionally by the same person—whose comment has been sought and conscientiously examined as being either excessively radical or as erring on the side of compromise to the point of being ingenious and purely nominal. However, unless the idea of an International Bill of the Rights of Man is to remain a vague phrase thinly covering the intention of doing away with such tangible safeguards of human rights as exist already, it is incumbent upon the student of the subject to put forward concrete proposals as a starting point for deliberation and discussion aiming at the incorporation of the International Bill of the Rights of Man as an integral part of the law of nations. In leaving the safer path of expounding the existing law and in choosing to propound schemes involving fundamental legal changes, the lawyer cannot legitimately complain of any trenchant criticism by the expert and the layman alike. I have deemed it my duty to incur that risk. The Dumbarton Oaks Proposals recognize the promotion of "respect for human rights and fundamental freedoms" as one of the objects of the Organisation of the United Nations and as one of the "conditions of stability and well-being which are necessary for peaceful and friendly relations among nations." Whether such recognition will be translated into effective legal institutions of international society will depend, to a substantial degree, upon the extent to which an attempt will be made to study the implications and possibilities, in terms of positive law, of that acknowledgment of human rights and fundamental freedoms as part of the future international order and as the foundation of its spiritual authority.

The publication of this book has been assisted by the American Jewish Committee. It is fitting, for many reasons, that the Committee should have actively interested themselves in the problem of an International Bill of the Rights of Man. No people in history has suffered more cruelly from a denial of elementary human rights. At the end of the first World War representatives of Jewish organisations, from the United States and elsewhere, played a prominent part in securing the adoption of the Minorities Treaties—a significant step in the direction of the general international protection of the rights of man. The Committee are not in any way associated with or responsible for the views expressed in this book. I wish to express my sincere thanks to Dr. Max Gottschalk, director of its Overseas Department, for assistance in many ways, including the arrangements for publication, and to Mr. Milton Himmelfarb, of the Overseas Department, who helped see the book through the press.

The first part of this book, entitled "The Law of Nations, the Law of Nature, and the Rights of Man," has grown out of a paper read before the Grotius Society in November, 1942, and of a series of lectures delivered under the same title in the University of Cambridge in the summer of 1943. They form the doctrinal and jurisprudential basis of the practical proposals put forward in the book, and I hope to publish them separately in England, in an extended form, as soon as circumstances permit. In the meantime it has been considered convenient to publish the book in the United States. I wish to express my appreciation of the efficiency and of the courtesy of the director and staff of Columbia University Press who, in face of wartime communications, have borne with patience the delays of proofreading on the other side of the ocean. I am indebted to Mrs. G. Lyons, B.Sc., for most able secretarial assistance.

H. LAUTERPACHT

Cambridge, Eng.
October, 1944

CONTENTS

Part 1

THE LAW OF NATURE,
THE LAW OF NATIONS, AND
THE RIGHTS OF MAN

CHAPTER I

INTRODUCTION

THE INTERNATIONAL recognition and protection of the rights of man is, in strict juridical logic, independent of any doctrine of natural law and natural rights. In fact, it might be argued—and it has actually been maintained—that the main reason for the significant and revolutionary innovation implied in an International Bill of the Rights of Man is the realization of the utter inadequacy of the notion of natural rights to protect effectively the rights of man. The need, it would appear, is not for a controversial theory, but for specific rules of law and effective legal remedies. One explanation of the dry scorn and acid vituperation which Bentham poured upon the Declaration of 1789 was the belief that it might prove a useful instrument in the hands of those anxious to find in a high-sounding phrase an easy substitute for positive means of remedial legislation. Some of the recent attempts to revive the doctrine of natural rights, apparently conceived as a satisfactory alternative to reforms in internal and international law, may serve as a reminder that the contingency is by no means hypothetical. It might seem, therefore, that the protagonists of an International Bill of the Rights of Man would do well to steer clear of any elusive and illusory conceptions of the law of nature and natural rights.

To do that would be to misjudge alike historical experience and the essential requisites of a durable and effective protection of the human rights. The law of nature and natural rights can never be a true substitute for the positive enactments of the law of the society of States. When so treated they are inefficacious, deceptive, and, in the long run, a brake upon progress. But while they are bound to be mischievous when conceived as alternatives to changes in the law, they are of abiding potency and beneficence as the foundation of its ultimate validity and as a standard of its approximation to justice. Moreover, to eliminate the ideas of natural law and natural rights from the consideration of the protection of the rights of man is to renounce the faculty of understanding their growth in the course of history and their association with that law of nations which is now to become its ultimate physical sanction. Finally, to discard, in this context, the ideas of the law of nature is to deprive ourselves of that inspiration which lies in the continuity of legal and political thought on the subject, without which we cannot hope to overcome the seemingly insurmountable difficulties which confront any scheme for an International Bill of the Rights of Man.

The Constitution of Virginia of 1776, the American Declaration of Independence, and the French Declaration of the Rights of Man and of the Citizen were the first constitutional instruments of modern times to proclaim that the natural rights of man were, as such, part of the fundamental law of the State and that their protection was the reason for its existence. Since then, the theory of natural law, which had always been the main inspiration, if not the conscious instrument, of the doctrine of the rights of man, has suffered an eclipse in a century dominated by the historical and analytical trends of jurisprudence. The theory of the rights of man was itself assaulted from highly diverse quarters. It was attacked by those who were frightened by and hated the great revolutionary movements which proclaimed the rights of man. It was assailed, probably for the same reason, by those French authoritarians who saw in the supposed materialism of the doctrine of natural rights a threat to religious and spiritual authority and clamoured, as Lamennais did, for a Declaration of the Rights of God instead of a Declaration of the Rights of Man. It drew upon itself the condemnation, in terms of finality congenial to philosophers, of the idealistic school of philosophy, in Germany and elsewhere, which saw in the State the highest end and the ultimate value.[1] It came in for castigation and merciless dissection at the hands of those who, not without reason, identified the advocates of natural rights as determined opponents of

[1] "This question [the rights of individuals] is one which called for discussion a century ago, but at the present time it can be considered a question no longer. The rights of the individual are, in short, to-day not worth serious criticism. . . . The welfare of the community is the end and is the ultimate standard. And over its members the right of the moral organism is absolute. Its duty and its right is to dispose of these members as seems to it best. Its right and duty is, in brief, to be a Providence to itself."—F. H. Bradley, "Some Remarks on Punishment," *International Journal of Ethics*, April, 1894 (reprinted in *Collected Essays*, I [Oxford, 1935], 158). William Wallace, the Hegelian, spoke of the State as the ultimate creator, guardian, and guarantee of all rights in the world. Bosanquet wrote in a similar vein. The political philosophy of totalitarian regimes was, not unnaturally, highly critical of the emphasis upon rights at the expense of duties. Writers who were tempted to see in these regimes more than a passing wave of retrogression were inclined to the same view. See E. H. Carr, *Conditions of Peace* (New York, 1942), p. 122.

social progress in so far as it could be achieved by the regulative action of the State. Herbert Spencer was not alone in invoking natural rights against what he called meddling legislation and against the right of the State to tax the citizen for social services. In fact, there was repeated in the nineteenth century the perplexing spectacle, which had been witnessed before, of natural rights and natural law being invoked on behalf of both progress and reaction, on the side of both stability and change. But these vicissitudes of the theory of natural rights did not prevent the incorporation in the next hundred years of what hitherto had been merely natural rights of man as part of the constitutions of practically all States of the world.

There were tangible indications, expressed in a manner more eloquent than theoretical controversy, that the coming period was to be one of triumphant assertion of the rights of man. But this was not to be—for the reason that the rights of man were given a foundation no more solid or secure than the law of the sovereign State. They were denied the protection of that legal order which by virtue of its universality and of its potential supremacy over the State would alone be capable of safeguarding them against the tyranny of absolutism and the arbitrariness of majority rule. The sovereign State, in an exclusive and unprecedented ascendancy of power, became the unsurpassable barrier between man and the law of mankind. The human being became, in the offensive, but widely current, terminology of the experts, a mere object of international law. But even that was an overstatement of the existing position. In fact, the individual became only to an imperfect degree the object of the law of nations. Treaties of a humanitarian character were concluded for protecting the individual in some specified spheres. But the fundamental claims of human personality to equality, liberty, and freedom against the arbitrary will of the State remained outside the orbit of international law save for the precarious and controversial principle of humanitarian intervention.

The results of this self-imposed limitation of the law of nations are well known. They are expressed, by most compelling implication, in one of the three solemnly proclaimed purposes of the first and the second World Wars. These objects have been not only to repel an aggressive will for world domination and to build an international system of security. The third major object of the first World War was, in the words of one who, to a degree higher than most statesmen of modern times, possessed the gift of expressing the enduring ends of humanity, "to make the world safe for democracy," [2] that is, we may say, to render it a secure habitation for the fundamental right of man to be governed by rulers chosen by and accountable to him. The third major object of the second World War has been essentially the same. It has been given repeated expression not only by private individuals and organizations [3] but also in solemn pronouncements of the leaders of the United Nations, such as the formulation of the "four freedoms" by President Roosevelt in his Annual Message to Congress of January 6, 1941 [4] and their (incomplete and, in a material sense, self-contradictory) reiteration in the Atlantic Charter of August 14, 1941.[5] That major purpose is, in the words of Mr. Churchill, to ensure that the war ends "with the enthronement of human rights." [6]

In the course of the first World War the call to make the world safe for democracy was more than a convenient slogan of war propaganda. It was the outcome of the perception of two basic facts. It was realized, in the first instance, that the securing on the part of international society of inalienable human freedoms through democracy is an

[2] President Wilson referred to that phrase in insisting that its principle should be incorporated in the Covenant—as it was in fact in Article 1, paragraph 2 (see below, p. 7*n*). He said: "We have said that this war was carried on for a vindication of democracy. The statement did not create the impulse but it brought it to consciousness. So soon as it was stated that the war was being waged to make the world safe for democracy, a new spirit came into the world. People began to look at the substance rather than at the form. They knew that governments derived their just powers from consent of the governed. I should like to point out that nowhere else in the draft is there any recognition of the principle of democracy. If we are ready to fight for this, we should be ready to write it into the Covenant" (David Hunter Miller, *The Drafting of the Covenant*, I [New York, London, 1928], 165).

[3] See, *e. g.*, The Declaration of the Rights of Man proposed by H. G. Wells in *The New World Order* (London, 1940), pp. 139–143; C. K. Streit, *Union Now* (New York, 1939), p. 126; and, in particular, Quincy Wright, *Human Rights and World Order*, printed in the *Third Report of the Commission to Study the Organization of Peace*, February, 1943. The Commission has devoted exhaustive study to the question of an international bill of the rights of man. See also the statement, in the Fourth Report of the Commission, on "International Safeguard of Human Rights," published in *International Conciliation*, September, 1944, Pamphlet No. 403, pp. 552–574. And see the discussion on "New Rights of Man in an International Organization" in *The World's Destiny and the United States; a Conference of Experts in International Relations* (Chicago, 1941), pp. 101–137. See also G. Schwarzenberger, *Power Politics* (1941), pp. 389–390.

[4] See below, pp. 84–85.   [5] See below, p. 85.   [6] See below, p. 86.

indispensable condition of the peace of the world. Long before that, Emmanuel Kant expressed the same idea by postulating the republican form of government as one of the prerequisites of perpetual peace. It was along that line of thought that the League of Nations was originally conceived as an association of democratic States.[7] There are many who believe that the toleration of and the admission to membership of States in the constitution of which there was no room for human liberty in the accepted sense reduced the League to a mere shadow of its spiritual self. The second fundamental factor which underlay the association of democracy with the idea of a world secure under the reign of law was that no legal order, international or other, is true to its essential function if it fails to protect effectively the ultimate unit of all law—the individual human being. The two decades which followed the first World War lent weight, with ominous emphasis, to these now self-evident propositions. They have resulted, in the second World War, in the widespread conviction that some form of an International Bill of the Rights of Man is a major purpose of the war, inasmuch as it is an essential condition of international peace and international progress. Many believe that without some such expansion of international law the fabric of international society will be built on precarious foundations.

Alongside that main stream of thought, the idea of a universal guarantee of the rights of man has been given support or attention on the part of some European States bound by the obligations of the so-called minorities treaties. These States favour a solution which by virtue of the generality of its application would remove from them what they conceive to be a stigma of inferiority and which would also do away with the danger of the minorities forming a State within a State and looking for protection to foreign Powers of the same race or

[7] This seems to have been the original interpretation, according to the makers of the Covenant, of Article 1, paragraph 2, which provided for the admission as new members of "any fully self-governing State." The French text expressed that intention more clearly: "Tout Etat . . . qui se gouverne librement." President Wilson's understanding of the term "self-governing" appears clearly in his view expressed at the meetings of the Commission on the League of Nations. He said: ". . . No one would have looked at the German government before the war, and said that the nation was self-governing. We knew that, in point of fact, the Reichstag was controlled by the Chancellor, that it was an absolute monarchy": David Hunter Miller, *The Drafting of the Covenant*, I, 165. For an identical interpretation of the term see the views of Larnaude and Orlando, *ibid.*, II, 473.

language.[8] Finally, some of the minorities, conscious of the inadequacy of the protection hitherto afforded by the treaties, are inclined to see a more effective safequard in a universally applicable International Bill of the Rights of Man.

But what is an International Bill of the Rights of Man? The capacity of language for evasion or concealment of thought is infinite. This fact applies in particular to the language of international intercourse. International treaties have often been adopted as a mere appeal to the conscience of governments; as a bare statement of principle unaccompanied by any legal obligation; as a declaration deliberately deprived of any effective means of guarantee and enforcement. We remember, for instance, the thin semblance of obligation in the articles of the Hague Convention, in which arbitration, in questions of a legal nature, was "recognized by the signatory Powers as the most effective, and at the same time the most equitable, means of settling disputes which diplomacy has failed to settle," and in which, consequently, in the language of the Convention, it was thought desirable with regard to disputes thus qualified "to have recourse to arbitration, in so far as circumstances permit." [9] We recall the humanitarian and economic clauses of Article 23 of the Covenant of the League of Nations in which the members undertook, *inter alia*, "subject to and in accordance with the provisions of international conventions existing or hereafter to be agreed upon" to secure just treatment of the native inhabitants of territories under their control and to "make provision to secure and maintain freedom of communications and of transit and equitable treatment for the commerce of all Members of the League." The Permanent Court of International Justice interpreted that provision of the Covenant as

[8] For an emphatic expression of that view see the articles of President Beneš in *Foreign Affairs*, 1941, and in the *Czechoslovak Year Book of International Law*, 1942, pp. 1–6.
[9] Article 38 of the Convention on the Pacific Settlement of International Disputes of 1907. The principal Commission of the Second Hague Conference, in commenting on the impossibility of concluding a binding convention on these lines, stated that "nevertheless, the divergences of opinion which have come to light have not exceeded the bounds of judicial controversy, and that, by working together here during the past four months, the collected States of the world not only have learned to understand one another and to draw closer together, but have succeeded in the course of this long collaboration, evolving a very lofty conception of the common welfare of humanity." —J. B. Scott, *Reports to the Hague Conferences* (Oxford, 1917), p. 454. Baron Marschall von Bieberstein's unofficial comment on this resolution was: "It is difficult to say less in more words."—*Die grosse Politik der europäischen Kabinette*, XXIII (Part II), 346.

implying, in effect, no obligation whatsoever.[10] The Declaration of the Rights of Man adopted in 1929 by the Institute of International Law [11] was not intended to supply the basis of an enforceable international instrument. It was intended, if and when accepted by States, as relying on no other sanction than that of the public opinion of the world.

Should it be decided to reduce any international bill of human rights to a mere statement of political or moral principle, then, indeed, it would be most likely to secure easy acceptance; for any possible difficulty in agreeing upon its terms will be merged in the innocuous nature of its ineffectual purpose. But if the second World War ought to end, in the words of the British Prime Minister, "with the enthronement of human rights," then a declaration thus emaciated would come dangerously near to a corruption of language. By creating an unwarranted impression of progress it would, in the minds of many, constitute an event which is essentially retrogressive. For it would purport to solve the crucial problem of law and politics in their widest sense by dint of a grandiloquent incantation whose futility would betray a lack both of faith and of candour. In comparison, it is a matter of relatively minor importance that if the Bill of Rights thus devitalized were to replace the Minorities Treaties, religious and ethnic minorities would be deprived of the benefit of safeguards which in normal circumstances would have afforded a considerable degree of protection.

Yet, when all has been said, the fact remains that any attempt to translate the idea of an International Bill of the Rights of Man into a working rule of law is fraught with difficulties which disturb orthodox thought to the point of utter discouragement. The obstacles are immeasurably greater than the psychological impediment which expresses itself in some countries in the distrust of seemingly abstract pronounce-

[10] It held that Article 23 did not oblige Lithuania to keep open the railway communications with Poland. Any such obligation would have to be subject to and in accordance with a specific international convention. There was no such convention between Poland and Lithuania. Also, the court said, whatever may be the obligations of the members of the League under Article 23, it does not imply any specific obligation to open any particular lines of communication—*Advisory Opinion of October 15, 1931*, Permanent Court of International Justice, Series A/B, No. 42, p. 118.

[11] The Declaration is printed in *American Journal of International Law*, XXIV (1930), 560, and in *Annuaire de l'Institut de Droit International*, XXXV, No. 2 (1930), 298. For comment on the Declaration see André Mandelstam, in Académie de Droit International, *Recueil des Cours*, XXVIII, No. 4 (1931), 133–229, and J. B. Scott, *Le Progrès du droit des gens* (1934), 207–237.

ments. They are more serious than the association of a Bill of Rights with the much maligned natural rights and the law of nature. They are more intricate than the divergencies of rigid and flexible constitutions. They are even more relevant than the fact that in some countries the high tradition of personal freedom has been due not so much to the written letter of the law as to the wise restraint in enforcing it and that such countries may be reluctant to associate themselves with a formal codification of what has well proved its worth as a living tradition.

The first major difficulty appears clearly as soon as we pause to consider the substance of an International Bill of the Rights of Man. How far shall the Bill go, and how explicit shall it be in securing what is historically the first fundamental right, namely, that of freedom from arbitrary imprisonment and other physical restraint? What shall be the nature of the procedural and substantive safeguards in criminal trials, and how, if at all, ought we to reconcile the discrepancies of legal systems in the matter? Ought we to postulate the writ of habeas corpus, trial by jury, and the prohibition of retroactivity of laws as universal legal institutions? Shall the recognition of the fundamental right of personal freedom go to the length of accomplishing—what the international community has so far conspicuously failed to accomplish— the absolute abolition of slavery? To what extent ought we to go in prohibiting forced labour both in colonies and in the metropolitan territory? How far ought the recognition of the other aspects of personal freedom—freedom of religion, of speech and other forms of expression of opinion, of association and assembly, as well as the sanctity of the home and the secrecy of correspondence—to leave room for the unavoidable latitude of the law in safeguarding the recognized legal interests of the members of the community and the welfare of the State as a whole? Shall the Bill stop short of ensuring the right of every individual to a nationality and of doing away with the legal and moral monstrosity of statelessness? Shall it postulate the right of emigration, and, if it does so, shall it ignore the corresponding, but much more intricate, question of the right to free immigration? What shall be the substance and the limits of the right of equality before the law? Shall it include the equality of the sexes and the right of aliens to be treated on a footing of equality with nationals? To what extent shall it and can it protect national and cultural minorities against discrimination? Shall it purport to embrace situations as delicate and baffling as the position of the native population in South Africa, of the Indian community in Kenya, or of the Negro race in the Southern States of the United States? Shall equality include the right of minorities to the unrestricted use of their language before the authorities of the State and the right to develop their native culture and institutions, with the assistance, on an equitable basis, of the finances of the State? Ought the fundamental right of political equality and liberty to include equality of opportunity and economic freedom in the sense of postulating the right to work, to social security, and to education? Ought the Bill of Rights to comprise the right to property—the right so sacred to the fathers of the American Revolution and of the French Convention, the right which Locke, to whom declarations of rights owe, perhaps, more than to any other thinker, treated with a reverence second to none? Ought freedom thus conceived to include the right of the individual to buy and to sell unhampered by State interference and restrictions? These queries still leave untouched what is perhaps the most difficult question of all. Can an International Bill of the Rights of Man leave out that most fundamental of all freedoms, namely, that persons and groups of persons who have reached the requisite stage of development shall not be governed except by their consent in the wider sense, that is, by rulers freely chosen by them and accountable to them through the regular processes and safeguards of responsible government? If that apparently inescapable principle is accepted, will not the International Bill of the Rights of Man be tantamount to an international guarantee of democratic rule? Similarly, it is not possible to admit that the application of that principle is not relevant to the position of peoples under colonial and mandatory tutelage. Indeed, it is not by any process of logic that all these emanations of the basic rights of freedom and equality can be ignored in an international bill of human rights.

These questions suggest that the idea of an International Bill of the Rights of Man may be plausible and attractive so long as we do not pause to enquire into the substance of its provisions. However, the contents of that fundamental international instrument do not represent the most difficult aspect of the matter. For assuming, as we must, that its enactment is intended as a significant contribution to the soluion of a crucial problem of law, politics, and international peace, there arises the question of the enforcement and of the guarantees of that universal charter of human rights.

To the unsophisticated it would appear, in the first instance, that these imply the setting up of an international machinery of judicial review, through an appropriate tribunal, having jurisdiction to nullify executive action, decisions of courts, and the legislation of States as does, for instance, the Supreme Court of the United States. It is proper to refer to that court by way of example. For it is a court which, more widely than any tribunal in the world, has been called upon to protect the rights of the individual as guaranteed by the Constitution. Yet the very mention of the Supreme Court of the United States as an organ acting in that capacity reveals instantaneously the extreme complexity of the problem involved. For although no court has performed this task with greater authority, none has incurred more intense criticism on that account. No tribunal of similar standing has drawn upon itself to a comparable extent the charge that its activity has tended to produce a government of judges, not of law. It has exposed itself to the accusation that in discharging the task of protecting the rights of the citizen guaranteed in the Bill of Rights and in the other clauses of the Constitution it has deprived the states of their legislative sovereignty; that by its reliance upon the inalienable rights of the individual it has often impeded vital measures of social reform intended to protect the individual against the soulless iniquity and inhumanity of modern economic power; that it has interpreted the rights of the individual in terms of outworn philosophies and its own social prejudices; that to the safeguards of the Constitution it has added a "higher law," law of nature, of its own; and that it has even attempted to set a limit to the right of the people as a whole to shape its destiny by way of constitutional amendment. These charges go beyond that expressed in the epigram that the Constitution of the United States means what the Supreme Court says it means.

These criticisms and difficulties with which that august tribunal of the United States has had to contend are almost trifling when compared with the situations with which an international tribunal, endowed with similar powers, would be confronted. The powers of any court, national or international, are, in theory, rigidly circumscribed by the duty to apply existing law. But that law is indefinite and elastic in proportion to the generality of its content—such as is implicit in the guarantee of the inherent rights of man against the State. In relation to such matters it is of special significance that the judicial duty of applying the law must be fulfilled by human beings with their own philosophies and prejudices. There is no means of excluding the operation of that human element. Within the same national group there exist restraints upon the unavoidable power of judges: these are the community of national tradition, the overwhelming sentiment (from which judges are not immune) of national solidarity and of the higher national interest, the corrective and deterrent influence of public opinion, and, in case of a clear abuse of judicial discretion, the relatively speedy operation of political checks and remedies. None of these safeguards exist, to any comparable extent, in the international sphere. All these difficulties reveal the implications of the proposal to confer such powers, in relation to the very basis of the national life of sovereign and independent States, upon a tribunal of foreign judges.

It may be said that some such powers have occasionally been exercised by international and quasi-international tribunals. In 1935 the Permanent Court of International Justice was asked to give, and gave, an Advisory Opinion on the constitutionality of certain amendments to the Penal Code of the Free City of Danzig, which, in effect, violated the provision of the Danzig Constitution prohibiting the retroactive operation of the criminal law.[12] However, it must be borne in mind that, normally, the Constitution of Danzig was placed under the guarantee, not of the Court, but of the Council of the League, a flexible political organ. Neither is it without importance that the State in question was a small semi-independent community set up to meet a complex political situation. The position is different when it is proposed to confer jurisdiction of that nature upon an international court with regard to Great Powers, such as the United States of America, Great

---

[12] *Advisory Opinion of December 4, 1935*, Permanent Court of International Justice, Series A/B, No. 65.

Britain, and Russia, in the matter of the most intricate, most intimate, and practically indefinable aspects of their national life. The same applies to the suggestion of an international writ of habeas corpus before a tribunal of foreign judges sitting at a distance of three thousand miles or more. This, too, is not inconceivable. The Supreme Court of the United States exercises such jurisdiction in exceptional cases. So do the courts of the British Empire. In August, 1939, a High Court Judge, sitting as a Vacation Court in London, decided, in the case of *Ning Yi-Ching and Others*, on a summons for a writ of habeas corpus to prevent four Chinese prisoners in the British Concession at Tientsin from being handed over to the Japanese authorities.[13] But there is little persuasive power in these examples.

Undoubtedly, direct international judicial review is not the only conceivable effective procedure for implementing an international charter of human rights. There may be the alternative method: the obligation of the signatories may be limited to incorporating the International Charter as part of their constitutional law and to conferring upon their highest tribunal the full right of judicial review of legislative and other acts contrary to the Charter. But judicial review of legislation is not an innovation likely to prove acceptable to some States, including Great Britain. Moreover, such an obligation, to be practicable, would have to include submission to some manner of international supervision, aided, in controversial matters of importance, by an opinion given by an international tribunal. There may be no half-way house between a mere declaration of principles and a revolutionary departure in the status of human personality in the constitutional and international spheres. This being so, the question arises once more whether we are entitled to expect governments to acquiesce in restrictions of sovereignty more far-reaching in their implications than any yet propounded in the annals of international utopias.

Finally, we must not lose sight of the major—and, again, apparently insoluble—political difficulty. How far is an International Bill of the Rights of Man compatible with the principle that each State must be left free to determine its system of government? That principle

[13] *Annual Digest and Reports of Public International Law Cases*, 1938–1940, Case No. 44.

was proclaimed in the Atlantic Charter alongside the enunciation of some of the "freedoms." This was done, apparently, in order to allay the susceptibilities or apprehensions of actual and potential allies as well as of other States. But can we in the same breath assert the right of interference, by making human freedoms a matter of international interest, and the principle of non-interference by laying down that the system of government upon which these freedoms depend is not of effective international concern? A purely verbal solution as adopted in the Atlantic Charter may be legitimate in the circumstances. It may also be the expression of the hope, which is probably not devoid of foundation, that the economic and social system of Soviet Russia, a country upon whose active coöperation the great reform would depend to a substantial degree, may not be intrinsically irreconcilable with a full recognition of human rights.[14]

In any case, if an international bill of rights is to form part of a system of a wide and comprehensive association of States, the problem will arise whether the comprehensiveness and the strength—or the apparent strength—of the association is to yield to the revolutionary departure embodied in the idea of an International Bill of the Rights of Man. We are not at liberty to assume lightly that the problem will or can be solved.

In view of all these difficulties, it may be felt that indulgence in the idea of an International Bill of the Rights of Man is a regrettable dispersion of effort, of the futility and utter impracticability of which the student of law and politics ought to warn both governments and public opinion at large. It may be his business to do so. At the same time, however, it is his duty to assist in uncovering the hidden springs and the enduring core of the matter—a matter which is the abiding theme of political and legal thought throughout the ages. It is possible that in the contemplation of the continuity of ideas and aspirations on the subject we may find assistance in approaching the solution of that persistent problem of law and government.

[14] The chapter on the "Fundamental Rights and Duties of Citizens" in the Constitution of Soviet Russia of December, 1936, is no less emphatic in the recognition of the rights of man than the most progressive modern constitutions. There is no reason why with the passing of the revolutionary period of transition in Russia and with the normalization of international relations the use of extraordinary powers inimical to individual freedom should not tend to diminish.

CHAPTER II

THE IDEA OF NATURAL RIGHTS IN LEGAL AND POLITICAL THOUGHT

THE RELATION of the individual to the State has always been the main problem of law and politics. That problem has consisted in the reconciliation of two apparently conflicting factors. The first is that the State, however widely its object may be construed, has no justification and no valid right to exact obedience except as an instrument for securing the welfare of the individual human being. The second is that the State as a political institution has come to be recognized as the absolute condition of the civilized existence of man and of his progression towards the full realization of his faculties. It is a matter of absorbing interest to note that in the history of political and legal thought and action the conflict between these two factors has been bridged by the notion, appearing under various disguise, of the fundamental rights of the individual, of the natural, or inherent, or inalienable rights of man. These are the limits which, it has been asserted, the Leviathan of the State must not transgress. That assertion has not been limited to those who, as in Gierke's scathing comment, reduced the State to the level of an insurance society for securing the liberty and the property of the individual.[1] With isolated, though important exceptions, the idea of the inherent rights of man is the continuous thread in the pattern of history in the matter of that weighty issue of the relation of man and State.

It is true that, whereas the idea of the law of nature dates back to antiquity, the notion and the doctrine of natural, inalienable, rights preëxistent to and higher than the positive law of the State is of more recent usage. As will be suggested presently, the law of nature itself, unconsciously or by design, was often merely a cloak concealing the desire to vindicate the rights of man. However, quite apart from that

---

[1] O. F. von Gierke, "Die Staats- und Korporationslehre der Neuzeit," in his *Das deutsche Genossenschaftsrecht* (Berlin, 1913), IV, 407—a paraphrase of Vico's reference to Spinoza. "Spinoza," says Vico, "speaks of the state as if it were a trading partnership" (as quoted by E. F. Carritt, *Morals and Politics* [Oxford, 1935], p. 46).

fact, in order to judge the antiquity of the idea of the natural rights of man we must look to their substance rather than to their designation. Their substance has been the denial of the absoluteness of the State and of its unconditional right to exact obedience; the assertion of the value and of the freedom of the individual against the State; the view that the power of the State and of its rulers is derived ultimately from the assent of those who compose the political community; and the insistence that there are limits to the power of the State to interfere with man's right to do what he conceives to be his duty.

But all this is not new. It dates back to Greek and Roman political philosophy. It has become almost a commonplace to maintain that any such political ideas were foreign to the Greek conception of the State, which, it is said, looked to expediency, whereas we look to legitimacy, and which confounded politics and morals. We find a German writer [2] of authoritarian tendencies contrasting the conception of fundamental rights of man in the liberal bourgeois State with the austerity of the Greek city-state:

The antique State knew of no rights of freedom. A private sphere with an independent right against the political community seemed to it inconceivable. The idea of individual freedom independent of the political freedom of people and State was regarded as absurd, immoral, and unworthy of a free man.

It is possible that some German writers in the nineteenth and twentieth centuries adapted their interpretation of Greek political philosophy in this matter to the urge to find an impressive precedent for their authoritarian conception of the State. It is probable that that interpretation found an unduly ready acceptance on the part of some writers in England and in the United States. Lord Acton's essay on "Freedom in Antiquity" [3] and Ritchie's account of the Greek idea of the law of nature [4] are typical of this assessment of the position. But this view, so widely held, needs revision.

[2] Carl Schmitt, *Verfassungslehre* (Munich, Leipzig, 1928), p. 158.
[3] *The History of Freedom and Other Essays* (edited by J. N. Figgis and R. V. Laurence, London, 1907), pp. 1–29.
[4] *Natural Rights* (London, 1895), pp. 20–33. Professor A. E. Zimmern's account of the politics of fifth-century Athens gives, it is believed, a more adequate picture: *The Greek Commonwealth* (5th ed., Oxford, 1931), pp. 125–197.

It was no mere national complacency which made Herodotus point to the Greek *isonomia*, equality before the law, as contrasted with arbitrary Persian rule, to Greek *isotimia*, equal respect for all, and to Greek *isogoria*, equal freedom of speech. One may discover a logical distinction between all these and the idea of inherent rights in the moden sense, but it is, in many respects, a distinction without substantial difference. The same applies to the references to equality of opportunity in Pericles's funeral speech. Neither is it without importance that the Greek *nomos* signified primarily, not a legislative enactment by the State, but custom grown out of the consciousness and free life of the community. The supremacy of custom is not consistent with the picture of an omnipotent State riding roughshod over the rights of the individual. There is evidence that the constitution of the Greek State knew of some kind of distinction between fundamental and ordinary laws, inasmuch as action was permitted against proposers of laws in derogation of the basic constitution of the State. When, in the *Crito*, Socrates, awaiting execution and refusing the help of friends who provided means for his escape, gives reasons for his duty to obey the unjust sentence of the State, he bases that obligation, not on the absolute claim of the State to obedience, but on an implicit contract—a contract which, in turn, presupposes the duty of the State to allow freedom of speech and the right to emigrate. In the *Apology*, Plato goes much farther. He makes Socrates not only defend freedom of speech but also proclaim that a man ought not to obey laws which treat him unjustly. And although Plato distrusted democratic rule, in the *Politicus* he made Protagoras pronounce a most striking defence of democracy: While men differ in their aptitude for arts and professions, they have all been assigned a share of justice and fairness which are necessary for the art of government. The anguished defence which Sophocles put into the mouth of Antigone has often, and justly, been quoted in this connection. She may have transgressed Creon's decree; but she did not overstep the law of Zeus or the eternal precepts of justice. This, in essence, is the assertion that the individual is governed by a rule of conduct superior to the arbitrary decrees of the earthly authority. Nor, finally, is it irrelevant to point to the Stoic philosophy, in which the equality of man was extended beyond the confines of the State and made the principal manifestation of the universal dominion of reason and of law, higher in authority than the collective will of man acting through the laws of any single State. It was that immutable law, that inward voice of God, in the eyes of whom all men are free and who knows of no distinction between rich and poor, or Greek and barbarians, before which all outward authority must, in the view of the Stoics, find its ultimate justification.

It is true that the precepts of philosophers were more advanced than the practice of the Greek State. But we are concerned here with the growth and the influence of ideas. Moreover, that practice, though it did not protect the freedom of human personality against the intolerance of democratic majorities, gave to the individual that paramount share in the creation of the common will which made him identify himself with the State even when it contrived to compass his destruction. The martyrdom of Socrates was, in its tragic climax, a self-imposed ordinance. The tyranny of Athenian democracy was in the same category as the Whig doctrine of the absolute supremacy of Parliament—which is the modern constitutional doctrine of England.

The Stoic philosophy was largely responsible for the continuation of the tradition of freedom and equality in Roman political and legal philosophy. We find it in the writings of Cicero, who left upon ancient and medieval thought a deep and beneficent impress out of all proportion to his originality as a thinker. He followed the Stoics closely in stressing the fundamental resemblance and equality of men given by the fact of their common possession of reason and of the capacity to develop and to attain virtue notwithstanding differences in learning and ability.[5] We see Seneca insisting that virtue can be attained both by the slave and the free and that slavery affects the body only, while the mind is of necessity the slave's own and cannot be given into bondage.[6] We find the same line of thought in the work of many Roman jurists at the full height of absolutist imperial rule. We see Ulpian explaining the absolutist doctrine of "quod principi placuit, legis habet vigorem" by the qualifying statement that this is so only because the people had conferred legislative authority upon the ruler.[7] For he, like Cicero,

---

[5] *De legibus* i. 10.   [6] *De beneficiis* iii. 19. 20. 28.   [7] *Digest* i. 4. 1.

thought that no man is free unless he has a share in political authority. And it was Ulpian who, in company with other Roman lawyers of the Empire, taught that whatever may be the position of the slave in civil law, slavery is not so by natural law, for by it all men are equal.[8] The exact meaning of these and similar statements has been disputed, but there ought to be no doubt that they served a purpose in affirming the ideas of the freedom and the equality of man. They explain the humanitarian decrees of the Emperors for the protection of slaves in a way amounting to a measure of incipient recognition of the personality, in the accepted sense, of the slave in Roman law.[9]

There is a striking continuity of thought between the Stoics and the most representative political literature of the Middle Ages in the affirmation of the principle of the higher law—which is the law of nature—as the source of the rights of freedom and of government by consent. St. Thomas Aquinas defined natural law as "the participation in the eternal law of the mind of a rational creature."[10] He was reproducing the central idea of the Stoics, the idea of a law superior to the external authority of the State. The State, according to St. Thomas Aquinas, is subject to that higher law which determines the relation of the individual to the State. The justification of the State is that it serves the individual; a king who is unfaithful to his duty forfeits his claim to obedience. It is not rebellion to depose him, for he is himself a rebel; all political authority is derived from the people, and laws must be made by the people or their representatives. Marsilius of Padua used almost identical language. In fact, the view that the ruler is under the supremacy of the law is the principal feature of the political theory of the Middle Ages. By the end of the Middle Ages the substance of the doctrine of the natural rights of man was well established. They flowed from the conception of the law of nature conceived as a higher law superior to the State. They included the right to government by consent, the right to freedom from taxation without representation, the

---

[8] *De legibus* i. 10. 12.

[9] *Ibid*. i. 17. 3. 2. See the decrees of Antonius providing that an owner who killed his slave without just cause is accountable to the law and that the master who treats his slave with cruelty may be compelled to sell him: Caius, *Institutes* i. 53. See also *ibid*. i. 62, for the edict of Claudius to the effect that if a slave has been deserted by his master in grave illness, he should be set free.

[10] *Summa*, 1a, 2ae, qu. 94, art. 2.

right to freedom from arbitrary physical constraint (the principle of the Habeas Corpus Act latent in the 39th Clause of the Magna Charta was acknowledged in 1188 by Alfonso IX at the Cortes of Leon). Custom, not the fiat of the State, was regarded as the typical manifestation of the law binding upon the individual. This was a doctrine propounded not only by leading continental jurists, such as Beaumanoir and Gratian. We find it also in St. Germain's *Dialogus de fundamentis legum Angliae;* [11] in Bracton's statement that "all pleas are determined by the Customs" which the King is bound to keep and to cause to be kept; [12] in Hooker's affirmation that popular consent is the basis of all law.[13]

After the temporary wave of retrogression, which in the sixteenth century was the twin and not unnatural result of the vogue of the teaching of Machiavelli and of the absolutism of the nascent national State, two factors combined to revive and to strengthen the idea of natural rights of man. The first was the direct outcome of the Reformation and of the religious struggle which followed it. Religious intolerance and persecution brought forth the insistence, with a fervour not inferior to the religious impulse itself, on the natural right of freedom of conscience and religious belief. Erasmus gave that movement an impetus which left an indelible impress on the European tradition of tolerance.[14] The Puritans and the Levellers in England inscribed it in the tenets of their political faith as the foremost inalienable right. Matters of religion were the first subject with regard to which the Revolutionary Army of 1648 set a definite limit to the sovereignty of Parliament: "We do not empower our Representatives to continue in force, or make, any laws, oaths, covenants, whereby to compel by penalties or otherwise any person to anything in or about matters of faith, religion, or God's worship." [15] Twelve years prior to the Agreement of the People, the Puritan colonists who, under the inspiration of Roger Williams founded Rhode Island, adopted in their compact a declara-

[11] iv. 8. [12] *De legibus* i. 1. 2.
[13] *The Laws of Ecclesiastical Polity* i. 10. 4; i. 10. 5; viii. 2. 13.
[14] See Lord Acton, *History of Freedom*, p. 50, and *Lectures on Modern History* (ed. J. N. Figgis and R. V. Laurence), p. 105.
[15] From the Second Agreement of the People (1648), *Puritanism and Liberty; Being the Army Debates (1647–9) from the Clarke Manuscripts* (edited by A. S. P. Woodhouse, London, 1938), p. 361.

tion truly revolutionary in character which excluded matters of religion from the purview of the legislature.

The second factor that helped to keep alive and to instill fresh vigour into the idea of natural rights was the theory of the social contract, which arose in the Middle Ages and remained predominant up to the commencement of the eighteenth century. The very notion of the social contract implies, it will be noted, the existence of rights which the individual possesses before entering organized society. Most of the propounders of the doctrine of the social contract taught that there were insurmountable limits to the power of the State not only on account of the terms of the contract but also for the simple reason that some rights, because of the nature of man, are inalienable. This, indeed, was not the invariable teaching of the school of the social contract. The appeal of the blessings of peace and the terrors of anarchy consequent upon resistance were such that some construed the social contract as an instrument of unconditional, total, and irrevocable subjection. Even Grotius was not, subject to considerable exceptions,[16] far removed from that way of thinking. He argued that if according to Roman and Hebraic law a man could sell himself irrevocably as a slave, there was no reason why a people as a whole should not be able to do so. The dialectical quibble by which Hobbes arrived at the same result, without any exceptions, is well known. The social contract was in his view a compact only between subject and subject, not between the community and the ruler. The latter received all the power, but contracted no obligation. Yet this was not the typical application of the theory of the social contract. The typical use of that theory took place under the influence of Locke, who excluded the inalienable rights from the scope of rights relinquished in the social contract. It was Locke's conception of the social contract that struck the deepest note in contemporary thought and that exercised a powerful influence on the early American declarations of rights and on the French declarations of 1789 and 1791 in which, more emphatically than anywhere else, the principle was proclaimed that society is set up for the defence of certain inalienable rights.

[16] See below, p. 44.

The claim to religious toleration and the theory of the social contract were not the only sources of the renewed vitality of the notion of the natural rights of man. Witness Milton's appeal to the natural freedom of man as the basis of his right to be ruled by law, not by the arbitrary whim of man; or the insistence, in the course of the Puritan Revolution, on natural rights in support of political freedom, social equality, and universal suffrage; or the place which Blackstone in his exposition of the laws of England assigned to the natural rights of man —an exposition which, at least in its influence, was not impaired by the seemingly unqualified acknowledgment of the supremacy of Parliament.

The Virginian Declaration of Rights of 1776; the similar constitutional enactments, in the same year, of Pennsylvania, Maryland, Delaware, New Jersey, and North and South Carolina; the constitutions of New York and of New Georgia of 1777 and that of Massachusetts of 1780; the Declaration of Independence, 1776, and the Bill of Rights in the form of the first ten Amendments to the Constitution of the United States; the Declaration of the Rights of Man and of the Citizen adopted in 1789 by the French National Assembly and prefixed to the Constitution of 1791; and the Declarations prefixed to the French constitutions of 1793 and 1795—all these mark the radical innovation of the acknowledgment of the inherent rights of man in the constitutional law of modern States. It was not, as is widely believed,[17] a case of shifting from natural law to natural rights. For that process, as has been pointed out, is coeval with political and philosophical thought dating back to antiquity and the Middle Ages. The notion of human nature as a source and standard of political rights is older than the end of the eighteenth century. What was new was the formal incorporation of these rights as part of the constitutional law of States and their consequent protection not only against the tyranny of kings but also against the intolerance of democratic majorities. What was new was the rejection by positive enactment—for the idea itself went back to the Middle Ages and Bodin [18]—of the idea of the ultimate and uncontrolled sover-

[17] See John Dewey, *Freedom and Culture* (New York, 1939), p. 103.
[18] See below, pp. 29–30.

eignty of the sovereign people itself.[19] The sovereign was subjected to the higher law conceived as the guarantor of the inalienable rights of man.

Since then the recognition of the fundamental rights of man in the constitutions of States has become, in a paraphrase of Article 38 of the Statute of the Permanent Court of International Justice, a general principle of the constitutional law of civilized States. In the nineteenth century it became part of the law of nearly all European States. Sweden adopted it in 1809; Spain, in 1812; Norway, in 1814; Belgium, in 1831; the Kingdom of Sardinia, in 1848; Denmark, in 1849; Prussia, in 1850; [20] Switzerland, in 1874. The French Constitution of 1848 recognized "rights and duties anterior and superior to positive laws." After the first World War it was adopted by Germany and all the new European States, with the exception of democratic Austria (where the omission was due not to reasons of substance, but to the peculiarities of the legal theories of some of the draftsmen of the Constitution). Even when some of these States subsequently succumbed to the wave of totalitarianism, their revised constitutions—like that of Poland of 1935 and of Rumania of 1938—did not dispense with a list of (attenuated) fundamental rights. The Latin American States followed in the nineteenth and twentieth centuries the general trend practically without exception. They amplified the scope of fundamental rights by enlarging on the duties of the State in the social and economic spheres and by adding considerably to the guarantees of their enforcement. States on the Asiatic continent followed suit. Thus, for instance,

[19] It will be noted that, in No. 84 of *The Federalist*, Hamilton objected to a Bill of Rights on the ground that the people is sovereign, that it cannot be limited, and that, accordingly, the sovereign authority cannot be limited. That view did not prevail. When in 1778 Theophilus Parson objected to the proposed Constitution of Massachusetts on the ground that it contained no Bill of Rights, he considered as firmly established the principle that "the supreme power is limited and cannot controul the unalienable rights of mankind." See C. H. McIlwain, *Constitutionalism and the Changing World* (Cambridge, 1939), p. 66. In 1768, in the *Massachusetts Circular Letter*, Samuel Adams, while still referring to the sovereign as supreme, spoke of man's right to retain what is his own as "an essential, unalienable right, in nature, engrafted into the British constitution as a fundamental law, and ever held sacred and irrevocable by the subjects within the realm" (*ibid.*, p. 71).
[20] The Bismarck Constitution of 1871 contained no list of fundamental rights, but these were included in the constitutions of the states members of the Bund. The All-Russia Congress proclaimed, in January, 1918, a "declaration of the rights of the toiling and the exploited peoples" which was incorporated as Part I of the Constitution of July 5, 1918. That declaration was considerably extended in the Constitution of 1936.

within a period of two years we see the adoption of chapters on the rights and duties of the people in the Provisional Constitution of China of May 12, 1931, on the rights and duties of the Siamese in the Constitution of the Kingdom of Siam of December 10, 1932, and on the rights of Afghan subjects in the Fundamental Principles of the Government of Afghanistan of October 31, 1931. In 1933 the Kingdom of Tonga amended its Constitution, in which the first chapter, on the declaration of rights, begins significantly as follows: "Since it appears to be the will of God that man should be free, as He has made all men of one blood, therefore shall the people of Tonga and all who sojourn or may sojourn in the Kingdom be free forever." The Turkish Constitution of 1928 did not refrain from similar terminology, vividly reminiscent of the Declaration of 1789: "Every Turk is born and lives free. . . . The limits, for every one, of freedom, which is a natural right, are the limits of the freedom of others." [21]

Two facts emerge from the survey undertaken in this Chapter. The first is the antiquity of the notion of the innate rights of man appertaining to him as a human being and constituting what may be called the higher law. The second is the close association of these rights with the doctrine of the law of nature. The character and the meaning of that association may now be considered.

[21] For a valuable survey of the relevant constitutional provisions of various countries see *Constitutional Provisions concerning Social and Economic Policy*, Montreal, International Labour Office, 1944.

CHAPTER III

THE LAW OF NATURE AND THE INHERENT RIGHTS OF MAN

IT HAS BEEN SHOWN that the notion of the natural rights of man is of great antiquity and of significant continuity. It is now enshrined in the constitutional law of most States. But the progress of the idea and of the practice of inherent rights of man in the nineteenth and twentieth centuries has only been achieved in face of constant and trenchant criticism. They have been described as fanciful, elusive, and double-edged. They have been assailed as individualistic and antisocial. With these strictures we are not concerned here. But we cannot ignore one objection which, far from invalidating the essential idea of natural rights, is nevertheless in a sense unanswerable. It is a criticism which reveals a close and, indeed, an inescapable connection between the idea of fundamental rights on the one hand and the law of nature and the law of nations on the other. That criticism is to the effect that in the last resort such rights are subject to the will of the State; that they may —and must—be regulated, modified, and if need be taken away by legislation and, possibly, by judicial interpretation; that, therefore, these rights are in essence a revocable part of the positive law and of a sanctity and permanence no higher than the constitution of the State either as enacted or as interpreted by courts and by subsequent legislation. This objection was, indeed, present to the minds of the authors of the Declaration, of August 4, 1789, of the Rights of Man and of the Citizen. For the Assembly decreed that the Constitution should be *preceded* by the Declaration. The intention, apparently, was to endow the latter with an authority superior even to that of the Constitution. In the words of Thouret, the *rapporteur*, when a new constitution was being framed in 1791, the Declaration was left intact on the ground that it "had acquired, in a sense, a sacred and religious character." Or, as Dupont de Nemours put it, it was in the minds of its authors "the fundamental law of the laws of our own and of other nations which ought to last as long as time itself." For this reason Duguit and other French constitutional writers have deemed it fit to proclaim a significant hierarchy of obligations. The legislator, in this view, is bound by the Constitution, but the authors of the Constitution and of its future changes are bound by the most fundamental instrument— the Declaration of Rights. He does not state what is the legal basis and the legal sanction of that supreme Declaration of Rights—unless it be the right of revolution.[1] A somewhat pathetic intimation of the same problem appears in the concluding passage of the Statute of Virginia for Religious Freedom of 1786. In that passage it is conceded that it is not possible for the Assembly to secure the Bill for all time by declaring it irrevocable.

Yet we are free to declare, and do declare, that the rights hereby asserted are of the natural rights of mankind, and that if any act should be hereafter passed to repeal the present act or to narrow its operation such act will be an infringement of a natural right.

This difficulty reveals the Achilles heel of the notion of natural rights of man so long as they depend for their validity and their practical recognition upon the uncontrolled will of the sovereign State and so long as the ultimate sanction of their being is grounded exclusively in the law of the State. Where else can that ultimate sanction be found? It must rest in a legal source superior to that of the State. That superiority may be of two kinds. It may be that of the law of nature conceived as a limitation inherent in the nature of all rational law and as a standard of justice and fitness the disregard of which must reduce law to a mere form of arbitrary power. That law of nature is not without its sanctions. For it is a factor whose operation shapes the habitual obedience which is at the basis of all positive law; it moulds the minds of rulers and legislators by instilling into them that degree of reasonable-

---

[1] *Traité de droit constitutionnel* (2d ed., Paris, 1923), III, 562–567. Similarly, with regard to the German Weimar Constitution of 1919, Professor Carl Schmitt, an able, though not sympathetic, commentator on that document, denied that fundamental rights, for instance, those of personal freedom, were of the same degree as the other provisions of the constitution and that they could be altered by the regular procedure provided for changes in the constitution: "No German law must be interpreted or applied in derogation of it [the Weimar Constitution]. No German law must destroy a real fundamental right. These basic principles cannot be abolished either by ordinary law or by a law changing the constitution as provided in Article 76, but only by a new fundamental constitutional law of the German people."—*Verfassungslehre* (Munich, Leipzig, 1928), p. 161.

ness and restraint which constitutes the barrier between compliance and rebellion; and no law or legal theory can exclude it from the province of judicial interpretation of the positive law. The other legal source which is above the supreme authority of the State and in which lie the ultimate safeguards of the rights of man is the law of nations, or, as it is more often called, international law. It is, predominantly, the body of rules, voluntarily accepted or imposed by the existence of international society, which govern the conduct of States and are subject to enforcement by external sanction. The rights of man cannot, in the long run, be effectively secured except by the twin operation of the law of nature and the law of nations—both conceived as a power superior to the supreme power of the State.

This being so, it is of more than purely historical interest to trace the interaction and the inward connection of these two limiting forces, on the one hand, and the notion of the rights of man, on the other hand —a connection as old as the philosophy of the Stoics. For, indeed, it was only within the immeasurable confines of the cosmopolis of the City of God in which the law of reason, being the law of nature, reigns supreme, that the Stoics envisaged the common law of humanity based on the most fundamental of all human rights, the principle of equality. It is almost as if they perceived the equality of man as imperfect and precarious unless apprehended as part of an oecumenical international order. It is in this sense that Seneca insisted that all men are akin by nature, which has formed them of the same elements and placed them in the world for the same end. Marcus Aurelius elaborated on the same theme: "The common possession of reason is synonymous with the necessity of a common law. . . . That common law makes fellow-citizens of all men. If this is so, we are members of some political community in the sense that the world is in a manner a State." There is, in fact, an intimate and, on reflection, unavoidable connection between the notion of the law of nature as the true source of legal justice and the notion of all humanity as a community of citizens equal in the eyes of nature. It is only within the structure of a wider system in which the State has ceased to be an absolute law unto itself and an absolute purpose unto itself that the inviolate character of inherent human rights can receive adequate legal expression and that the sanctity of the individual human being as the ultimate subject of all law asserts itself in full vigour.

But the Stoics marked the beginning, not the end, of that inevitable association between inherent human rights, the law of nations as the expression of a universal order, and the law of nature. For, as already intimated,[2] it is a suggestive fact of history that in the development of the idea of the fundamental rights of man the notion of the law of nature played the paramount and the principal part. With the Stoics, Greek and Roman, with Cicero, and, subsequently, with the Christian Fathers, it was natural law, as lying behind and above all positive law, which was the transcending authority delimiting the earthly power of the State in relation to the individual. From the very beginning the law of nature was brought into being for judging the legitimacy of the acts of the rulers—which means their conformity with human rights. From man's essential nature, which is reason and which he shares with God, Cicero deduced not only a common law but also a common share in justice.[3] He and Roman lawyers—Ulpian in particular—appealed to the law of nature as the supreme and final authority for the proposition that the slave and the free man were equal, any positive law notwithstanding. So did the Greek Stoics before him and Seneca, the Roman Stoic, after him. So did Philip the Fair of France in 1311, who, when proposing to liberate the serfs, insisted that "every human creature formed in the image of our Lord ought by natural law to be free." Four years later, Louis X of France, in an ordinance, exhorted the serfs to purchase their freedom "comme selon le droit de nature chacun doit naistre franc." The extent to which the issue of slavery prompted the assertion of a law of nature even by those who, like Aristotle, denied any inconsistency between the two is not uninstructive with regard to the question of the influence of the claims of freedom upon both the rise and the growth of the theories of the law of nature.

The idea of the law of nature underlay most of the political and the legal speculation of the Middle Ages inasmuch as it laid emphasis upon the subordination of the ruler to the rule of law, which emphasis was its predominant theme. For when at that time the law of nature came to be identified with the law of God it did not become a bulwark of

---

[2] See above, pp. 18–19. [3] *De legibus* (Loeb edition), p. 323.

established authority. It continued to be invoked as the authority for the subjection of rulers to principles of justice, for respect for the sanctity of human personality, and for the right of the individual to defend himself against the abuses of absolutism by rebellion and by tyrannicide if need be. Thus, at a later date the law of nature played a prominent part in writings of the monarchomachs. In the *Vindiciae contra tyrannos* we find the author asserting that "the law of nature teaches and commands us to maintain and to defend our lives and liberties, without which life is scant worth the enjoying, against all injury and violence." Even Bodin, who laid the foundations of the modern theory of indivisible and absolute sovereignty as the essential characteristic of the State, illogically but significantly subjected that supreme sovereignty to the law of nature.[4] The theory of natural law—"radical to the very core" as Gierke put it—accompanied the birth of the modern State. It supplied the material by means of which Locke, strongly influenced by the natural-law doctrines of Grotius and Pufendorf, propounded with a weighty simplicity his views on the inalienable rights of man. It had previously been invoked by Sir Matthew Hale and other English lawyers who asserted the rule of law against the arbitrariness of the executive. Hale described as wild and "against all natural justice" the proposition that the king may make, repeal, or alter laws as he pleases. It was appealed to by the Puritans, the Levellers, and the leaders of the Revolutionary Army; it was invoked by Milton; it was relied upon by Blackstone. It was that armory of natural law which, in Bryce's telling phrase, "had been for nearly two thousand

[4] In addition to the law of God and the fundamental laws of the Kingdom, such as the "Salic" law (*De republica* i. 8). He was not unduly concerned with the objection, which had clearly occurred to Althusius, that an authority subject to the law of nature and the law of God cannot properly be called supreme (*Politica methodice digesta* [1603], ed. 9, No. 20). That aspect of the problem is discussed by Loyseau in his *Traité des seigneuries*, ch. ii, p. 8 (*Les Œuvres de Maistre Charles Loyseau* [1678]), with a clarity which warrants quotation: "As there can be no crown if its circle is not complete, so there is no sovereignty if it lacks anything. Still, since God alone is all-powerful and the power of man cannot be entirely absolute, there are three sorts of laws, which limit the power of the sovereign without being concerned with the sovereignty; namely, the laws of God, for that the Prince is not less sovereign for being subject to God; the rules of justice natural and not positive, because, as has been said before, it is essential to the *seigneurie publique* that it be administered by justice and not at discretion; and finally the fundamental laws of the state, in that the Prince is bound to exercise his sovereignty according to its inherent nature and in the form and with the conditions under which it is established." (As translated in McIlwain, *Constitutionalism and the Changing World* [1939], p. 41.)

years a harmless maxim, almost a common place of morality" and "became in the latter part of the eighteenth century a mass of dynamite which shattered an ancient monarchy and shook the European Continent." [5] As we have seen, it was not, perhaps, quite so harmless a maxim in the centuries which preceded the American and French revolutions. It merely gathered strength. The doctrine of inherent rights as expressed in the American Declaration of Independence, in the first American constitutions, and in the French Declaration of the Rights of Man was not an original invention. It put to revolutionary use the accumulated power of what had been for a long time the backbone of the doctrine of the law of nature on which James Otis, Samuel Adams, Jefferson, and the other Fathers of the Revolution leaned so heavily. In the realm of thought—in the realm of political and legal theory—the association of the law of nature and of the natural rights of man goes back to antiquity. The terminological connection in the sphere of constitutional law as expressed in 1776 and 1789 took place almost at a time when the law of nature was beginning to lose its appeal.

In the nineteenth century that particular function of natural law was rendered unnecessary, for the simple reason that, apart from the fact that the doctrines of natural law found themselves in a defensive position, that century was assimilating and putting into practice the accomplishments of the law of nature as expressed in the great American and French constitutional pronouncements. When in the twentieth century that achievement was put in jeopardy, the law of nature resumed, as we shall see, its historic function as the champion of the rights of man.

What was and is that law of nature which throughout the ages proved to be the principal bearer of the idea of the indefeasible rights of man? It would seem that nothing short of an exposition of the successive theories and the subjective ideas of writers and scholars can supply an adequate answer to the question. However, there is in the theories of the law of nature, from Greek philosophy until modern times, a firm core of method and substance which bears directly, though partly in a somewhat negative fashion, upon the issue before us.

We cannot hope to understand adequately the law of nature unless

[5] *Studies in Law and Jurisprudence* (Oxford, 1901), II, 163.

we disabuse our minds of the idea that it has been exclusively, or predominantly, speculative, deductive, and fanciful; that it has been divorced from experience; and that its exponents have attempted to engraft upon the living body politic the products of abstract *a priori* speculation. Nothing could be farther from the truth.

From the very inception the theories of natural law have been generalizations from actual experience. They have been attempts to put in the form of general law the fact of a uniformity as ascertained by observation and study of evidence—although it has not always been the kind of evidence that would satisfy the modern mind. Their authors have endeavoured to form laws of conduct by reference to the nature of man, to his physical and mental constitution as they saw it, and to his station and purpose in the scheme of creation as they perceived it from contemplating the world around them. No doubt all this was speculation, but that is unavoidable whenever the human mind is at pains to forge a link of orderliness, cause, and purpose between seemingly disconnected phenomena.

Witness, for instance, the way in which Aristotle arrived at the conception of natural law. For him [6] it was synonymous with the legal experience of all or most peoples as contrasted with the law of one country. He distinguished between law which is in accordance with nature because it is recognized by all and the peculiar law of individual peoples. The laws and customs followed by the generality of mankind must, in his view, be regarded as a manifestation of a common moral and mental constitution exhibiting a uniformity and regularity which nature shows in other realms of existence.

The Stoic conception—both Greek and Roman—of the law of nature was on the face of it more abstract. Actually, it was grounded on what the Stoics believed to be the fundamental fact of the common origin of man and of his common possession of and subjection to reason conceived as the central and ruling power of the world. In that sense human relations are governed by a law coeval with man, in its essence unalterable, anterior to the State, and of necessity incorporated in the law of any State worthy of the name. In the Epicurean philosophy we

[6] In addition to his conception of nature as implying a rational design in the universe manifested, though never fully realized, in the material world.

find a conception of the law of nature which is almost utilitarian in character. Inasmuch as natural justice prescribes what is good for the greatest number, the law of nature was identified with the common good. Some of the imperialist jurists of the Middle Ages followed the same line of utilitarian reasoning when they taught that as God wills the happiness of those whom he has created, utility is the best standard of right conduct, since it is in conformity with the law of nature and the law of God.

Cicero's conception of natural law was, in the same sense, inductive: "Universal consent is the voice of nature." [7] "In every matter the consent of nations is to be considered as the law of nature." [8] His influence on later Roman jurists is undeniable in this matter, as in other respects. For the *jus naturale* of the Roman jurists was not a mere abstraction. It was the right law, the law appropriate to the individual and the social nature of man, deduced, not from a speculative void, but from the general condition of mankind at large. The *jus gentium*, with a fair admixture of equity, was positive law. But it was often described as that part of natural law which had been accepted and acted upon by the civilized communities of the Mediterranean world. The actual difference between *jus gentium* and *jus naturale* was not considerable. They often merged one into the other. The institution of slavery, which must be alien to any law of nature that is not an abuse of language (though Aristotle and others tried to justify it by reference to natural law), prevented any such identification. But *jus gentium* and *jus naturale* came sufficiently close together to act as a reminder that the notion of the law of nature was not pure speculation.

The position was essentially the same in the Middle Ages and in the period which followed them. When the upholders of the law of nature propounded that it was established by the reason of the thing, they did not refer to the reason of the thing as conceived by their own speculation and their own individual opinion. Evidence of constant and immemorial usage was required—though opinions differed as to the kind of evidence needed. There is not much difference between

---

[7] "Omnium consensus naturae vox est" (*Tusc.* i. xv. 35).
[8] "Omni autem in re consensio omnium gentium lex naturae putanda est" (*ibid.*, i. xiii. 30).

founding the law of nature on the animal and social nature of man, as Grotius did, and basing it on social solidarity, as does the modern jurist Duguit.

There is nothing necessarily arbitrary about the law of nature. On the contrary, it has been a constant challenge to arbitrariness in the name of what is in the long run universal—because generally accepted —and commendable to reason and to the nature of man, including his sense of justice. Its essence is not, as some have thought, the opposition of the ideal law to the law as actually in operation. Far from it. Actual law is often the full embodiment of natural law or approximates it (which is merely another way of saying that law is the realization of the maximum of socially obtainable justice). It is only when the positive law of any given time and place departs from what reason, the senti-ment of right, and the general legal experience of mankind make to constitute the law of nature that the latter assumes the character of a challenge and a protest. It is in this sense that the law of nature is both an expression of reality and a standard of fitness. This is the true mean-ing of the view of St. Thomas Aquinas that God himself is subject to the law of nature and of the opinion of Grotius that natural law "would have a degree of validity even if we should concede that which cannot be conceded without the utmost wickedness, that there is no God, or that the affairs of man are of no concern to Him." [9]

The law of nature has incurred the charge of being fanciful and speculative. Undoubtedly, it is not capable of exact demonstration in the same way as a clear rule of positive law (although we often find that a rule of positive law is less clear than it appears and that it leaves room for, or calls for, interpretation by reference to that indefinite law of nature). It is certainly less precise and less amenable to proof than laws in the domain of physics or mathematics. This is so for the reason that it applies to the more complicated sphere of human nature and of social relations of man. Thus Locke was of the opinion that the natural constitution of man—of man in the state of nature—was one of equal and peaceful individuals who submitted themselves to the rule of the

[9] *Proleg.* 11. Elsewhere—in i. i. x. 5—he says: "The law of nature, again, is unchange-able—even in the sense that it cannot be changed by God. Measureless as is the power of God, nevertheless it can be said that there are certain things over which His power does not extend."

State because of the inconvenience which would result from the fact
that in the state of nature every person preserves the right of judgment
in disputes with others.[10] Hobbes, on the other hand, was of the view
that the natural constitution of man was one of aggressive and vicious
enmity towards others and that consequently any form of tyranny is
preferable to the state of natural anarchy. But these differences do not
affect the reality of the law of nature; they do not reduce it to a mere
postulate or presumption. The social nature of man; his physical and
mental constitution; his sentiment of justice and moral obligation; his
instinct for individual and collective self-preservation; his desire for
happiness; his sense of human dignity; his consciousness of man's station and purpose in life—all these are not products of fancy, but objective factors in the realm of existence. As such, they are productive of
laws which may be flouted by arbitrariness, ignorance, or force, but
which are in conformity with the more enduring reality of reason and
the nature of man. This, then, is the law of nature which has acted as
the justification of the positive law and as the principal instrument of
the legal and political notion of the rights of man.

It is true that that law of nature has often fulfilled other and opposite functions. Aristotle justified slavery as a natural institution on
the ground that some men are by nature free and capable of guiding
their lives towards a rational end, while others are by nature slaves
capable of just enough reason to comprehend it in others. The barbarians were by nature slaves. The slave has by nature no sense of
freedom and no understanding of the higher art of existence in political society. His purpose and destiny is to serve others. Only the
Greeks had by nature the physical and mental qualities required for
political existence.[11]

[10] An inconvenience not so great, however, as to justify submission to a tyrannical
rule. This would mean "to think, that men are so foolish that they take care to avoid
what mischiefs may be done them by polecats or foxes, but are content, nay, think it
safety, to be devoured by lions" (*Second Essay of Government*, VII, 93).
[11] *Politics* i. 1. 5. He says: "Inferior kinds of men are by nature slaves, and it is better
for them, as for all inferiors, to be under the rule of a master. For that man is by
nature a slave who can be, and therefore is, the property of someone else, and has
sufficient intelligence to understand, but not to reason. The lower animals however,
do not even understand; they merely obey their instincts. As a matter of fact, the
use of slaves and of domestic animals does not differ much: from the physical labour
of both are obtained the services necessary for life." Aristotle deplored the fact that
there was no certain distinguishing mark to serve as an infallible index of the slave,

This appeal to the law of nature as justifiying legal and, subsequently, economic slavery is a frequent occurrence. In 1785 we find the Reverend John Townsend, in *A Dissertation on the Poor Laws*,[12] voicing the same view: "It seems to be the law of nature that the poor should be to a certain degree improvident, that there may always be some to fulfil the most servile, the most sordid, and the most ignoble offices in the community. The stock of human happiness is thereby much increased." He was not unmindful of the lot of the poor: "As to the lowest poor . . . the desire of obtaining bread will quickly dispose the mind to undergo the greatest hardships, and will sweeten the severest labours. The peasant with a sickle in his hand is happier than the prince upon his throne." At various periods upholders of economic stability appealed to natural law as the basis of the sanctity of contracts and property; the critics of the prohibition of usury found in it a useful argument. So did the opponents of State interference in the economic sphere. In 1604 a Committee of the House of Commons asserted that since merchandise was the principal trade of the country it was "against the natural right and liberty of the subjects of England to restrain it into the hands of some few." [13] Adam Smith availed himself of it in advocating "the obvious and simple system of natural liberty." This reliance upon natural law on the part of vested interests inimical to the economic freedom of man was destined to prove a persistent feature of the nineteenth century. It was especially in the United States, in the

---

although he thought that in general this might be observed in the cringing manner of the inferior. Equality, says Aristotle, can apply only to those equal by birth and power. "Equality is regarded and is just not for all, but for equals. Similarly inequality is regarded, and is so by nature, as just, but not for all, but only for those who are not equal" (*Politics* iii. 5. 8). Neither was he at a loss to answer the embarrassing question as to the noblest families being made prisoners of war and sold as slaves. His answer was: "Victory is always owing to some superior advantage: so that it seems that violence does not prevail without ability." Nearly two thousand years later Sir Thomas Smith, in *The Commonwealth of England* (published first as *De Republica Anglorum* [1567] and reprinted in 1589 under the English title), wrote in a similar vein: "A bondman or a slave is as it were (saving life and humane reason) but the instrument of his Lord, as the axe, the saw, the chessyll and gowge is of the charpenter." Between the master and his slave "there is no mutual societie or portion, no law or pleading between thone and thother . . . there is no right, law nor commonwealth compact, but only the will of the Lord and segnior."

[12] Quoted in Sidney and Beatrice Webb, *English Poor Law History*, Part II, Vol. I (London, 1927), p. 8.

[13] Quoted by R. H. Tawney, *Religion and the Rise of Capitalism* (London, 1926), p. 179.

second half of the nineteenth century, that the ideas of the law of nature and of natural rights were resorted to in an attempt to curb State interference with rights of private property and with freedom of contract. The Fourteenth Amendment to the Constitution, adopted in 1868, provided that "no State shall deprive any person of life, liberty, or property without due process of law; nor deny to any person within its jurisdiction the equal protection of the laws." The expression "due process of law" became henceforth the pivotal constitutional problem of the United States. The Amendment was passed largely for the protection of the Negro population. But the Supreme Court soon held that the safeguards of the Amendment extended only to such rights, and these were few, as the Negroes enjoyed by virtue of their general citizenship of the United States; it did not protect them against State legislation in other spheres. While thus the main purpose of the amendment suffered a restriction which defeated its apparent purpose, the amendment became, by an unexpected turn of judicial interpretation, to a considerable extent an instrument for the protection of vested interests and of economic stability against social legislation and economic change. The Supreme Court interpreted the concept of "due process of law," not as a restriction of a procedural character, but as a substantive limitation intended to secure respect for the inalienable natural rights—of which that of private property was foremost—and for the fundamental unwritten principles of the Constitution and of government as determined by the inherent rights of the individual expounded in the Declaration of Independence. The ideas of natural law and of natural rights were revived and endowed with fresh vigour for that purpose. By reference to the natural right of man courts in the United States often declared to be unconstitutional legislation for securing humane conditions of work, for protecting the employment of women and children, for safeguarding the interests of consumers, and for controlling the powers of trusts and corporations. This explains why natural rights have been regarded in some quarters in the United States with suspicion and bitterness and why writers affirming the supremacy of a higher law over the legislature have nevertheless spoken with impatience of the *damnosa hereditas* of natural rights.

It was not only in the economic sphere that natural law was found convenient as a fertile source of reasoning. In the Middle Ages it was relied upon by the supporters both of the Empire and of the Papacy— both sides claiming the right and the capacity to give a more correct interpretation of the law of nature. It was identified with the law of God; as such, it was a weapon for establishing the supremacy of the Church. Catholic writers invoked it as supporting the view that the Scriptures cannot be taken literally, as claimed by the reformers, but must be interpreted in the light of reason and of the law of nature. In general, it was grossly exploited for various reasons. Sir John Fortescue, in a learned and highly laboured argument in his *De natura legis naturae*, availed himself of it as a plea for the Lancastrian title of the Crown of England. It has been invoked by enemies of political freedom and champions of absolutism. While Bossuet, for that purpose, derived all political authority from God, Filmer relied on natural law. Paternal authority was to him the only inalienable natural right; it was preserved in every State with a monarchical form of government. "There is," he said, "a natural right of a supreme father over every multitude, although many at first do most unjust to obtain the exercise of it." [14] There are few more serviceable instruments of dialectics than reliance upon natural law. Recently it has been invoked to justify interference with personal liberty on eugenic grounds because the unborn have their natural rights as much as the living.[15] The abuse of the idea of natural law in the defence of causes both paltry and iniquitous has caused many to reject it with impatience. This is, perhaps, the principal reason why a practical reformer like Jeremy Bentham, a great judge like Mr. Justice Holmes,[16] and a legal philosopher like Hans Kelsen [17]—all believers in progress—have treated the law of nature with little respect. However, the rejection of an actually or potentially beneficent notion because it may be and has been abused savours of a kind of realism which has often led mankind to defeat. It may be doubted whether in our impatience

[14] *Patriarcha; or, The Natural Power of Kings* (1680), Chapter I, 10.
[15] Dean W. R. Inge, *Liberty and Natural Rights* (Oxford, 1934), p. 33.
[16] See below, p. 87*n*.
[17] In a challenging contribution entitled "Die philosophischen Grundlagen der Naturrechtslehre und des Rechtspositivismus," Kelsen has gone to the length of asserting that the typical function of the theory of natural law has been to supply a justification of the positive law and that there is no substance in the view that it has been essentially of revolutionary character (*Philosophische Beiträge*, Kant Gesellschaft, No. 31 (1928), pp. 37–41).

with the *"damnosa hereditas"* of natural rights we really advance matters by asserting that the sovereign power is limited, not by any higher law of the natural rights of man, but by the nature of law itself and by its inherent limitations. For this is a circumlocution. There is no such thing as the nature of law as distinguished from the nature of man. Moreover, it is not only the law of nature which has been exposed to the gross exploitation of special pleading. There is, in the realm of ideas, no higher tribunal, other than the ultimate test of experience, to which appeal can be made against the ingenuity of partisanship.[18] In a sense the very misuse of the notion of natural rights has been a tribute to the vitality and the inner worth of the law of nature. Witness the embarrassed abundance of argument by dint of which Aristotle attempted to prove that slavery was consistent with nature. Above all, the impatience with the misuse of the notion of the law of nature fails to see that this has not been the typical service which it has been called upon to perform. The typical and, in point of time, anterior use to which it was put was the assertion and the defence of the imprescriptible rights of the liberty and the equality of man.

This fact reveals a further significant link in the chain of political and legal thought. The doctrine of the law of nature was, as we have seen, the bulwark and the lever of the idea of the natural rights of man. But it was the latter which, in a most substantial sense, called the doctrine of the law of nature into being. Legal and political theories are not as a rule leisurely speculations of philosophers unrelated to human needs and aspirations; neither are they in the same category as the calm and detached generalizations through which the scientist masters the phenomena of the physical world. They are pragmatic and

[18] Bentham's irritation at the vagueness and inconclusiveness of the appeal to the abstract principles of the law of nature was most emphatic. Such appeal, he said, is "but womanish scolding and childish altercation, which is sure to irritate and which never can persuade,—*I* say that the legislature *cannot* do this—*I* say, that it *can. I* say that to do this, exceeds the bounds of its authority—*I* say, it does *not*. It is evident that a pair of disputants setting out in this manner may go on irritating and perplexing one another for everlasting, without the smallest chance of ever coming to an agreement. It is no more than announcing, and that in an obscure and at the same time, a peremptory and captious manner, their opposite persuasions, or rather affections, on a question of which neither of them sets himself to discuss the grounds": ("A Fragment on Government," *Works*, ed. John Bowring [Edinburgh, 1843], pp. 126, 127). In comparison, Bentham thought, somewhat naïvely, that no disagreement is possible so long as the argument proceeds from the principle of utility.

teleological; they serve a purpose. That purpose of the theory of the law of nature, to which it owed its origin to a large extent, its sustenance throughout centuries, and its periodic revivification has been the vindication of the rights of man. Historically the doctrine of natural law is rooted deeply in the claims of freedom against the tyranny of the State and the injustice of its institutions.

The doctrine of natural law thus called into being and periodically resuscitated by its parent, progeny, and ally—the rights of man—in due course fulfilled functions other than to buttress the claims of the indestructible human rights. But the original connection never disappeared. The doctrine of the fundamental rights of the individual owed as much to the idea of natural law as the latter owed to the former. The interaction was constant and mutually beneficial.[19] That drama in the realm of thought was re-enacted, under the impact of the same dynamic cause, at the beginning of the twentieth century, during and after the first World War, and in the course of the rise of totalitarianism in the decade preceding the second World War. The renaissance of the law of nature at the beginning of the twentieth century was not yet another theory of the judicial function. It was the unmistakable result of the urge to find the spiritual counterpart to the growing power of the modern State. In so far as that power increasingly assumed the menacing shape of unbridled sovereignty of the State in the international sphere, it became the promoter of international anarchy and threatened, through the spectre of modern war, both the rights of man and the heritage of his civilization. The movement towards the revival of natural law after the first World War was the manifestation of the resulting widespread sense of danger. When, in the following decade, pagan absolutism as perfected in the German State threatened to engulf man, in countries opposed to that ideology the tradition of the law of nature became once more a vital element in affirming the sanctity of the individual and in the craving to find a basis for law more enduring than the enforceable will of the sovereign. Only so can we explain the fervour and the intensity of the periodic resurgence of the idea of natural law in the twentieth century.

[19] Sir Henry Maine appears, so far as I have been able to ascertain, to have been the only writer who has shown an understanding of that mutuality of influence: "It is chiefly . . . by allying themselves with political and social tendencies that the doctrines of Nature and her law preserved their energy" (*Ancient Law*, 1920 edition, p. 95).

CHAPTER IV

THE LAW OF NATIONS, THE LAW OF NATURE, AND THE INALIENABLE RIGHTS OF MAN

THE INTIMATE RELATION between the law of nature and the notion of the inherent rights of man has not been a one-way movement of ideas. It has been shown that, in their rise and in their growth, the doctrines of natural law owed as much to the ideas of the inalienable rights of man as the latter owed to the former. We can trace the same mutuality of influence in the relations of international law and the law of nature. The modern law of nations as it came into being after the Reformation and as it was formulated by Grotius and his immediate predecessors, owed its origin to the historic necessity of regulating the relations of the new sovereign States which arose on the ruins of the temporal unity of Christendom. But the manner, the speed, and to a high degree the substance of the transformation of that historic necessity into a working body of rules were determined to a large extent by the doctrine of the law of nature as modernized and secularized by Grotius, to whom many refer as the father of international law. Grotius called in the law of nature, to which he gave fresh vitality and authority, in order to found the modern system of international law. But much of the new vigour and dignity which he imparted to the law of nature came from the fact that it was made the basis for that so much needed law governing the relations of sovereign States. International law, by thus endowing the law of nature with a great historic function, gave it a new lease of life and a new significance.

But here, again, in a different sphere and to a different degree, was repeated the phenomenon which we observed in the relation of the law of nature and in the ideas of the rights of man. One of the factors which in the seventeenth and eighteenth centuries gave new vitality to the law of nature was the need for a law of nations. Subsequently the law of nature gave as much as it had received—and much more. Students of international law know that it is difficult to exaggerate the part which the law of nature played in the creation and in the development of the law of nations. It did so not only *eo nomine* but also through the constant influence of Roman Law, the written reason, the *ratio scripta*. When Vattel was calling his treatise *Le Droit des gens; ou, Principes de la loi naturelle appliqués à la conduite et aux affaires des nations et des souverains*, he was giving expression to one of the salient features of modern international law. In this respect—in the recourse to natural law —there was only a difference of emphasis between so-called naturalists, Grotians, and positivists. The rigid distinction between the three groups was an afterthought of the positivist period in the twentieth century— a period which was of but short duration. With the Statute of the Permanent Court of International Justice which declared "general principles of law as recognized by civilized States"—a modern version of the law of nature—to be one of the primary sources of international law, the law of nature came once more into its own. It was elevated, not to the dignity, for it had an abundance of dignity in its own right, but to the formal status of a source of the law of nations. We may now recall that the law of nature which has thus acted through the ages as the principle vehicle of the development of international law owed much of its appeal, of its *raison d'être*, and of its very origin to its connection with the affirmation of the rights of man. International law is thus indirectly under an obligation to the notion of inherent human rights.

However, the relation is more significant than one of indebtedness. For international law has in this matter given more than it has taken. In the first instance, the founders of modern international law were, in various and often circuitous ways, instrumental in stressing the value and the importance of the natural rights of man. The issue presented itself in a clear-cut form to Franciscus de Victoria, perhaps the greatest of the scholastic writers who preceded Grotius in the sixteenth century. In his work *De Indis recenter inventis*, published in 1532, he propounded the view that the primitive peoples of America were entitled to the protection of the rules of law and justice applicable to all the peoples of the world. Even after Christianity had been proposed to them with simple proof and they refused to accept it, this would not make it lawful to wage war upon them and to deprive them of their possessions.

Grotius, it is true, seemed in one vital respect to have adopted an attitude inconsistent with the recognition of the inherent rights of man. For he seemed to deny the right of resistance—a right which, in the final resort, is the supreme assertion of the inalienable rights of man. That right of resistance, he says, although following from the natural right to ward off injury, is limited within the State in the interest of public peace and order. It would seem that to his mind most evils were preferable to civil strife. He adduced some specious arguments based on the contention that by Hebraic and Roman law a person could sell himself irrevocably as a slave. But it would be misleading to judge the attitude of Grotius to the ideas of political freedom by his views on the right of resistance. This is so not only because of the personal circumstances in which he found himself when writing *De jure belli ac pacis.* He was at that time in France—a fugitive from a temporary eruption of Calvinistic intolerance in Holland. He lived under the protection of Louis XIII, the powerful monarch to whom he dedicated his work. It is understandable, if not pardonable, that he made a point of denying to peoples the right to punish and coerce kings. But there is more to it than an explanation in terms of personal circumstance. For while Grotius denied the right of active rebellion, he was emphatic that there was no duty to carry out orders which were contrary to the law of nature or to the commandments of God.[1] Secondly, even with regard to active resistance, Grotius admitted of exceptions which to a large extent nullified his principal thesis, such as the case of "rulers who are responsible to the people, whether such power was conferred at the beginning or under a later arrangement as at Sparta." [2] "If such rulers transgress against the law and the State, not only can they be resisted by force, but in case of necessity, they can be punished to death." The passage is obscure; it is entitled "that the right to make war may be conceded against him who has the chief authority among a free people." [3] If the passage means anything at all, it largely nullifies his

[1] *De jure belli ac pacis* i. iv. i. 3.   [2] *Ibid.,* i. iv. viii.
[3] *Jus belli dari posse in principem populi liberi.*

sweeping denial of the right of resistance. It would mean that that right is excluded only with regard to absolute monarchies in which the people surrender unconditionally all their rights. Grotius also admits of other weighty exceptions to this principle of non-resistance. These include the wide and elastic case of resistance against extreme oppression; for this, he says, is a case of self-defence: "I should rarely dare indiscriminately to condemn either individuals or a minority which at length availed itself of the last resource of necessity." [4] Thirdly, we must remember that on a wider view it is not the principle of non-resistance, explained to some extent by the personal circumstances of the great jurist and attenuated by the elastic exceptions, which is the proper measure of his attitude. That measure is the fact that the human being is the centre of the Grotian system, both in the internal and in the international sphere. He identifies the law of nature with the nature of man conceived both in abstract isolation and as a social being. "For the very nature of man, which even if we had no lack of anything would lead us into the mutual relation of society, is the mother of the law of nature." [5] And it will be noted that one of the main features of his teaching is the insistence that the standards of justice applicable to individuals are valid in relation to States,[6] which, he maintains, in relation to mankind at large occupy the position which individuals occupy within the State.[7] Finally, in assessing the place of Grotius in the matter of the fundamental rights of man we must not forget that it is to him that dates back the idea of international humanitarian intervention for the protection of these rights. He claimed for rulers the right to demand punishment "not only on account of injuries committed against themselves or their subjects but also on account of injuries which do not directly affect them, but excessively violate the law of nature or of nations in regard to any person whatsoever." [8] And he lays it down elsewhere that when a tyrant practises against his subjects atrocities which no just man can approve, "the exercise of the right vested in human society is not precluded." [9] It was this conception of the law of nature, with man and his welfare occupying the centre of the system—

---

[4] i. iv. vii. 4. [5] *Proleg.* 16. [6] *Ibid.*, 21.
[7] "Populi respectu totius generis humani privatorum locum obtinent," *Mare liberum*, ch. v.
[8] *De jure belli ac pacis* ii. xx. xl. i. [9] ii. xxv. viii. 2.

a direct link with the Thomist view of natural law—which passed from Grotius to Locke and, through him, to the wider scene of the revolutionary declarations of 1776 and 1789.

Vattel, second only to Grotius in authority and influence, went beyond the founder of modern international law in defending the fundamental rights of man. He insisted that obedience ought not to be absolute or blind and that no agreement can bind or even authorize subjects to violate the natural law. It is convenient to quote his words in full: [10]

It is taken for granted that every citizen impliedly agrees to this diminution of his rights, because without it society could not exist. But when it is a case of clear and glaring wrongs, when a prince for no apparent reason attempts to take away our life, or deprive us of things without which life would be miserable, who will question the right to resist him? The care of our existence is not only a matter of natural right but of natural obligation as well; no man may give it up entirely and absolutely; and even though he could give it up, is it to be thought that he has done so by the compact of civil society when he entered into it for the sole purpose of obtaining great security for his personal safety? The welfare of society does not indeed demand such a sacrifice. As Barbeyrac has well said in his notes on Grotius, "if it is in the interest of the public that those who obey should put up with some inconveniences it is none the less for the public interest that those in authority should fear to test their patience too severely."

Neither is his insistence on the freedom of philosophical discussion without interest; [11] nor his distinction between ordinary laws and the fundamental laws of the constitution which, he says, even the nation as a whole ought not to change lightly; [12] nor his denial that the Prince can change or be absolved from obedience to fundamental laws even if he is generally invested with legislative power.[13] His person is sacred and inviolable, but only for so long as he does not transgress the fundamental law. "The moment he attacks the Constitution of the State the Prince breaks the contract which bound the people to him, and the people become free by the act of the sovereign and henceforth they

[10] *Le Droit des gens*, Book I, sec. 54 (as translated by C. G. Fenwick in the Carnegie Endowment edition, Washington, 1916).
[11] Book I, sec. 114.   [12] Book I, sec. 35.   [13] Book I, secs. 46, 47.

regard him as an usurper seeking to oppress them." [14] In elaborating this right of resistance Vattel uses language substantially reminiscent of that of Locke. He goes clearly beyond Grotius in admitting the right of resistance regardless of whether the Prince is an absolute ruler or not, for even if the people have surrendered their rights without express reservation there is always the implied reservation of the supreme right of resistance. Moreover, he says, when the ruler gives his subjects a lawful cause for resisting him, any foreign power may rightfully assist the oppressed people.[15] Here, once more, we have the recognition— especially significant in the case of Vattel, whose respect for the sovereignty of States otherwise knows few limits—of the right of international intervention for safeguarding the fundamental rights of the individual. It is not surprising that Vattel became a popular source of quotation by the theorists of the American Revolution.

The contribution of the writers on international law to the stock of ideas of the rights of man came also by way of the elaboration of the doctrine of equality of States. The analogy of the equality of individuals proved a fertile source of argument, and there was no hesitation in relying on it on a liberal scale.

Just as the tallest man [says Wolff] is no more a man than the dwarf, so also a nation, however small, is no less a nation than the greatest nation. Therefore, since the moral equality of men has no relation to the size of their bodies, the moral equality of nations also has no relation to the number of men of which they are composed.[16]

And it was not without an eye on the question of equality of States that Pufendorf wrote his well-known chapter on the natural equality of man.[17] However, Pufendorf's more direct contribution lay in his affirmation of the subjection of the legislator to the higher law of human nature and of reason. In this, his influence upon Locke was second only to that of Grotius.

Was it a mere coincidence that the three greatest figures in the literature of international law in the seventeenth and eighteenth centuries were the three principal writers who, through Locke and independently of him, exercised a powerful influence upon the growth

---

[14] Book I, sec. 51.   [15] Book II, sec. 56.
[16] *Jus gentium methodo scientifica pertractatum* (1764), Proleg., sec. 16.
[17] *De jure naturae et gentium libri octo* (1688), Book iii, ch. ii.

and the acceptance of the ideology of the inalienable rights of man? One explanation, as already suggested, is that the law of nature, which was one of the starting points of that ideology, itself acquired a fresh vigour by having become the basis of the system of international law. By dint of that renewed vitality, purged by Grotius and others of its clericalism, it was enabled to continue with added vigour its age-old function of supplying the foundation and the stimulus for transforming, at the end of the eighteenth century, the idea of natural rights into a dynamic political principle. Another, and perhaps more fundamental, explanation is that the law of nations, in itself conceivable only as being above the legal order of sovereign States—just as the higher law of nature is superior to it—is not only a law governing their mutual relations but also, in the final analysis, the universal law of humanity in which the individual human being, as the ultimate unit of all law, rises sovereign over the limited province of the State.

Secondly, international law has contributed in a more direct way to the maintenance of the rights of man and the protection of his welfare by the hesitating and infrequent, but significant, practice of humanitarian intervention, such as that on behalf of the Greek people in 1827 and subsequently of the oppressed Armenians and Christians in Turkey; by the custom which began in the middle of the seventeenth century of safeguarding through treaties the rights of religious freedom; by the long series of treaties of a humanitarian character, ranging from slavery conventions to the imposing structure of international legislation concluded under the aegis of the International Labour Organization; and by minorities treaties entered into after the first World War. In fact, we can trace two strains in modern international law. One has been concerned with the relations between States as such: with the law of treaties, with the jurisdictional immunities of diplomatic representatives and of foreign States generally, with acquisition of territory, and with the rules governing the conduct of war. The other has used international law to promote and protect, through international co-operation and institutions, the interests and the welfare of the individual. The great and increasing volume of what is conveniently described as international legislation has been largely devoted to this latter aspect.

Thirdly, although international law does not at present recognize, apart from treaty, any fundamental rights of the individual guaranteed and protected by international society as against the State of which he is a national, it does recognize some of the principal fundamental rights of the individual in one particular sphere, namely, in respect of aliens. These are entitled to treatment which conforms with a minimum standard of civilization, regardless of how the State where they reside treats its own nationals. That minimum standard of civilization comprises in particular the right of personal liberty and, generally, to equality before the law. International tribunals have repeatedly declared it to be a rule of international law. The result, which is somewhat paradoxical, is that the individual in his capacity as an alien enjoys a larger measure of protection by international law than in his character as the citizen of his own State. In current theory and terminology these are not the rights of the alien; they are the right of his State to insist that its nationals should be treated in accordance with certain principles. But this is a not necessarily accurate generalization of the procedural incapacity of individuals in existing international law—an incapacity which has already been overcome in many spheres. Moreover, under the practice of the system of protection of minorities and, even more so, of mandatory government, the procedural capacity of the individual received incipient recognition by the admission of petitions which, while conferring no legal *locus standi* upon the individual, set in motion the appropriate international procedure. Under the Upper Silesian Convention of 1922 the arbitral tribunal constituted thereunder affirmed the right of a national of a State to bring an action against it before an international tribunal.[18] The Permanent Court of International Justice held, in a case of great significance, that there is nothing in international law to prevent individuals from acquiring direct rights under a treaty if this be the intention of the signatories.[19]

This, then, is the past contribution of the law of nations to the idea and the actual protection of the rights of man. It has expressed itself

[18] See the decision of the Upper Silesian Arbitral Tribunal in *Steiner and Gross v. Polish State; Annual Digest of Public International Law Cases*, 1927–1928, Case No. 188, and the remarks thereon by Dr. Georges Kaeckenbeeck, President of the tribunal, in *The International Experiment of Upper Silesia* (London, New York, 1942), pp. 50–54.
[19] *Advisory Opinion No. 15 of March 3, 1928, on the Jurisdiction of the Courts of Danzig:* Series B, No. 15.

in the work and in the influence of the great publicists, in the practice of safeguarding the rights of man through humanitarian intervention and in a variety of treaties, and in the recognition of the rights of aliens. However, in relation to the rights of man the true part of international law lies, not in its contribution in the past, but in the potentialities of its function in the future. In order to realize fully the implications of that function we must have before our mind's eye the intricate picture, which it has been attempted to sketch in this Chapter, of the inward relation and mutual influence of the law of nature, the law of nations, and the rights of man. We have seen how the notion of the rights of man derived its strength and sustenance from the law of nature. We have ascertained how the law of nature owed much of its vitality and growth to its association with the notion of the rights of man. We have followed the part which the law of nature played in the creation of modern international law and the accession of strength it in turn acquired from the law of nations. We have traced the benefits which international law received—indirectly, through the law of nature— from the notion of the rights of man and what it has contributed to it. Each of the three has been in relation to the two others the recipient and the benefactor, the master and the tool, the originator and the product.

This picture of the most intimate connection between the rights of man, the law of nature and the law of nations may appear to some to be dialectical to the point of ingenuity. Nevertheless, it is this picture which probably represents a true account of the history of political and legal thought on this central issue. Moreover, it is believed to be expressive of a deeper unity. In the theories of the law of nature the starting point and the irreducible element has been the individual human being. The law of nations and, we may say, the law of nature, by denying, as they needs must do, the absolute sovereignty of States, give their imprimatur to the indestructible sovereignty of man. It is probably the natural law of humanity—as it is certainly its moral duty —to develop its capacities to all attainable perfection. That duty man has a natural right to fulfill—through freedom. Inasmuch as freedom means the fullest development of the possibilities of human personality, it is not a means of the very highest order, but an end in itself.

The State is to ensure that freedom. The law of nations, conceived in the fullness of its proper function, exists for the purpose of accomplishing that object by making man's freedom secure from the State and by rendering the State secure from external danger. It is only within the scheme of an overrriding international order that we can give reality to the otherwise contradictory notion that the supreme authority of the State is limited and that the rights of man must be based on that limitation. It is not enough to say that the law of the State is circumscribed by its purpose and by the external nature of its power. Democracy, although an essential condition of freedom, is not an absolute safeguard of it. That safeguard must lie outside and above the State.

In that scheme of things the sovereign national State, whether or not it be the permanent form of political organization of man, is not an end unto itself but the trustee of the welfare and of the final purpose of man. In that scheme of things it would be for international society to ensure the fulfilment of that trust through a fundamental enactment—an International Bill of the Rights of Man—conceived, not as a declaration of principles, but as part of positive law, as part of the constitutional law both of States and of the society of States at large. In relation to the national Declarations of 1776 and 1789, and to the constitutional practice of the nineteenth century which followed them, an International Bill of the Rights of Man would constitute an advance commensurate with that which the Declarations of 1776 and 1789 marked upon the law of the eighteenth century. These Declarations drew upon themselves a volume of criticism hardly surpassed in passionate condemnation and in the ingenuity of its dialectics. Yet in retrospect the strictures of Burke,[20] of Bentham,[21] and of Von

[20] Burke, who described the Declaration of 1789 as a "digest of anarchy," was more temperate in his criticism than Bentham. He did not deny "the real rights of man"; he did not even deny that they can be discerned. But he challenged the wisdom of defining them. "If civil society be made for the advantage of man, all the advantages for which it is made become his right." Many years before he attacked the theorists of the French Declaration he invoked, in his great speech on the American rebellion, "the natural rights of mankind." These, he said, "are indeed sacred things, and if any public measure is proved mischievously to affect them, the objection ought to be fatal to that measure, even if no charter at all could be set against it. Only a sovereign reason, paramount to all forms of legislation and administration, should dictate." This language is not far removed from that of the French Revolution.
[21] In 1795 Bentham collected his critical observations on the subject in some manuscripts entitled "Anarchical fallacies: being an examination of the Declaration of Rights issued during the French Revolution" (*Works*, ed. John Bowring [Edinburgh, 1843], II, 491 ff.). One line of Bentham's criticism was that if the purpose of the

Gentz [22]—as well as of modern critics, such as Ritchie [23]—appear petty and petulant. The cautious faith of Jefferson [24] and of Sir James Mackintosh [25] stands out by comparison as a more accurate expression of the enduring strivings and accomplishments of humanity and justifies

declaration was to limit the power of the representative bodies elected by the people, that object was not possible of achievement. For the legislature was elected by the people, and the people could not bind itself—a view clearly set forth by Hamilton in his opposition to the Bill of Rights. Bentham's main argument (lucidly summarized by Elie Halévy, *The Growth of Philosophic Radicalism* [English translation, London, 1928], pp. 175 ff.) was that the declaration amounted to saying that "every law, or other order, divesting a man of the enjoyment of life or liberty is void," and that consequently all penal laws are void. There was no law which, in his view, could not be met by the unanswerable argument that it has abrogated the Declaration of Rights. Some of Bentham's criticism is due to an ultrapositivist view of the law of the clear Austinian brand: "Right is the child of law; from real laws come real rights, but from imaginary law, from laws of nature, come imaginary rights, a bastard brood of monsters. . . . Natural rights is simple nonsense; natural and imprescriptible rights (an American phrase) rhetorical nonsense, nonsense upon stilts." Much of his opposition, as may be seen from the preceding passages, is explained by the sincere apprehension of the practical reformer lest mere talk about natural rights be regarded by some as a sufficient substitute for legislation.

[22] *Ueber die Deklaration der Rechte* (1792), republished in Friedrich von Gentz, *Ausgewählte Schriften* (Stuttgart, 1837). But it is indicative of the temper of the period that Gentz fully accepted the doctrine of natural rights and the theory of the social contract. He says: "That man, when he enters the world, brings with him rights of which nothing but his own free will may deprive him even to the smallest extent— this nowadays no person doubts who has devoted some passing thought to man conceived as a moral entity and properly described as a human being" (*ibid.*, p. 64). But after describing the declaration as "one of the most important documents in the history of this century," he subjected it to destructive criticism on the lines of Burke and Bentham. His conclusion was that "the system of the French rights of man combines all errors which can possibly underlie a constitution, in particular a systematic constitution. It is inaccurate in itself; it is inapplicable; it is destructive of its own purposes. Even the greatest admirer of the highest good of humanity, even the warmest friend of the people, can hardly suppress a smile on beholding the caricature drawn up by the French legislature under the title of rights of man" (*ibid.*, p. 108).

[23] *Natural Rights.*

[24] In a letter to Madison, written in 1789, he said: "The declaration of rights, is, like all other human blessings, alloyed with some inconveniences, and not accomplishing fully its object. But the good in this instance, vastly overweighs the evil." In another letter to Madison, written in the same year, he said: "Experience proves the inefficacy of a bill of rights. True. But though it is not absolutely efficacious under all circumstances, it is of great potency always, and rarely inefficacious. . . . There is a remarkable difference between the characters of the inconveniences which attend a declaration of rights, and those which attend the want of it. The inconveniences of the declaration are, that it may cramp government in its useful exertions. But the evil of this is short-lived, moderate and reparable. The inconveniences of the want of a declaration are permanent, afflicting, and irreparable."—S. K. Padover, ed., *Democracy*, by Thomas Jefferson (New York, London, 1939), pp. 76, 77.

[25] *Vindiciae Gallicae* (London, 1791), Section IV. For a sound assessment of the value of the Declaration of Rights see A. V. Dicey, *Lectures on the Relation between Law and Public Opinion in England during the Nineteenth Century* (London, New York, 1905), p. 171. See also Harold Laski, *Liberty in the Modern State* (London, 1930), p. 52; G. P. Gooch, "The French Revolution and World Force," in *The Evolution of World Peace*, ed. F. S. Marvin (2d ed., London, 1933), pp. 98–104.

Lord Acton's judgment that the single confused page of the Declaration of 1789 outweighs libraries and is stronger than all the armies of Napoleon. At the same time the lesson of the century and a half which have followed these Declarations shows that the rights of man are beset by mortal dangers and must largely remain in the realm of theory unless they are grounded in the firm anchorage of the international legal order. Only so can we resolve the contradiction, which has always been the favourite theme of the opponents of declarations of rights of man, between the supremacy of the law within the State and the notion of fundamental human rights.

Any such consummation, in which the rights of man will form part of the positive law of the society of States, will not mean that the law of nature has played its part in the matter and must henceforth be consigned to the province of historical research. The law of nature must, as it has done in the past, supply much of the spiritual basis and much of the political inspiration of that elevation of the rights of man to a legal plane superior to the will of sovereign States. Nothing short of that spiritual basis will be of sufficient authority to lend permanent support to an innovation so significant and so far-reaching. The view that the rights of man are grounded solely in positive law is mischievous when related to the positive law of the State; it is equally objectionable in relation to the positive law of international society. The law of nature is in no sense a substitute for positive law; it cannot by itself supply the solution of the problem of the rights of man. Whenever that happens the doctrine of natural rights degenerates into a doctrine of vested rights. Whenever the law of nature is treated as an alternative to changes in existing law it ceases, on balance, to be a beneficent force and becomes a check upon progress; if the enthronement of the rights of man is to become a reality, then they must become part of the positive law of nations suitably guaranteed and enforced. Of that law, the law of nature will continue to be an ever-present impulse and a fertile source of vitality and improvement.

For that reason what has been said here about the part which the law of nature has played in the matter in the past is not of mere historical interest. If we are to face with any hope of success the bewildering and seemingly insoluble problems of an international charter of human rights, it is proper that we should seek assistance in the contemplation of the continuity of human thought on this matter and of the true objects of international law. Statesmanship may recoil from the revolutionary immensity of the task. And it is certainly the duty of the student of international law to bring into relief the complexities of any such innovation in the constitutional law of mankind. At the same time it is within his province to attempt to prove that any such departure in the law would not be in the nature of a break with what is truly permanent in the legal tradition of Western civilization and that it would be in accordance with the purpose of the law of nations. That purpose cannot be permanently divorced from the fact that the individual human being—his welfare and the freedom of his personality in its manifold manifestations—is the ultimate subject of all law. A law of nations effectively realizing that purpose would acquire a substance and a dignity which would go far towards assuring its ascendancy as an instrument of peace and progress.

CHAPTER V

NATURAL RIGHTS IN BRITISH CONSTITUTIONAL LAW AND POLITICAL THEORY

THE EXTENT of the British contribution to the theory and the practice of fundamental rights of man is not a matter of mere historical interest. It is of some relevance to the question of the attitude of this country to any proposals to make an International Bill of the Rights of Man part of international law as well as of the constitutional law of England. Great Britain has remained outside the orbit of the almost universal trend of safeguarding the fundamental rights of the individual in a written constitution. This is not so for the reason that Great Britain does not possess a written constitution. For much of her constitutional law is in fact reduced to writing. The reason is that Great Britain is a country with a flexible as distinguished from a rigid constitution. The Habeas Corpus Act, as, indeed, any other part of statutory or customary common law relating to the so-called liberties of the subject, can be changed overnight by the ordinary process of legislation, that is, by a simple majority of both Houses of Parliament assented to by the King.

It is also true that, with weighty exceptions, the doctrine of natural rights found no favour with English political and legal thinkers from Burke till the end of the nineteenth century. However, this is only one half of the story. For it is not the formal structure of the English constitution, or the impatient refutations of the Declarations of Rights by Burke and Bentham, or the negative and complacent attitude of the analytical school in the matter that has become the common heritage of the world, but the long list of English constitutional charters of liberty: the works of Prynne, of Milton, of Sidney, of Halifax, and, above all, of Locke; the doctrines of the Puritans and of the Cromwellian revolution; and the veneration of fundamental rights of freedom by the great lawyers from Bracton through Coke to Blackstone, whose chapter on the "Absolute Rights of the Inidvidual" was not inferior in its influence to the sonorous solemnity of the language in which he extolled them.

The English contribution to political thought and practice on this matter may best be gauged by its influence on the successive American declarations of the rights of man. The American declarations of rights —and these were the principal source of the French declarations [1] and, with them, of the constitutional practice of most States—owe their origin, in varying degrees of importance, to the following causes and influences: There was, first, the English constitutional practice of safeguarding the rights of the subject by way of general statutory enactment, begining with the Magna Charta and its successive confirmations, continuing through the Habeas Corpus Act and the Petition of Right, and ending with the Bill of Rights and the Act of Settlement. The second was the influence of the English political doctrines of freedom and toleration, especially those of the Puritan revolution and of the writings of Milton, Locke, and Blackstone. The third lay in the precedents of the early history of the American colonies, with their own Puritan tradition of toleration and the first political compacts which they set up as the basis of their political life. The fourth was the influence of continental thought in the domain of political theory, particularly of Montesquieu. The fifth was the desire of the authors of the American Bill of Rights to safeguard freedom not only against the encroachments of the executive but also against the tyranny of the legislature and of its majorities. Finally, at the time of the rise of American independence the doctrine of natural rights was, as it had always been, the handmaid of political necessities and aspirations; it was the appointed weapon of a nation in revolt.

Closer investigation of all these sources of the American declarations of rights cannot be attempted here. They have been summarized in order to throw into relief the part played by British political thought and practices. For of all the factors mentioned, the British contribution

[1] Of this, Condorcet's writings bear convincing testimony. In his work *On the Influence of the American Revolution in Europe,* published in 1786, he set out a list of the rights of man which included the security of the person, the security and the free enjoyment of property, and the participation, directly or through representatives, in legislation. In his "Instruction by the Provinces to their Representatives at the Estates General of 1789" the list was enlarged to include the right to be tried by judges appointed according to law and control of taxes and expenditure.

was the most direct and the most easily ascertainable. But this is not generally admitted. Many have doubted whether there is any material connection between the English charters of liberty and the doctrine of fundamental rights as adopted in the American and the French declarations. They have pointed to the now generally adopted view that the first historic document of the liberty of the subject, the Magna Charta, was never what tradition and popular understanding believed it to be, namely, a vindication of the liberties of the people as a whole. It is now commonly accepted that the crucial Clause 39 of the Charter was a partisan instrument extorted from the King for the benefit of the feudal claims and privileges "inimical alike to the Crown and to the growth of popular liberties." [2] It excluded the jurisdiction of the King's justices and stipulated for the trial of the feudal barons by their equals. This is now the recognized interpretation of Clause 39 of the Magna Charta which provided that no free man can be taken or imprisoned or, generally, his person interfered with, except by the lawful judgment of his peers or of the law of the land. When in Darnel's Case, John Selden argued that since Magna Charta no freeman ought to be imprisoned except according to the law of the land, not by special command of the King, he pointed out that this right was limited to freemen; villains, bound to the land under feudal law, had no remedy against arbitrary imprisonment.

And yet the fact remains that in the history of fundamental rights no event ranks higher than that charter of the concessions which the nobles wrested from King John. This is not merely a case of a *communis error facit jus*.[3] The outstanding feature of that event is the limitation of the power of the supreme authority. The exclusion of the ar-

---

[2] W. S. McKechnie, *Magna Carta* (Glasgow, 1905), p. 387. See also Frederick Pollock and F. W. Maitland, *History of English Law* (2d ed., Cambridge, 1923), I, 173n: "Even in the most famous words of the Charter we may detect a feudal claim which will only cease to be dangerous when in the course of time men have distorted their meaning:—a man is entitled to the judgment of his peers; the King's justices are no peers for earls or barons." See also McIlwain, *Constitutionalism and the Changing World*, p. 87.

[3] The critical interpretation of the Magna Charta is not of recent date. In 1646 we find William Walwyn saying: "Magna Carta hath been more precious in your esteem than it deserves; for it may be made good to the people and yet in many particulars they may remain under intolerable oppression" (*England's Lamentable Slavery* [1645], p. 5). At the same time Richard Overton referred to it as "being but a beggarly thing, containing many marks of intolerable bondage" (*A Remonstrance of Many Thousand Citizens* [1646], p. 15).

bitrary power of man over man is the essence of freedom. The jurisdictional privilege which the barons secured, not without the support
of other classes of the people, was not an exemption from the ordinary
and regular processes of the law; it was a security against the arbitrary
proceedings of the King's justices, against a tyrannical *droit administratif*. In this respect the meaning of the Magna Charta is today essentially what it was in 1215. It is of no decisive significance that, in the
main, only one class of the people benefited directly from that limitation of the royal power; what matters is the fact of the limitation. It is
this aspect of the Magna Charta that became part and parcel of general
consciousness. The vindication of human liberties did not begin with
their complete and triumphant assertion at the very outset. It com-
menced with recognizing them in *some* matters, to some *extent*, for
some people, against *some* organ of the State. Milton's defence of
freedom is a landmark in the history of the rights of man; but the limitations which he put on that freedom are utterly unacceptable to the
modern conception. He excluded from toleration

popery and open superstition which, as it extirpates all religions and civil
supremacies, so itself should be extirpated, provided first that all charitable
and compassionate means be used to win and regain the weak and misled;
that also which is impious or evil absolutely either against faith or man-
ners no law can possibly permit, that intends not to unlaw itself.[4]

The Puritans who founded some of the American colonies were the
champions of religious tolerance and of democratic rule; but they were
not unduly particular in setting a limit to either. According to many
of the emigrants in the Mayflower "good and religious man had a right
to rule the evil and irreligious." Neither were they too liberal in conceding the attributes of a "good religious man." In 1656 some of the
colonies decided on the exclusion of all "Quakers, Ranters, and notorious heretics." John Cotton limited religious toleration to "circumstan-
tials as distinguished from fundamentals." [5] In his opinion and that of
many other Puritans "freedom was the prerogative of righteousness;
the well-being of society required that the sinner should remain subject

[4] *Areopagitica (in fine).*
[5] A limitation which was refuted by Roger Williams in *The Bloudy Tenent, of Persecution, for cause of Conscience, in a Conference between Trvth and Peace* (1644).

to the saint." [6] Locke excluded from the principle of toleration opinions contrary to human society or to the moral precepts which are necessary to the preservation of civil society; "those who attribute unto the faithful, religious, and orthodox, that is, in plain terms, to themselves, any peculiar privilege or power above other mortals, in civil concernments; or, who, upon pretence of religion, do challenge any manner of authority over such, as are not associated with them in their ecclesiastical communion"; and "those who deny the being of God" for the "taking away of God, though but even in thought, dissolves all." [7] The authors of the French Declaration of the Rights of Man did not consider freedom of association to be a necessary consequence of individual liberty.

These examples, which could be multiplied, show that the historic value of any single pronouncement affirming the rights of man as against authority is not dependent upon the degree of its completeness. Of this truth the Magna Charta, even as rediscovered in its limited objective, is a paramount illustration. Its repeated confirmation, the Habeas Corpus Act, the Petition of Right, the Bill of Rights, and the Act of Settlement drew their strength and continuity from the original document. What was of decisive and, ultimately, of permanent significance was that for the first time, in a basic constitutional document, a restraint was put upon the supreme power. It was this idea, not its temporary limitation to the charmed circle of the barons, that became a power in history. For that circle was destined to expand. In the course of time the original limitation became a dim memory, which nothing but the industry of modern scholars would have resuscitated. The Bill of Rights of 1688 suffered, in a different sphere, from similar limitations. It was described by Burke and Macaulay as conservative. It was the work of Churchmen and of the rich Whig gentry who perpetuated their hold on the country to the exclusion of the masses of the people. It contained no reference to the liberties of the subject. And yet by submitting the Crown to the supremacy of Parliament and by enthroning the right of resistance—which Locke, the theoretician of the Whig revolution, regarded as operative against Parliament it-

[6] V. L. Parrington, *Main Currents in American Thought* (New York, 1927), I, 33.
[7] *A Letter Concerning Toleration* (the first letter).

self—as part of a fundamental constitutional document it accomplished, in the perennial struggle for freedom, what Lord Acton described as "the greatest thing done by the English nation." [8]

Neither is the importance of the English contribution seriously influenced by the fact that the rights secured by the successive charters of liberty were not treated as inherent rights belonging to the Englishman as a person. They were asserted to be based on statute, on grant, on long practice; they invoked prior laws, customs, and established liberties. The appeal was to the native rights of the Englishman, not to the natural rights of man. This, of course, was not invariably so. The language of the Levellers and of the Puritans and the names Milton,[9] Algernon Sidney,[10] Locke,[11] and Blackstone [12] forbid any such generalization. But on the whole it is true that appeals to the law of nature in support of the freedom of the individual were less frequent in England than elsewhere. This was so for the very good reason that once the claims of freedom assumed the complexion of statutory enactment and of a tradition of the common law, it was easier and more plausible to invoke these rather than the precepts of the law of nature and the principle of inalienable rights.

[8] *Lectures on Modern History* (ed. Figgis and Laurence), p. 231.
[9] *The Tenure of Kings and Magistrates* (1649; *Prose Works*, ed. J. A. St. John [London, 1868–72], II, 8): "No man who knows aught, can be so stupid as to deny, that all men were naturally born free. . . . It being thus manifest, that the power of kings and magistrates is nothing else but what is only derivative, transferred, and committed to them in trust from the people, to the common good of them all, in whom the power yet remains fundamentally, and cannot be taken from them, without a violation of their natural birthright."
[10] *Discourse Concerning Government* (1698), ch. i, sec. 2: "that man is naturally free, that he cannot be justly deprived of his liberty without cause, and that he does not resign it nor any part of it, unless it be in consideration of a greater good which he proposes to himself." God had implanted the principle of liberty in the breast of man, and the rights of the people proceed from nature.
[11] "To understand political power right, and derive it from its original, we must consider what state men are naturally in, and that is a state of perfect freedom to order their actions . . . within the bounds of the Law of Nature, without asking leave, or depending upon the will of any other man. A state also of equality, wherein all the power and jurisdiction is reciprocal, no one having more than another, there being nothing more evident than that creatures of the same species and rank, promiscuously born to all the same advantages of nature, and the use of the same faculties, should also be equal one amongst another, without subordination and subjection": (*Second Treatise of Government*, ch. ii, sec. 4). "Men, being, as has been said, by nature all free, equal and independent, no one can be put out of his estate, and subjected to the political power of another without his own consent . . . by agreeing with other men to join and unite into a community" (*ibid.*, ch. viii, sec. 95). And see below, pp. 62–63.
[12] See below, p. 61.

Finally, we cannot hope to gain a proper understanding of the English contribution to the common stock of the constitutional doctrine of the rights of man without a critical appreciation of a view which, if accepted, would substantially reduce the significance of that contribution. It has been maintained that the very conception of inalienable and fundamental rights superior to the State was unknown to English legal and political tradition for the reason that the rights of the Englishman were secured only against the executive, not against the legislature; that the successive crises and revolutions made little difference in this respect; and that what happened in 1688 was merely that the absolutism of the Whig Parliament replaced the absolutism of the King. Neither, it has been said, knew or recognized the indefeasible rights of man. This view is only partly true; and that part is not wholly relevant to the issue. In the first instance, the doctrine of the absolute supremacy of Parliament, unrestricted by a higher law, is of comparatively recent origin. It is not a doctrine which Bracton, or Hooker, or Sir Matthew Hale would have accepted.[13] Secondly, that assertion of the supremacy of Parliament must be treated in its historical context. In its primary sense it was a vindication of the right of the subject to be governed, not by the arbitrary power of the King, but by the people through its freely elected representatives; it was one stage in the long process of asserting the right of man to freedom. What, from the point of view of the historian in the twentieth century, may have been the replacement of one kind of arbitrariness by another was an essential stage in a historical process—not to mention the fact that the arbitrariness of Parliament is preferable to the arbitrariness of a king or of a dictator.

Moreover, it is of interest to note that, even in the seventeenth and eighteenth centuries, when the doctrine of the supremacy of Parliament was asserted apparently without reservation, it was often qualified in the writings of the foremost lawyers and political thinkers by the overriding authority of a higher law. Coke laid down in clear terms the doctrine of the supremacy of Parliament: "Of the power

---

[13] "The omnipotence of Parliament was not the orthodox theory of English law, if orthodox at all, even in Hale's time. It was formally adopted, and then not without lip-service to natural law, in Blackstone's Commentaries": Sir Frederick Pollock, in *Law Quarterly Review*, XXXIX (1923), 165.

and jurisdiction of the Parliament, for making laws in proceeding by Bill, it is so transcendant and absolute, as it cannot be confined either for causes or persons within any bonds." [14] But in Doctor Bonham's case he qualified the supremacy of Parliament by making the interpretation of statutes subject to an overriding law of nature. There has been controversy as to whether the precedents on which Coke relied in Doctor Bonham's case justified his conclusion. Some have doubted whether the relevant passage in the judgment of the great lawyer was in fact intended to deny the absolute supremacy of Parliament. But the very controversy is significant.

It is even more so in the case of Blackstone. Was his homily on the law of nature which rendered void an Act of Parliament inconsistent therewith merely lip service, seeing that no lawyer before him had affirmed so emphatically that "the power of parliament is absolute and without control"? [15] Parliament, according to Blackstone, can do "everything that is not naturally impossible." But he thought that to refer to that power as "the omnipotence of parliament" was "a figure rather too bold." And, possibly, his reference to Parliament as being empowered to "do everything that is not naturally impossible" ought to be interpreted in the light of his statement in the preceding chapter that "the principal aim of society is to protect individuals in the enjoyment of those absolute rights which were vested in them by the immutable laws of nature." Is it "naturally possible" for Parliament to divest the subject of rights vested in him by the "immutable laws of nature"? It may not be profitable to engage in a textual interpretation of Blackstone. His insistence on the absolute supremacy of Parliament was probably due to the realization, with which no lawyer can lightly dispense, of the necessity of a supreme power "which must in all government reside somewhere." Blackstone's glorification of the supremacy of Parliament may have been invoked by those in England who sought for legal arguments supporting the claim to impose the will of the Parliament at Westminster upon the rebellious American colonies in matters of taxation and otherwise. But those rebellious colonies relied repeatedly upon Blackstone in asserting those inalienable and absolute rights of man which in his words "the first and primary

[14] *Institutes*, edition of 1671, Part IV, ch. i.   [15] *Commentaries* I. ii. 3.

end of human laws is to maintain and regulate." These rights are the right of personal security, the right of personal liberty, and the right of property. With regard to the latter, the colonies were specially interested in the principle that "no subject of England can be constrained to pay any aids or taxes, even for the defence of the realm or the support of government, but such as are imposed by his own consent, or that of his representatives in parliament." [16] The great constitutional charters of liberty, from the Magna Charta to the Act of Settlement, Blackstone described as a "declaration of our rights and liberties" which, in fact, is the phraseology of the Bill of Rights.[17]

Unlike Blackstone, Locke showed no ambiguity in his position, and to him the American and other declarations of rights are more indebted than to any other writer. His is not merely a defence of freedom against the arbitrariness of the Executive.[18] It is a vindication of the rights of man against the legislature, against the State itself; it is a denial of the ultimate legal sovereignty of the State; it is an assertion of the legal right of rebellion against the State encroaching upon the natural rights of man. These views he does not put forward lightly and without having faced the necessity of a supreme centre of authority within the State.[19] And he puts them forward with a clarity which discourages any attempt at paraphrasing his exposition. He says in his *Second Treatise on Civil Government:*

Though the legislative power, whether placed in one or more, whether it be always in being or only by intervals, though it be the supreme power in every commonwealth; yet, first, it is not, nor can possibly be absolutely arbitrary over the lives and fortunes of the people. For it being but the joint power of every member of the society given up to that person or assembly which is legislator, it can be no more than those persons had in a state of Nature, before they entered into society and gave up to the community; for nobody can transfer to another more power than he has

[16] I. i. 3.
[17] "An Act, declaring the Rights and Liberties of the Subject, and settling the Succession of the Crown."
[18] He had previously been dismissed from Oxford by Charles II.
[19] That necessity was vividly present before the minds of the political thinkers prior to the Revolution of 1688, as may be seen from the emphatic observation of Halifax: "I lay down then as a fundamental, first, that in every constitution there is some power which neither will nor ought to be bounded" ("Political and Miscellaneous Thoughts and Reflections," in his *Works* [London, 1715], pp. 213-214).

in himself, and nobody has an absolute arbitrary power over himself, or over any other, to destroy his own life, or take away the life or property of another. A man, as has been proved, cannot subject himself to the arbitrary power of another; and having in the state of Nature, no arbitrary power over the life, liberty, or possession of another, but only so much as the law of nature gave him for the preservation of himself and the rest of mankind, this is all he doth or can give up to the commonwealth, and by it to the legislative power, so that the legislative can have no more than this.[20]

And he says again, in the same work:

Though in a constituted community standing upon its own basis and acting according to its own nature—that is, acting for the preservation of the community—there can be but one supreme power, which is the legislative, to which all the rest are and must be subordinate, yet the legislative being only a fiduciary power, to act for certain ends, there remains still in the people a supreme power to remove or alter the legislative, when they find the legislative act contrary to the truth reposed in them . . . And thus the community perpetually retains a supreme power of saving themselves from the attempts and designs of any body, even of their legislators, whenever they shall be so foolish or so wicked as to lay and carry on designs against the liberties and properties of the subject. . . . And thus the community may be said in this respect to be always the supreme power, but not as considered under any form of government, because this power of the people can never take place till the government be dissolved.[21]

Paine's disquisition on the Rights of Man is in its essential aspects little more than a repetition or elaboration of the teaching of Locke:

Men are all of one degree and consequently all men are born equal, and with equal Natural Rights. . . . Natural Rights are those which appertain to man in right of his existence. Of this kind are all the intellectual rights, or rights of the mind, and all those rights of acting as an individual for his own comfort and happiness, which are not injurious to the natural right of others.[22]

From these premises two or three certain conclusions will follow: First, that every civil right grows out of a natural right; or, in other words, is a natural right exchanged. Secondly, that civil power properly considered

[20] Ch. xi, sec. 135.   [21] Ch. xiii, sec. 149.
[22] *Rights of Man*, in his *Writings*, ed. M. D. Conway (New York, 1894), II, 311.

as such is made up of the aggregate of that class of the natural rights of man which becomes defective in the individual in point of power, and answers not his purpose, but, when collected to a focus, becomes competent to the purpose of every one. Thirdly, that the power produced from the aggregate of natural rights, imperfect in power in the individual, cannot be applied to invade the natural rights which are retained in the individual, and in which the power to execute is as perfect as the right itself.[23]

However, Paine's contribution lies outside the survey of the English influence upon the American formulations of the rights of man in the early constitutions of States and in the Bill of Rights. Of these American instruments it may be said, without fear of exaggeration, that while their philosophy had largely been formulated by the English exponents of the notion of natural rights, there are few passages in them, especially in the Bill of Rights, which are not either strikingly reminiscent or a practically literal reproduction of some of the English constitutional charters of liberty.[24]

This somewhat detailed discussion of one aspect of the English share in the development of the doctrine of the rights of man is admittedly in the nature of a digression. It was necessary in order to show that the degree of the English influence was not determined by such factors as the absence of an express legal doctrine of natural rights, or the paucity of reliance upon natural law, or the absence of a written constitution, or the eventual acceptance of the doctrine of the supremacy of Parliament. It was determined by causes more fundamental and more enduring. These were a powerful political tradition of freedom conceived, in the words of the Act of Settlement, as "the birthright of the English people"; the enunciation of the principle of natural rights of man by men of the Puritan revolution and by writers of the calibre of Milton, Locke, and Blackstone; and, above all, a succession of statutory charters of personal freedom which, any constitutional doctrine notwithstanding, acquired the character of fundamental laws of the kingdom and which enabled Blackstone to say that "the absolute rights of every

[23] *Ibid.*, p. 307.
[24] In particular in the Bill of Rights. The provision as to the independence of judges derived from the Act of Settlement of 1701 which laid down that judges' commissions should for the future be made *quam diu se bene gesserint* and not *durante beneplacito*.

Englishman (which, taken in a political and extensive sense, are usually called their liberties) as they are founded on nature and reason, so they are coeval with our form of government." [25] They made it possible to secure in practice the rights of man at the time when at the height of the Cromwellian dictatorship the acquittal of Lilburne made Cromwell remark that he regarded the outcome of the trial as a severer blow than a lost battle.

It is reasonable to assume that these fundamental aspects of the English constitutional doctrine may in the long run prove decisive for determining the attitude of this country to an International Bill of the Rights of Man, and not the supposed or actual difficulties such as result from the absence of a written constitution in England or from the doctrine of the absolute supremacy of Parliament. The absence of a written constitution is hardly relevant. The question of codifying the entire constitutional law in the form of a written document does not arise. Parts of it may be and have been frequently reduced to writing, not only in the sphere of the liberties of the subject but also with regard to the very highest matters of the legislative power proper, as in the Parliament Act of 1911 or in the Statute of Westminster of 1931. The supremacy of Parliament and the absence of judicial review of legislation from the point of view of its conformity with the constitution or with the international obligations of Great Britain are factors to be considered in connection with the proposal of an International Bill of the Rights of Man forming an integral part of the law of States. But this is no reason why the implementation of the Bill of Rights within each State should not, if necessary, take place in accordance with the constitutional forms and the traditions of the country concerned. It is possible that the supremacy of Parliament may be deliberately made to yield to the significant innovation implied in an International Bill of the Rights of Man. For the notion of natural and inalienable human rights, to which such a bill would give expression, is in fact a denial of the absolute supremacy of any earthly legislative power.

[25] *Commentaries* i. i.

Part II

THE INTERNATIONAL BILL
OF THE
RIGHTS OF MAN

CHAPTER VI

THE TEXT OF THE BILL

PREAMBLE

WHEREAS the enthronement of the rights of man has been proclaimed to be the purpose of the war waged by the United Nations;

Whereas the United Nations have declared that they were waging war for the defence of life, liberty, independence, and religious freedom, as well as for the preservation of human rights and justice;

Whereas the United Nations have expressed their desire to establish a peace which will assure to all freedom from fear and want;

Whereas the respect of the natural rights of man to freedom and equality before the law is the primary and abiding condition of all lawful government;

Whereas the denial of these rights is and has proved to be a danger to the peace of the world;

Whereas the natural right of man to freedom comprises the right of self-government through persons chosen by and accountable to him;

Whereas, for that reason, the observance of the principles of democracy must, irrespective of the form of government and of the economic system, be placed under the protection and the guarantee of international society;

Whereas the equality of man regardless of nationality, race, and colour demands an equal opportunity of self-government and cultural development;

Whereas the dignity of man, the dictates of justice, and the principle of social solidarity in modern society require that no person shall suffer undeserved want and that the State shall safeguard effectively the right to work under proper conditions of employment, to education, and to social security;

Whereas the sanctity of human personality and its right and duty to develop in freedom to all attainable perfection must be protected by the universal law of mankind through international enactment, supervision and enforcement;

The United Nations of the World now adopt this International Bill of the Rights of Man as part of the fundamental constitution of International Society and of their own States:

PART I

Article 1

The liberty of the person shall be inviolate within the limits of the law.

No person shall be deprived of liberty save by a judgment of a court of law or pending trial in accordance with the law. Detention by purely executive order shall be unlawful in time of peace.

There shall be protection from arbitrary and unauthorized arrest.

The law shall provide against prolonged detention preceding trial, against excessive bail or unreasonable refusal thereof, against denial of adequate safeguards of evidence and procedure in criminal cases, against the refusal of protection in the nature of the writ of habeas corpus, against the retroactive operation of criminal laws, and against inhuman and cruel punishment.

Article 2

No State shall permit slavery, or traffic in slaves, or compulsory labour in any form other than public service, equally incumbent upon all, or as part of punishment pronounced by a court of law.

Article 3

There shall be full freedom of religion.

Article 4

The freedom of speech and expression of opinion in writing and by other means shall not be denied or impaired.

Article 5

There shall be full freedom of association and assembly.

Article 6

The sanctity of the home and the secrecy of correspondence shall be respected.

Article 7

All nationals of the State shall enjoy full equality before the law and equal treatment in all respects by the authorities of the State. In particular, there shall be no discrimination on account of religion, race, colour, language, or political creed.

Aliens shall not be denied the full and equal protection of the preceding articles of this Bill of Rights and of other rights granted to them by the law of the State in which they reside. No alien legally admitted may be expelled except in pursuance of a judicial decision or recommendation as a punishment for offences laid down by law as warranting expulsion.

Article 8

Every person shall be entitled to the nationality of the State where he is born unless and until on attaining majority he declares for the nationality open to him by virtue of descent.

No person shall be deprived of his nationality by way of punishment or deemed to have lost his nationality except concurrently with the acquisition of a new nationality.

Article 9

The right of emigration and expatriation shall not be denied.

PART II

Article 10

No State shall deprive its citizens of the effective right to choose their governments and legislators on a footing of equality, in accordance with the law of the State, in free, secret, and periodic elections.

Article 11

Whenever the political condition or the stage of development of a community which has not yet obtained full political independence or which constitutes a colony or a mandated territory require the continued application of the principle of trusteeship or of mandatory tutelage by another State, such modification of the right of self-government shall be subject to the supervision of and to ultimate control by international authority. There shall be formed for that purpose an International Statute of Peoples under Colonial and Mandatory Government.

Article 12

In States inhabited by a substantial number of persons of a race, language or religion other than those of the majority of the population, persons belonging to such ethnic, linguistic or religious minorities shall have the right to establish and maintain, out of an equitable proportion of the available public funds, their schools and cultural and religious institutions and to use their own language before the courts and other authorities and organs of the State.

Article 13

States shall, within the limits of their economic capacity and development, make effective provision for securing the right to work, to education and to public assistance in case of unemployment, old age, sickness, disablement and other cases of undeserved want.

Article 14

States shall, in co-operation with other States and with the International Labour Organization, make provision for securing just and humane conditions of work.

PART III

Article 15

Every State shall, by appropriate constitutional means, adopt Part I of this International Bill of the Rights of Man as part of its domestic law and constitution. The effect of such adoption shall be to abrogate any existing statute or any other rule of law inconsistent with these Articles of the International Bill of the Rights of Man. They shall not be abrogated or modified, by legislative action or otherwise, save in pursuance of international agreement or authorization.

Article 16

The enforcement of any law safeguarding the legal rights of others or providing for the safety and the welfare of the community shall not be deemed to be inconsistent with the guarantee of the fundamental rights proclaimed in Part I of this International Bill of the Rights of Man.

Article 17

In every State the highest judicial tribunal of the State or a special Constitutional Court of Liberties shall have jurisdiction to pronounce judgment upon the conformity of legislative, judicial or executive action with the provisions of Part I of this International Bill of the Rights of Man.

Article 18

This International Bill of the Rights of Man is hereby declared to be an integral part of the Law of Nations. It is placed under the guarantee of the United Nations of the World. Its observance shall be a matter of concern to all the United Nations.

Article 19

There shall be established within the framework of the political organization of the United Nations of the World a High Commission for the supervision of the observance of the International Bill of the Rights of Man.

The Commission shall consist of independent persons of the highest distinction appointed by the Council of the United Nations. The Commission shall be assisted by a Secretariat appointed by the President of the Commission.

The Commission shall collect information and receive petitions and representations bearing on the observance of the International Bill of the Rights of Man. The Commission shall, in the matter of such petitions and otherwise, communicate with and receive observations from the States concerned. The Commission shall submit annual reports to the Council of the United Nations and, whenever necessary, draw the attention of the Council to such infractions of the Bill of Rights as may call for action by the Council of the United Nations.

The right of individuals and organizations to petition the High Commission in the matter of the observance of this Bill of Rights shall not be denied or impaired.

Article 20

The Council of the United Nations shall be the supreme agency for securing the observance of the International Bill of the Rights of Man.

It shall be the right of any of the United Nations to call the attention of the Council to any infraction of the Bill of Rights.

The Council shall frame such rules of procedure as will best enable it to fulfill its duties as the supreme agency for the enforcement of the International Bill of the Rights of Man.

The Permanent Court of International Justice shall at the request of the Council give an advisory opinion on any question of law relating to the observance of the International Bill of the Rights of Man.

If the Council finds by a majority of three-fourths of its members that there has taken place an infraction of the International Bill of the Rights of Man such as to warrant action by the United Nations, the Council shall make a pronouncement to this effect. If the State in question persists in its refusal to remedy the situation violative of this Bill of Rights, the Council shall take or order such political, economic, or military action as may be deemed necessary to protect the rights of man.

CHAPTER VII

THE LEGAL NATURE OF THE BILL

The International Bill of the Rights of Man as a legal instrument.—
An International Bill of the Rights of Man can be conceived either
as a political declaration embodying a philosophy and principles
of government for the guidance of States and of public opinion or as
a legal instrument creating definite and enforceable legal rights and
duties between States and their nationals and between States themselves. The present Draft of the International Bill of the Rights of Man
is based on the latter conception. An impressive case may be put forward for the adoption of an International Bill of the Rights of Man
as a mere declaration of principle or of policy not intended as a source
of legal obligation. It is arguable that, though lacking in the binding
force of a legal rule, it would still possess the unrivalled authority of a
solemn re-statement of high purpose repeatedly affirmed at a supreme
hour of trial as the main spiritual motive of the greatest war in history;
that it would act as a rallying point for the public opinion of the world;
that it would supply the moral standard of actions and omissions of
governments in coming generations; and that it would be a guide and
beacon in the constant endeavour to maintain the rights of man and to
improve his status. Similar arguments have been put forward in favour
of the American and the French declarations of rights even by those
who were not otherwise impressed by their revolutionary fervour.[1]

It may be questioned whether the undoubted influence of these
instruments can accurately be adduced as pointing to the feasibility
of an International Bill of the Rights of Man conceived as a mere statement of policy and moral purpose. For it was of the essence of the
American and French declarations that, however incompletely realized, they constituted and were intended to constitute the highest
law of the State binding upon its supreme legislative and executive

---

[1] See Dicey, *Lectures on the Relation between Law and Public Opinion in England
during the Nineteenth Century* (1914), p. 309, who points out that although these instruments did not deliver a single Negro from slavery and that although they did not
save a single victim of the terror of the Revolution, they influenced public opinion by
dint of their formal acknowledgment that the sovereign cannot convert might into right.

organs. They were a denial, expressed in terms of law, of the arbitrary supremacy of the State itself. No such effect can be expected from a political declaration, however lofty. Moreover, it may appear doubtful to many whether a declaration affirming the rights of man in terms of principle can be a substantial contribution to the common stock of political and moral ideas. These doubters will insist, not without a show of reason, that the basic ideas of a Declaration of the Rights of Man have become part of the civilized world; that though they have been made temporarily to yield to the tyranny of dictatorship in some countries, they are in no need of any theoretical or formal reaffirmation and that what is required are legal guarantees, embedded in the institutions of positive law and superior to the law of any individual State, against the arbitrariness of power within the State. The criticism from that quarter is likely to go to the length of asserting that a political declaration, however impressive, would constitute a retrogressive step by reason of the inadequacy of its probable effect when compared with the need which gave rise to it. In view of the dangers to which, in the light of experience, the rights of man have been exposed; in view of the menace to which their suppression or danger of suppression exposes the peace of the world; in view of their solemn affirmation as being a major purpose of the war; and in view of the part which they play in the solution of the problem of minorities—a mere declaration, unaccompanied by adequate guarantees of supervision and enforcement, is likely to be regarded as yet another example of the evasion and the concealment typical of international intercourse.

It is possible that that criticism would be less emphatic with regard to what may be called social rights, namely, the right to work, to adequate conditions of work and pay, to education, and to economic security, as set forth in Articles 13 and 14 of the draft. The claim to a legal recognition of these rights is of more recent origin, and their solemn affirmation by the United Nations might be regarded as an advance, even if it were not accompanied by specific international guarantees by way of enforcement. But even in that case the advantage would be regarded by many as questionable unless the declaration were accompanied by an affirmation of an international interest in its fulfillment, of the right of international discussion, of the duty of

States to co-operate in good faith whenever such co-operation is necessary for the upholding and the progressive development of these rights, and of the ultimate right of the society of nations to ensure such co-operation.

The critics of an International Bill of the Rights of Man confined to a declaration of human rights, however widely and generously conceived, would be able to point to a series of solemn declarations of principle which were embodied in international conventions and which gave expression to a general recognition of vital principles, but which have failed to influence the actual practice of States. The solemn declarations of the First and Second Hague conferences in the matter of pacific settlement,[2] of the Covenant of the League of Nations with respect to obligatory arbitration [3] and to freedom of trade and communications,[4] and of the Slavery Conventions of 1919 and 1926 [5] would tend to substantiate that criticism. Past experience would, in the opinion of these critics, lend weight to the assertion that an International Bill of the Rights of Man adopted as a political declaration of principle would be a purely formal and unsubstantial fulfillment of a great principle proclaimed as a major purpose of the War and an easy device for States hitherto bound by minority treaties to achieve freedom from an embarrassing and, in their opinion, humiliating obligation.

It cannot be the object of the comments on the present draft to assess the value and the justification of such criticisms. But the draft is based on the assumption that the International Bill of the Rights of Man can be framed as a legal instrument and that it can, in principle, form part of the international legal order. An analysis of its provisions must contain an incidental, though substantial, answer to the question as to

---

[2] See above, p. 8.

[3] Although the Covenant recognized in Article 12 that the comprehensive categories of disputes enumerated therein were "generally suitable for arbitration," it was the considered view of the Council and of the Assembly that that provision in no way implied an obligation to submit these disputes to the compulsory jurisdiction of the Permanent Court—a view which was contrary to that adopted by the authoritative Committee of Jurists who drafted the Statute of the Court.

[4] See above, p. 8.

[5] In the latter convention the parties, recalling the intention of the signatories of the Convention of Saint-Germain of 1919 to secure the complete suppression of slavery in all its forms, undertook "to bring about progressively and as soon as possible, the complete abolition of slavery in all its forms" (Article 2(b): Manley O. Hudson, *International Legislation* (Washington, 1931), III, 2014.

the extent to which it is calculated to secure acceptance by government.

The International Bill of the Rights of Man as an instrument creating legal rights and obligations.—The International Bill of the Rights of Man is, with regard to the contemplation of the present draft, a legal instrument asserting legal rights and obligations. The obligations are, primarily, those of the States accepting the Bill and binding themselves to observe it. But they are also the obligations of the United Nations as a whole and of each of them separately in so far as they undertake to insist on the observance of the Bill of Rights and, if need be, to enforce it. To that extent the Bill constitutes the recognition not only of the legal interest of the signatories in the observance of its provisions but also of a most comprehensive right of collective supervision, intervention, and enforcement. The rights conferred by the Bill are, secondly, those of the individual. They are not only his rights under the law of his State—a law shaped, adopted, and enforced in accordance with the international obligations of the State. They are contemplated as his rights under international law. For one of the undoubtedly revolutionary innovations of the International Bill of the Rights of Man is to do away with the antiquated doctrine that the individual is the object, and not a subject, of the Law of Nations. Although the direct enforcement of these rights by the individual himself before international tribunals by way of judicial review is not considered feasible,[6] the international character of his rights under the International Bill is given expression both by way of their explicit recognition as an integral part of the law of nations [7] and by the conferment on the individual of another form of international procedural capacity as a means of the realization of the purpose of the Bill of Rights. Predominant among them is the right of petition, which must be safeguarded as a special right enshrined in the International Bill of the Rights of Man.[8]

The International Bill of the Rights of Man as an enforceable part of the law of nations.—Enforceability is of the essence of any rule of law; so is the principle that the person obligated cannot claim the exclusive right of determining whether and to what extent he has com-

------

[6] See below, pp. 184–185 ff.   [7] Article 18 of the Bill.   [8] Article 19, para. 4, of the Bill.

plied with his obligation. This being so, the International Bill of the Rights of Man, if it is to be conceived as an instrument creating legal rights and obligations in the international sphere, must be ultimately enforceable by international remedies. In the present, still rudimentary, stage of international law its obligations are often enforced by the individual action of the aggrieved State, but it follows clearly from the nature and the purpose of the Bill of Rights that its enforcement must, in the last resort, be international in character. This aspect of the Bill of Rights is compatible with the normal and regular enforcement of its clauses by the ordinary agencies of the State.

Secondly, it follows from the legal nature of the Bill of Rights that the question of its observance must ultimately be determined through an international procedure and machinery. It is this feature of the International Bill of the Rights of Man which renders the consideration of the substance of its provisions, as distinguished from their enforcement, a matter of difficulty and delicacy. For it is clear that governments will show less hesitation about the recognition of human rights which are not ultimately subject to international supervision and enforcement. This is also the reason, although in this draft and comment the substance and the enforcement of the Bill of Rights are dealt with separately, these two aspects are interdependent and why they cannot always be discussed one apart from the other.

The legal character of the International Bill of the Rights of Man and the generality of its provisions.—This requirement of enforcement and of ultimate international supervision and control demands and is consistent with the fact that the International Bill of the Rights of Man must to a large extent consist of provisions which are general in character and whose detailed application must be left to the legislation and to the judiciary of the individual State. The International Bill of the Rights of Man cannot prescribe detailed rules of law. It cannot lay down minutely either the procedure or the substantive law by which such rights as the liberty of the person, equality before the law, freedom of association, or the secrecy of correspondence, shall be safeguarded. This must be left to the law of the States. In fact, the constitutions of States leave these details to ordinary legislation. An International Bill of the Rights of Man must follow the same course for the added reason that it applies to a multiplicity of States of differing legal systems, of divergent legal tradition, and of varying stages of development. The wider the circle of States adopting the International Bill of the Rights of Man the more general must be its clauses. The result must be that the degree of protection afforded to the rights of man will differ in various States in such matters as arrest without warrant, liability to search, length of detention pending trial, and so on. Thus, for instance, the writ of habeas corpus has now been adopted in countries other than those within the orbit of Anglo-American common law. But that particular form of protection is unknown in a number of States, and it would be unnecessary and impracticable to impose it upon them. The same applies to the introduction of terminology and concepts peculiar to one country or group of countries like the notion of due process of law—even if the controversy surrounding the latter were not in itself a sufficient deterrent. Some countries may regard the abolition of titles of nobility to be an essential corollary of the principle of equality, but there is no reason for attempting to achieve a uniformity of practice in the matter. Some States, while adhering to the principle of freedom of religion, may, for reasons peculiar to their own history or on general grounds, deem it necessary to impose special restrictions on officers of religion or religious organizations. Such restrictions have often been imposed in order to prevent religion from being used as a cloak for or an instrument of political activity.[9] It could not be the legitimate object of an International Bill

---

[9] The Swiss Constitution of 1874 (as revised up to the end of June, 1921) stated, in Article 50, that the free exercise of religion is guaranteed "within limits compatible with public order and morality." It then proceeded to lay down that the cantons and the confederation may take measures to prevent encroachments by ecclesiastical authorities upon the rights of citizens and of the State; that no bishopric may be created within Swiss territory without the approval of the Confederation; that the Order of Jesuits, and societies affiliated with it, may not be admitted into any part of Switzerland, and that all activities in church and school are forbidden to their members (Article 51); and that the founding of new religious houses or religious orders, and the re-establishment of those which have been suppressed, are forbidden (Article 52). The Mexican constitution of 1917 provides not only that churches, irrespective of creed, shall in no case have legal capacity to acquire, hold, or administer real property or loans made on such real property (Article 27); it prohibits ministers of religion to criticize, either in public or in private, the fundamental laws of the country, or to vote, or to be eligible for office, or to assemble for political purposes. It is of interest to note that Duguit (*Traité de droit constitutionnel*, V [1925], 591–592) and others assert emphatically that the right of religious bodies to acquire property for the purpose of fulfilling their legitimate tasks is of the essence of religious freedom.

of the Rights of Man to forbid such measures of protection deemed necessary by the State.

It will be clear from what has been said above that, so long as the general and ultimate power of international supervision and enforcement is recognized, neither the generality of the provisions of the International Bill of the Rights of Man nor its normal application by the agencies of the State, would derogate from its character as an instrument embodying legal rights and obligations.

The Bill of Rights as a codification of generally accepted principles of law.—Neither would the legal nature of the International Bill of the Rights of Man be open to question for the reason that many of its clauses do not imply any limitation of the sovereignty of States, inasmuch as these are declaratory of what may be described as the general principles of constitutional law of civilized States in the matter of the rights of man. There ought to be little doubt that there already exists a body of law which may properly be so described. A survey of the constitutions of most countries shows that in the matter of the recognition of the fundamental rights of the individual there is a wide uniformity of law and practice. This applies in particular to provisions safeguarding personal liberty, freedom of religion, of speech, of opinion, and of association, and equality before the law. That uniformity is often shown in almost identical terminology.

The International Bill of the Rights of Man as a radical innovation in international law.—Although the International Bill of the Rights of Man, as here proposed, is to a large extent an affirmation of the general principles of constitutional law of civilized States in the matter of the fundamental rights of man, it is not exclusively so. In part, it amounts to a radical innovation in international practice and to a surrender—more formidable in formal appearance than in substance—of the sovereign rights of the State. The main features of that innovation may be here conveniently noted:

a) Even with regard to those parts of the Bill which do not go beyond a declaration of the existing law, States would agree to a limitation of their sovereignty inasmuch as they would deprive themselves of the faculty of abrogating or modifying unilaterally what will henceforth have become part of international law.

b) Similarly, even with regard to those parts of the Bill of Rights which are in fact declaratory of the existing law and which would normally be administered by the agencies of the State, the Bill would signify a measure of surrender of sovereignty, inasmuch as States would consent to international supervision and enforcement. The most intricate and the most intimate aspects of national life would become the subject matter of international concern and of international guarantees.

c) The Bill of Rights would include provisions going beyond a solemn registration and affirmation of an existing body of law. In virtue of the acknowledgement of the right to self-government conceived not only as an expression of the principle of democracy, but also as referring to entire peoples and communities under colonial and mandatory government, it would amount to an abdication, on the part of the governing States, of their right to exclusive and permanent political control. It would include the duty to treat cultural and linguistic minorities in accordance with definite principles. Moreover, the Bill would contain an explicit, though necessarily elastic, recognition of obligations in the field of economic and social rights.

d) Finally, the International Bill of the Rights of man would include the obligation to participate in the international supervision and enforcement of its clauses.

It is clear, therefore, that the International Bill of the Rights of Man, conceived as one of the bases of the future international order, cannot be accepted without a substantial sacrifice by States of their freedom of action. The problem which it would purport to solve is nothing short of the twin tasks of protecting human freedom against the State and of securing international peace by ensuring lawful government within the State. Such an end cannot be achieved at a nominal price.

CHAPTER VIII

THE BASES OF THE BILL

PREAMBLE

WHEREAS THE ENTHRONEMENT of the rights of man has been proclaimed to be the purpose of the war waged by the United Nations;

Whereas the United Nations have declared that they were waging war for the defence of life, liberty, independence, and religious freedom, as well as for the preservation of human rights and justice;

Whereas the United Nations have expressed their desire to establish a peace which will assure to all freedom from fear and want;

Whereas the respect of the natural right of man to freedom and equality before the law is the primary and abiding condition of all lawful government;

Whereas the denial of these rights is and has proved to be a danger to the peace of the world;

Whereas the natural right of man to freedom comprises the right of self-government through persons chosen by and accountable to him;

Whereas, for that reason, the observance of the principles of democracy must, irrespective of the form of government and of the economic system, be placed under the protection and the guarantee of international society;

Whereas the equality of man regardless of nationality, race and colour demands an equal opportunity of self-government and cultural development;

Whereas the dignity of man, the dictates of justice, and the principle of social solidarity in modern society require that no person shall suffer undeserved want, and that the State shall safeguard effectively the right to work under proper conditions of employment, to education, and to social security;

Whereas the sanctity of human personality and its right and duty to develop in freedom to all attainable perfection must be protected by the universal law of mankind through international enactment, supervision, and enforcement;

The United Nations of the World now adopt this International Bill of the Rights of Man as part of the fundamental constitution of International Society and of their own States.

THE Preamble to the International Bill of the Rights of Man, as here set forth, may appear to some to be of forbidding length. But it has seemed proper that an international enactment of this character should propound in some detail the philosophy on which it is based. When the American colonies declared their independence in 1776, the authors of the declaration deemed it wise, out of respect for the "decent opinion of mankind," to set forth what they declared to be the self-evident truths from which they derived the right to act.[1] The principles which they formulated proved to be a factor of a significance transcending the historic event which gave rise to their enunciation. The effective international recognition of the rights of man would be a landmark in human history. It would be proper that it should be preceded by a statement of the philosophy underlying the fundamental enactment bearing on the relation of man and State in the new international order.

The declarations of the United Nations.—The first three paragraphs of the Preamble are a paraphrase and a recapitulation of some of the principal pronouncements of the governments and of the leaders of the United Nations defining the major purposes of the struggle in which they have been engaged. The case for an International Bill of the Rights of Man rests on considerations more permanent and more persuasive than declarations of war and peace aims made by governments during the period of hostilities. But such declarations are inspired by ideas and ideals whose validity is higher than that of legal promises and obligations and which are expressive of aspirations of individuals and of peoples more enduring than advantages of political strategy in any given war.

The first authoritative pronouncement made in the course of the war and directly relevant to an international enactment of the rights of man is contained in the Annual Message of President Roosevelt to Congress of January 6, 1941, in which he formulated the four freedoms. These were:

---

[1] "We hold these truths to be self-evident, that all men are created equal, that they are endowed by their Creator with certain unalienable Rights, that among these are Life, Liberty and the pursuit of Happiness. That to secure these rights, Governments are instituted among Men, deriving their just powers from the consent of the governed."—From the American Declaration of Independence.

The first is freedom of speech and expression—everywhere in the world.

The second is freedom of every person to worship God in his own way—everywhere in the world.

The third is freedom from want—which translated into world terms, means economic understanding which will secure to every nation a healthy peace-time life for its inhabitants—everywhere in the world.

The fourth is freedom from fear—which, translated into world terms, means a world-wide reduction of armaments to such a point and in such a thorough fashion that no nation will be in a position to commit an act of physical aggression against any neighbor—anywhere in the world. . . .

In the Atlantic Charter, August 14, 1941, the Prime Minister of Great Britain and the President of the United States made known "certain common principles in the national policies of their respective countries on which they base their hopes for a better future of the world." In this document they proclaimed, among other things:

5. They desire to bring about the fullest collaboration between all nations in the economic field, with the object of securing for all improved labour standards, economic advancement and social security.

6. After the final destruction of Nazi tyranny, they hope to see established a peace which will afford to all nations the means of dwelling in safety within their own boundaries, and which will afford assurance that all the men in all the lands may live out their lives in freedom from fear and want.

The Atlantic Charter was not intended as an exhaustive formulation of the rights of man to be secured by the peace settlement. It was supplemented, in part, in the Presidential Message to Congress of September 2, 1941. The President said:

It is also unnecessary for me to point out that the declaration of principles includes of necessity the world need for freedom of religion and freedom of information. No society of the world organized under the announced principles could survive without these freedoms which are a part of the whole freedom for which we strive.

The Declaration of the United Nations of January 1, 1942, in which they pledged themselves to a common prosecution of the war and to a common peace, gave expression, in its recitals, to the conviction of the United Nations that "complete victory over their enemies is essential to defend life, liberty, independence and religious freedom, and to preserve human rights and justice in their own lands as well as in other lands."

The wording of the first paragraph of the Preamble follows the phraseology of a Message addressed on October 29, 1942, by the Prime Minister of Great Britain to a meeting of protest organized by the World Jewish Congress. He spoke of the time "when this world's struggle ends with the enthronement of human rights." [2]

The International Bill of the Rights of Man as a declaration of the natural rights of man.—The reference, in paragraphs 4 and 6 of the Preamble, to the natural right of man to freedom and equality, may appear to some to introduce an unnecessary element of theoretical controversy. It is likely to give rise to the objection that there are no rights of man apart from the positive law of the State. An attempt to answer this objection was made in the introductory part of this book, where the reciprocal relations of the law of nature, of the law of nations, and of the rights of man were discussed at some length. The denial of the proposition that the fundamental rights of man come from the State and the State only is one of the basic assumptions of the philosophy underlying the International Bill of the Rights of Man. Its very essence is to secure their survival even if the State should become minded to trample upon them. The notion that all rights come from the State and that there are no rights unless they are recognized by it may be sufficient and convenient for the limited purposes of argument before municipal courts—for it may, on the whole, be true that only such law as comes from the State is enforceable by municipal courts. But that notion is as utterly inadequate as a general jurisprudential proposition as it is inacceptable in the sphere of morals and politics. The view that there is no higher law above the State—and it matters little whether we refer to that higher law as the law of nature or by any other name—is, in the long run, a glorification of force. It reduces the State—and law—to a mere instrumentality of power free from the

---

[2] *The Times*, London, October 30, 1942. It is of interest to note the use of the same turn of phrase by Gladstone. He said: "The greatest triumph of our time will be the enthronement of the idea of public right as governing the idea of European politics" (as quoted in *Speeches by the Earl of Oxford and Asquith* [New York, 1927], p. 218).

bonds of any overriding moral norm.[3] It is, of course, in the long run incompatible with any working or consistent conception of international law.

There are reasons which explain the opposition to the notion of the natural rights of man. One of them is that it has often been used as a cloak to conceal the advocacy of vested interests against the cause of progress. The answer to this criticism is that this has been the fate of many other beneficent ideas; there is no court or authority which can prevent that. The second, and more weighty, objection is that the idea of natural rights has often been treated as an alternative to changes in the law and that it has caused a vague, confused, and controversial form of words to be regarded as a convenient substitute for remedial legislation. This objection cannot apply to the reference, in the International Bill of the Rights of Man, to the natural rights of man. For it is the very purpose of the Bill of Rights to translate the natural rights of man into positive law of a high degree of effectiveness. The law of the State is not a purpose unto itself, but an instrument for realizing the welfare of the individual as the ultimate unit of all law. It is proper that international law, in embodying the rights of man in the form of a positive international enactment, should give recognition to that ultimate source and justification of legal authority.

These are the reasons which have prompted the insertion in the Bill of Rights of the reference to the natural rights of man. This is a case in which the advantages of an express recognition of a principle outweigh the drawbacks of any resulting controversy. In acknowledging that "the respect of the natural right of man to freedom and equality before the law is the primary and abiding condition of all lawful government" the signatories of the International Bill of the Rights of Man would be making a powerful contribution to the restoration of the authority of the State as a moral agency. A gesture of this

[3] This subject was the cause of one of the very few disagreements between Sir Frederick Pollock and Mr. Justice Holmes. The former described the view, apparently held by Mr. Justice Holmes, that there is no natural law of which lawyers can properly take cognizance, as denying any moral basis of law: *The Holmes-Pollock Letters*, ed. M. De W. Howe (Cambridge, Mass., 1941), I, 274–275. It is perhaps proper to surmise that the "inarticulate premise" of the attitude of Mr. Justice Holmes was not due to any uncritical adherence to the tenets of analytical jurisprudence, but rather to his experience of the manner in which before the Supreme Court advocates of natural rights relied on them in opposition to progressive measures of social legislation.

kind would provide a suitable accompaniment to the liquidation of dictatorships whose philosophy of government was, actually and admittedly, based on the denial of the natural rights of man.

The international guarantee of the rights of man as a condition of the peace of the world.—The recognition and the guarantee by the society of nations of the fundamental rights of man would constitute not only an attempt of utmost significance to place the government of man on a basis more enduring and more consistent with the notion of right than the physical power of the State. An International Bill of the Rights of Man would have a more immediate purpose and implication. The Preamble puts on record the conviction, abundantly substantiated by experience, that the denial of the fundamental rights of freedom, of equality, and of government by consent "is and has proved to be a danger to the peace of the world." That experience was given expression by President Wilson in words which merit quotation. He said: "No peace can last, or ought to last, which does not recognize and accept the principle that governments derive their just powers from the consent of the governed." [4] It must now be regarded as axiomatic that tyranny and dictatorship are in themselves a danger to international peace. Their essence is a denial of law, as generally conceived, not only within their borders, but also outside the confines of their States. Law is for them essentially a function of politics; it admits of no universality such as is the basis of a peaceful international order. International law has been for the Germany of the Third Reich—and for some German writers before that—merely "external State law" (*äusseres Staatsrecht*). It was defined by German writers as an "intercorporative law of co-ordination" built on the principle of racial consanguinity.

Politically, aggression and concentration on supposed external danger is the natural ally of a system which lacks the natural cohesion of a law based on consent. It is not an accident that after the first World War the active refutation of obligations of pacific settlement and

---

[4] *President Wilson's State Papers and Addresses* (New York, 1918), p. 353. And see the passage in the historic address to Congress on April 2, 1917, in which he formally took up the challenge of Germany. He said: "The world must be made safe for democracy. Its peace must be planted upon the tested foundations of political liberty": *ibid.*, p. 379.

collective security came from Italy, Germany, and Japan. Democracies have so far lacked that sense of historical continuity and political foresight which are necessary for the organization of peace and of prevention of war. In the absence of clear and unequivocal international obligations democratically elected governments are prone to act on the words of the prayer: "Give us peace in our day, O Lord," without regard to the price in terms of future peace and security. But this recognition of the shortcomings of democratic States as active and conscious instruments of peace must not degenerate—as it often does —into the superficial assertion that in the matter of avoidance of war and the observance of international obligations of peace there is no difference between dictatorships and States based on freedom and government by consent. Overwhelming experience points to the contrary. The securing of the rights of man is an essential condition and requirement of international peace, and it would be proper to include in the Preamble to the Bill of Rights an explicit affirmation of that fact.

The right to self-government and the international guarantee of democracy.—The right of man to political freedom conceived as "the right of self-government through persons chosen by and accountable to him" is an assumption of freedom so fundamental that, in the words of the Preamble, "the observance of the principles of democracy must, irrespective of the form of government and of the economic system, be placed under the protection and the guarantee of international society." This guarantee is one of the salient features of the Bill of Rights. It applies, of course, to all provisions of the Bill. But an international guarantee of democratic rule—as distinguished from the guarantee of the stability of particular democratic governments—is an innovation so striking and radical that it must be expressed in the Preamble as one of the principal purposes of the Bill of Rights.

The right to political independence and the principle of trusteeship.—The same applies to the recognition of the eventual right to self-government of semi-independent communities and of peoples at present under colonial and mandatory tutelage—a recognition coupled with the acknowledgment of the position of trusteeship on the part of the States now governing these peoples. Freedom, political and other, cannot be limited to some peoples; its authority and validity depend upon the full admission of its universality. The recognition of these principles cannot, as will be seen, be a mere gesture. Although it does not imply the international administration of these territories, the principle of trusteeship implies the substantive factors of international supervision and of international interest in the gradual realization of self-government and, ultimately, of independence for the peoples in question.

The social and economic rights of man.—Finally, the International Bill of the Rights of Man must recognize the connection between political freedom and economic freedom, between legal equality and economic and social equality of opportunity. That connection has been gradually admitted since the French Revolution. It has formed, increasingly and conspicuously, part of the declarations and statements bearing on the final objects of the War. It was fully recognized as an essential condition of peace, at the end of the First World War, in the introductory part of the Statute of the International Labour Organization in Part XIII of the Peace Treaties. The words of Section I of Part XIII may be suitably recalled in this context:

Whereas the League of Nations has for its object the establishment of universal peace, and such peace can be established only if it is based upon social justice; And whereas conditions of labour exist involving such injustice, hardship and privation to large numbers of people as to produce unrest so great that the peace and the harmony of the world are imperilled. . . . The High Contracting Parties, moved by sentiments of justice and humanity as well as by the desire to secure the permanent peace of the world, agree to the following . . .

The agreement was to establish the International Labour Organization. In Article 23 (a) of the Covenant the Parties undertook to "endeavour to secure and to maintain fair and humane conditions of labour for men, women and children, both in their own countries and in all countries to which their commercial and industrial relations extend." The objects of the International Bill of the Rights of Man, as here proposed, go beyond these, in law, imperfect obligations. In the first instance, they are not limited to the improvement of conditions of work; their purpose is to safeguard man from undeserved want generally and to assure to him the right to work, to education, and to social security. Secondly, the Bill of Rights not only establishes the principle of international concern in the realization of these social and economic rights of man. It bases that international concern on the individual and collective right of the signatories of the bill to insist, within the framework of appropriate international organs of supervision and, if need be, of enforcement, upon the fulfilment of the social and economic clauses of the Bill of Rights.

The rights of man as the enforceable law of mankind.—The penultimate paragraph of the Preamble is intended to express the central philosophy and purpose of the Bill of Rights. In the last resort it is not an instrument either of the preservation of peace or of any individualistic view of politics and ethics. It is an affirmation of the highest duty of man "to develop in freedom to all attainable perfection." The rights of man follow from that most fundamental of all duties. That duty can only be fulfilled in and through freedom—legal, social, and economic. The purpose of the State is to realize that freedom. The highest function of international society is to ensure the fulfilment of that purpose on the part of the State. In this respect, more than in any other, will the new international law approximate to the law of humanity.

CHAPTER IX

THE SUBSTANCE OF THE BILL

THE SUCCEEDING PAGES contain a comment on the provisions of Parts I and II of the Bill of Rights. Part III is concerned with the implementation, supervision, and enforcement of the Bill of Rights both by national and international agencies. It is convenient here to draw attention to the major difference between Parts I and II. Part I enumerates those fundamental rights of freedom in the wider sense which the signatories undertake to incorporate as integral parts of their law and constitution (Articles 15 and 16) and which, subject to supervision and eventual enforcement by international organs (Part III), will be normally given effect by the municipal courts of States to the exclusion of any procedure of international judicial review. These are the rights of personal freedom (Article 1), the prohibition of slavery, of slave traffic, and of forced labour (Article 2), freedom of religion (Article 3), freedom of speech and opinion (Article 4), freedom of association and assembly (Article 5), the right to sanctity of the home and of freedom of correspondence (Article 6), the right to equality before the law (Article 7), the right to a nationality (Article 8), and the right of emigration and expatriation (Article 9). Part II enumerates what may be called the political, cultural, economic, and social rights of freedom. These include the right to free government, *i.e.*, to government by consent (Article 10), the rights of semi-independent peoples and of communities under colonial and mandatory government (Article 11), the cultural rights of national minorities (Article 12), and the economic and social rights to work under proper conditions of employment, to equal opportunity of education, and to security from undeserved want (Articles 13 and 14). These rights are not of the same nature as the rights of Part I, inasmuch as they are not normally either capable of or suitable for enforcement by legal action before municipal tribunals of States. The reasons for that differential treatment follow clearly from the character of the rights in question. They are explained in more detail in Part III.

PERSONAL FREEDOM

Article 1

The liberty of the person shall be inviolate within the limits of the law.

No person shall be deprived of liberty save by a judgment of a court of law or pending trial in accordance with the law. Detention by purely executive order shall be unlawful in time of peace.

There shall be protection from arbitrary and unauthorized arrest.

The law shall provide against prolonged detention preceding trial, against excessive bail or unreasonable refusal thereof, against denial of adequate safeguards of evidence and procedure, against the refusal of protection in the nature of the writ of *habeas corpus*, against the retroactive operation of criminal laws, and against inhuman and cruel punishment.

Personal freedom, that is, freedom from arbitrary physical restraint on the part of governmental authority, is the first claim of man in his struggle against the arbitrariness of the State. It is often maintained that the practice of declarations of rights and of bills of rights owes its origin to the claims of religious freedom in the seventeenth century and to the assertion, in this connection, of inalienable rights of man lying altogether outside the province of the State. This view is only partially true. In the history of fundamental rights and liberties the safeguards against arbitrary physical restraint occupy the first place. The principal clauses of the Magna Charta, whatever changes the assessment of its significance may have undergone in the course of time, were concerned with personal liberty. It is through them and because of them that the very notion of rights of the individual against the power of the State struck deep roots in European consciousness. It was not until 1679 that the ancient writ of habeas corpus became, in the Habeas Corpus Act, a powerful instrument of protection of the subject. But in the long period between the Magna Charta and the Habeas Corpus Act the idea of the liberty of the subject was kept alive in the repeated confirmations of the charter of 1215. It was only on that physical, but indispensable, foundation of security of life and limb that liberty of religion and of opinion could be successfully vindicated. The liberty of the person is the basis of other liberties; without it other freedoms, however eloquently proclaimed, must be unreal. The right to personal freedom figures invariably in the enumeration of fundamental rights in written constitutions, including those of States whose governments wield absolute powers.[1] For this reason the absence of any direct reference to personal freedom in the Atlantic Charter can be explained only on the assumption that that document was not intended as an exhaustive enumeration of the rights of man.[2] Recent history has shown that the necessity for safeguarding personal freedom in its primary and oldest connotation, namely, freedom from arbitrary physical restraint, is by no means obsolete. No passing delicacy or difficulty of the political situation or of internal policy of any given State ought to stand in the way of its solemn reaffirmation. Such reaffirmation must include, in such detail as the world-wide scope of the Bill of Rights permits, the principal safeguards of personal freedom. The Bill of Rights cannot prescribe the details of these safeguards. These must be a matter for the municipal law of States. There is no escape from the dilemma that the liberty of the person must, like any other fundamental right, be inviolate only within the limits of the law.

Prohibition of administrative detention.—The Bill of Rights must, in the first instance, enact an express prohibition of detention, in time of peace, by purely executive order. No civilized community ought, except in case of an emergency amounting to a state of war, to permit summary deprivation of liberty by the executive authority. The principle, which was unsuccessfully asserted in Darnel's case but which the Petition of Right transformed into a clear principle of law, that the "command of the King" is not a valid reason for detention, must be fully recognized by the law of all signatories of the International Bill of the Rights of Man. The same applies to so-called protective custody in the form of concentration camps or otherwise, decreed by the police or any other executive organ.

Although, as mentioned, the Bill of Rights cannot lay down detailed regulations, it would be in accordance with the spirit of the prohibition of purely administrative detention if such States as have not yet done

[1] Article 127 of the Constitution of Soviet Russia of 1936 provides: "The citizens of the U.S.S.R. are guaranteed inviolability of the person. No person may be placed under arrest except by decision of a court or with the sanction of a procurator." Article 8 of the Portuguese Constitution of 1933 lays down: "The following constitute the rights and individual guarantees of Portuguese citizens:—(1) The right to life and personal inviolability."
[2] See above, p. 85.

so were to substitute a judicial for an administrative procedure in connection with the law relating to lunacy, juvenile delinquency, and the regulation of prostitution.

Protection from arbitrary arrest.—While the prohibition of imprisonment by administrative action refers to detention of a continuous character, the Bill of Rights must also provide safeguards against arbitrary and unauthorized acts of arrest. These safeguards must be of a general nature not only because uniformity in this matter is neither existent nor necessary, but also because various countries may find it desirable in the future to adapt the law in this matter to rapidly changing social conditions. Thus, for instance, the common-law rule that an officer making an arrest by virtue of a warrant must be in possession of the warrant when making the arrest is obsolete under modern conditions; it has in many States in the United States been modified by the rule authorizing the officer to arrest any person for whose arrest he knows that a warrant has been issued. Similarly, the common-law rule that an officer can make an arrest without a warrant for a felony, but not for a misdemeanour (except for one amounting to a breach of the peace and committed in his presence) is clearly inapplicable to modern conditions.[3] In Great Britain statutes have been passed from time to time with regard to various misdemeanours giving the police the power to arrest without a warrant. In France the *juges d'instruction*, in apparent disregard of articles 95 and 96 of the *Code d'instruction criminelle*, which require that the warrant must name or clearly designate the person to be apprehended, have adopted the practice of issuing to police officers warrants signed in blank. Modern conditions, in particular the growth of vast and crowded cities, may necessitate an adaptation of the law of arrest in such a way as to reconcile it not only with the liberty of the person but also with requirements of security and suppression of crime. It is possible that the main aspect of protection of personal liberty may to a large extent shift from unauthorized arrest to illegal prolongation thereof and to administrative detention. For these reasons it is clear that, apart from laying down the principle that there shall be protection from arbitrary arrest, the Bill of Rights ought, subject to the residuary international safeguards, to leave to

[3] See S. B. Warner, "Modern Trends in the American Law of Arrest," *Canadian Bar Review*, XXI (1943), 124 ff.

national courts and national public opinion the task of protecting the
liberty of the citizen in this respect. There is evidence that in democratic countries the courts and other authorities are conscious of the
importance of this issue.[4] It is doubtful whether any useful purpose
can be served by prescribing in the Bill of Rights uniform procedural
and other details, such as the period which must elapse between arrest
and a formal charge. This ought to be and has, as a rule, been done
in national constitutions and ordinary laws.[5] The clause in the Bill of
Rights laying down that "there shall be protection from arbitrary and

[4] See, for an interesting example, *People* v. *Scalisi,* 324 Ill. 131, 148, decided by the
Supreme Court of Illinois, where the court, in a case involving notorious criminals,
upheld the common law rule that a person resisting illegal arrest is guilty of homicide,
not of murder. The court emphasized that "to most citizens the right of liberty is as
sacred as life itself" and referred to "these fervent words of Patrick Henry: 'Give me
liberty or give me death.'" In France the practice of magistrates in issuing warrants in
blank has been severely criticised. See Duguit, *op. cit.,* V, 33 ff. But it is significant
that judicial practice has given an extensive interpretation of Article 106 of the Code
which authorizes arrest without a warrant and by any person in case the culprit is
caught in the act of committing a felony or when pursued by a hue and cry—but, in
both instances, only in the case of a felony involving a penalty which is *afflictive et
infamante.* In practice the courts have dispensed with the latter requirement. Moreover, Article 10 of the *Code d'instruction criminelle,* which is regarded by many
writers as contrary to the guarantee of individual liberty in the Declaration of 1789
and is still in force, confers in effect wide powers of arrest upon departmental prefects
and the prefect of the police in Paris.
[5] Article 78 of the Constitution of Denmark of 1915 (as amended in 1920) provides:
"Every individual who is arrested shall, within twenty-four hours, be brought before
a judge. If he cannot be immediately released, the judge shall decree by an order stating
the reason and made as soon as possible, at the latest within three days, whether he
should be detained, and if he should be released on bail, the nature and the amount of
such bail shall be fixed by the judge.
"A special appeal by the interested party from the order so made by the judge may
at once be taken to the Superior Court."
Article 97 of the Polish Constitution of 1921 provides: "Limitations on liberty, particularly personal examination (*'la revision personnelle'*) and arrest, are only permissible in cases provided by law and according to the method fixed by law, and in
pursuance of a judicial order.
"If, in any case, the judicial order cannot be produced immediately, it must be
transmitted within forty-eight hours and must state the reasons for the examination or
arrest.
"Persons who have been arrested and to whom the reasons for arrest have not been
communicated within forty-eight hours in writing over the signatures of the judicial
authorities shall immediately be restored to liberty."
Article 56 of the Constitution of Peru of 1933 (as amended in 1936) provides: "No
one may be detained except on a written warrant, with a reason assigned, from a
competent judge or from the authorities entrusted with the preservation of public
order, except in cases of arrest *flagrante delicto,* and in any event the detained person
must be brought, within 24 hours or in the interval of time allowed for distance, before
the proper court, which shall order his release or issue a warrant of imprisonment in the
period which the law indicates."

unauthorized arrest" is intended to impose upon States the obligation to possess or to enact appropriate law or legislation.

Detention preceding trial.—The principle that no person shall be deprived of liberty except by virtue of a judgment of a court of law must obviously be subject to the exception of detention pending trial. But detention pending trail may become an instrument of oppression, and the International Bill of the Rights of Man, following the precedent of the Bill of Rights of 1689 and of the American Bill of Rights, must establish the principle, to be expressed in greater detail by national legislation, that bail must not be unreasonably withheld or excessive, when it can be granted, and that detention pending trial must not be unduly prolonged.[6]

The protection of the writ of habeas corpus.—The effective adoption of these safeguards against arbitrary and unauthorized arrest and against purely administrative imprisonment would, in essence, be tantamount to a large extent to securing the advantages of the old procedural remedy of the common law, namely, of the writ of habeas corpus. Ought that remedy to be incorporated *eo nomine* in the International Bill of the Rights of Man? A number of factors militate in favour of an affirmative answer to that question. These are, in particular, the historical influence of the writ of habeas corpus on the development of the idea of freedom in the world and the fact that a number of countries outside the common law system have adopted it expressly or in substance.[7] On the other hand, it would not be in accordance with the objects of the Bill of Rights to use it for the purpose of imposing upon States a uniformity of criminal procedure. These considerations explain the wording of

[6] The draft of a law which the French Government submitted in 1924 to the French Chamber shows the possibilities of a thorough legislative regulation of the subject. According to the draft, the accused is entitled to temporary release within five days after having been interrogated by the *juge d'instruction* unless the latter upholds the arrest by a decision for which reasons must be given and against which the accused can appeal. That decision is valid only for twenty days. Any further detention, for a period which in any case must not exceed six months, can only be ordered by a collective decision of a special judicial body (*chambre des mises en accusation*).

[7] See, for instance, Article 23 of the Brazilian Constitution of 1934: "Habeas corpus shall be granted wherever anybody shall suffer or be threatened with violence or coercion in his liberty, by illegality or abuse of power." Article 69 of the Peruvian Constitution of 1933 provides: "All individual and social rights recognised by the constitution admit of the action of habeas corpus." Article 20(4) of the Constitution of Portugal of 1933 provides: "The exceptional safeguard of habeas corpus may be used against an abuse of authority in the circumstances prescribed in a special law."

the draft, which lays upon the State the obligation to provide against the denial of the protection *in the nature of* the writ of habeas corpus.[8]

The right to trial by jury.—The same considerations would seem to apply to the right to trial by jury in criminal cases. That right, to an extent comparable with the adoption of the writ of habeas corpus, has become part of the judicial system of most countries. It is grounded in the view that the sanctity of human personality requires that life and freedom shall be protected by safeguards even higher than judicial impartiality. So widespread has been the adoption of the system of trial by jury that the question arises whether it ought not to be proclaimed as a general legal principle, equally binding upon all States, and whether States which have not for various reasons adopted it so far should not accept it as part of the system embodied in the International Bill of the Rights of Man. However, it must be remembered that the exclusion of trial by jury is not confined to countries which do not possess a democratic system of government. Thus, in Europe trial by jury has been abolished not only in Italy and Russia but also in Holland, in democratic Germany, in 1924, and in the Swiss cantons of Berne and Basel. For the purposes of the present draft the balance of advantage seemed to be in favour of not including trial by jury among the essential personal rights.

Safeguards of evidence and procedure in criminal trials.—The American Bill of Rights contained, in the fifth and sixth amendments, detailed provisions for adequate safeguards of evidence and procedure in the course of criminal trials. These included the right of the accused

[8] It must be a matter for consideration to what extent it would be feasible to insert in the Bill a provision such as that encountered in the American Bill of Rights and in the constitutions of many States of the Union against the abrogation or suspension of the Bill of Rights except when public safety so requires in case of rebellion or invasion. The abrogation or suspension, in time of peace, of that fundamental remedy is no mere procedural measure; it amounts to a challenge to a substantive right and to an attempt at an arbitrariness against which, it may be urged, the safeguards of the Bill may properly be invoked. However, the matter raises the difficult question of the relation between the declaration of martial law, an important feature of which is the power of arrest and detention without warrant, and the suspension of the writ of habeas corpus. It is also connected with the even more intricate problem of the temporary suspension of constitutional guarantees in general by a proclamation of a state of siege and otherwise. These matters have been omitted, not without some hesitation, from the present draft. It is clear, however, that the question of any permanent suspension of constitutional guarantees safeguarded by the Bill of Rights is ultimately within the province of international supervision as here envisaged.

to be informed of the nature and cause of the charge; to be confronted with the witnesses against him; to have compulsory process for obtaining witnesses in his favour; to have the assistance of counsel for his defence; not to "be subject for the same defence to be put in jeopardy of life and limb"; and not be compelled to be a witness against himself. Some modern constitutions contain similar provisions. These safeguards must naturally vary from country to country; they must be adapted to the peculiarities of evidence and procedure in each of them. But the general principle is capable of a uniform formulation as here proposed. Without it the safeguards of the Bill of Rights would be deficient in a vital respect.

Prohibition of retroactive operation of criminal laws.—The experience of dictatorships has shown that the reasons for the prohibition enacted in the French Declaration of 1789 and in the American Constitution against retroactive operation of criminal laws have not become obsolete. Retroactive legislation may, in the sphere of criminal law, become a powerful weapon of tyranny cloaking arbitrariness in the garb of law. It is especially violative of personal liberty when it is indefinite and when its application is left to the individual discretion of the judge. This happened in Germany, in 1933, when judges were empowered to punish not only actual violations of the law, but also acts which according to the healthy sentiment of the people, as interpreted by the judges, deserve punishment. Most modern constitutions include provisions against the retroactive operation of the criminal law.[9]

Prohibition of cruel and inhuman punishment.—Recent experience has shown that the prohibition, in the words of the Eighth Amendment

[9] For an emphatic statement of this principle see, for instance, Article 57 of the Peruvian Constitution of 1933: "No one shall be condemned for an act or omission which, at the time it is committed is not qualified in an express and unequivocal manner as a punishable offence . . ." See also Article 16 of the German Weimar Constitution. It is a reasonable interpretation of the prohibition of retroactivity of criminal legislation that it is intended to prevent probably only such retroactive criminal laws as are to the prejudice of the accused—except, perhaps, when the retroactive law is calculated to relieve a person from punishment for violating a fundamental right. Article 27 of the Brazilian Constitution of 1934 lays down expressly that penal laws shall have retroactive effect only if they benefit the accused. See also the Advisory Opinion of the Permanent Court of International Justice of December 4, 1935, concerning the consistency of certain Danzig legislative decrees with the Constitution of the Free City, where the Court had occasion to put on record the implications, destructive of the fundamental rights of the individual, of retroactive criminal legislation: Series A/B, No. 65.

to the Constitution of the United States, of cruel and unusual punishments is by no means unnecessary. It occurs in some modern constitutions. Although it is a prohibition which protects not so much personal liberty as the dignity of human personality, it may properly appear in this article of the Bill of Rights.

PROHIBITION OF SLAVERY AND OF FORCED LABOUR

Article 2

No State shall permit slavery, or traffic in slaves, or compulsory labour in any form other than public service, equally incumbent upon all, or as part of punishment pronounced by a court of law.

Prohibition of slavery.—The International Bill of the Rights of Man must be used as an opportunity—long overdue—for the final and absolute prohibition of the institution of slavery both in the domestic sphere and as a matter of international law. It is a grave reflection on the modern law of nations, in which the individual is said to be the mere object of the law, that the attempts to abolish slavery by international agreement and to vindicate the freedom of man in its primary and most fundamental aspect as part of international law have so far remained unsuccessful. It needed one of the most sanguinary wars in history—the American Civil War—to remove that blot from the face of a State which at the threshold of its national existence proclaimed the freedom and the equality of man as his inalienable birthright. After that issue had been settled on the field of battle in the greatest slave-owning State, there ought to have been no insuperable difficulty in obliterating that offensive anachronism by way of an international prohibition. In 1833 the British Parliament abolished slavery throughout the British Empire. In 1791 the French Assembly decreed a Law providing that "every person is free as soon as he enters France." In 1848 slavery was solemnly abolished in all French colonies.[10] When in 1896 Madagascar was declared to be part of France, the Chamber unanimously expressed the opinion that the automatic consequence of that declara-

[10] It may be of interest to recall the language of the Decree of April 27, 1848: "Whereas slavery is an affront to human dignity, inasmuch as in destroying the free will of man it destroys the natural principles of right and duty; whereas slavery is a flagrant violation of the republican maxims of Liberty, Equality, and Fraternity . . . slavery shall be totally abolished in all French colonies and possessions."

tion was to abolish slavery in Madagascar. But the history of the efforts to abolish slavery by way of international agreement has been a significant commentary on the shortcomings of international legislative processes and on the power of the respect for the sovereignty of States, however small and backward, to block the way of reforms deemed fundamental by the public opinion of the world. By 1926, when the Slavery Convention was adopted, hardly any civilized State recognized within its borders the institution of slavery.[11] And yet the Slavery Convention stopped short of total abolition of slavery. In Article 2 the Contracting Powers undertook "each in respect of the territories placed under its sovereignty, jurisdiction, protection, suzerainty or tutelage, so far as they have not already taken the necessary steps: . . . (*b*) to bring about, progressively and as soon as possible, the complete abolition of slavery in all its forms." They also agreed, in Article 4, to give one another every assistance with the object of securing the abolition of slavery. The International Bill of the Rights of Man must make these undertakings absolute and unqualified with regard to every signatory of the bill. No considerations of gradualness and no difficulties of execution ought to be allowed to stand in the way of a complete abolition and prohibition of the institution of slavery.

Prohibition of traffic in slaves.—The present draft of the Bill of Rights provides that "no State shall permit slavery, or traffic in slaves." Should the total abolition of slavery become part of the municipal law of the signatory States, the prohibition of traffic in slaves would appear to have become irrelevant. It may therefore appear doubtful whether, in strict logic, it ought to be included in the Bill of Rights. In a sense the prohibition of slave traffic derogates from the principal prohibition abolishing slavery. However, the duty of States not to

[11] By 1925 the legality of slavery was no longer recognized by any Christian State save Abyssinia. It was abolished in Siam in 1905, and in China in 1909. The status of slavery was legally recognized only in certain central Asiatic countries like Tibet and Nepal (where the liberation of slaves was completed in 1926) and in some minor Islamic countries such as the Arabian States and Afghanistan. Article 11 of the Constitution of the latter lays down that "the practice of slavery is forbidden in Afghanistan." For a survey of the existing position in the matter of slavery and of the problems which have arisen in various countries subsequent to the abolition of the legal status of slavery see *Report of the Committee of Experts on Slavery in Pursuance of the Resolution of the Assembly of the League of September 25, 1931:* Doc. C. 618. 1932. VI. See, in particular, pp. 17–19 on practices, short of slavery, restrictive of the liberty of the person.

permit slave traffic would impose upon them the further obligation to render trading in slaves a criminal offence for their nationals inside and outside their jurisdictions, and this fact, in addition to providing a suitable basis for international co-operation calculated to prevent traffic in slaves, renders desirable the inclusion of this undertaking in the Bill of Rights. In this respect the Bill would be largely declaratory of the existing international practice. The British-American Treaty of 1814, which declared traffic in slaves to be "irreconcilable with the principles of humanity and justice"; the Declaration of Vienna of 1815, in which the signatory States resolved to bring about through negotiations the universal abolition of slave traffic; the Agreement of 1841 between the European Great Powers providing for machinery, including wide powers of search conferred upon their warships, to implement that purpose; the General Act of the Berlin Conference of 1881 which declared traffic in slaves to be contrary to the law of nations; the Treaty of St. Germain of 1919, in which the African Colonial Powers agreed to endeavour to secure the abolition of the slave trade by land and by sea; and, finally, the Slavery Convention of 1926, in which the parties undertook without reservations "to prevent and suppress the slave trade"—all these show the widest measure of agreement on the subject.[12]

Prohibition of forced labour.—The securing of the right of the individual to be protected from forced labour would seem to be a self-evident provision of an International Bill of the Rights of Man. Forced labour is not only a denial of the dignity of human personality; in the words of the Slavery Convention of 1926, it has a tendency to develop "into conditions analogous to slavery." This being so, it is proper that no attempt should be made in the present Bill of Rights to treat differently involuntary labour generally and the more specific problem of

[12] The efforts to abolish the slave trade constitute one of the most impressive humanitarian chapters in history. It is reported that the British declaration of policy in 1815 with regard to the slave trade was received not only with enthusiasm; in the words of Wellington, it was received with frenzy. See W. L. Mathieson, *Great Britain and the Slave Trade, 1839–1865* (London, 1929), p. 7. In 1818 the British Government offered Spain a gift of £850,000 and a loan of ten million dollars as the price of immediate abolition of traffic in slaves; the offer was refused. At that time Marryat, the British agent for Trinidad, said with regard to the Spanish slave trade: "We should tell those slave-traders who come to ask our assistance that we would not fight for liberty with one hand and for slave trade with the other."

forced labour in the colonies. The law of civilized States has suppressed or discouraged involuntary labour in its various forms. The courts of the United States have interpreted the prohibition, in the Thirteenth Amendment, of slavery and of involuntary servitude as including peonage, the Chinese coolie trade, compulsory labour as a punishment for breach of contract, and specific performance of contracts of personal service. In England courts have developed the doctrine of contracts in restraint of trade and have refused to enforce specifically contracts of service. The French *Code Civil* prohibited, in Article 1780, contracts of service of indefinite duration or of indefinite character. For the prohibition of involuntary labour is an essential aspect of protection of human freedom. At the same time it is clear that even that prohibition must be subject to such exceptions as compulsory labour by virtue of a judicial sentence, the work of convicts, obligations of compulsory military service, service on juries, and labour on public works and roads, provided that in principle such services are equally incumbent on all. The latter exception might cover, in particular, the various forms of conscription of youth for compulsory labour in any general scheme of national civic and physical education. A number of States have adopted in their constitutions provisions of this nature. Thus Article 26 of the provisional Constitution of China of 1931 lays down that "all persons shall have the duty to perform military service and compulsory labour (for the State) in accordance with the law." At the same time, it might be a matter for consideration to what extent an International Bill of the Rights of Man ought to discourage or render illegal schemes of regimentation of large sections of the population, adopted under the influence of totalitarian ideas alien to the spirit of the Bill of Rights.[13]

The question of forced labour in colonial territories must come within the purview of the same principles and exceptions. The exception of public service may be capable of an interpretation rendered necessary by the special conditions of the territories in question, but determined at the same time by the general prohibition of forced labour

[13] On the other hand, the formation of camps of forced labour performed by the opponents of any political regime deprived of their liberty by a decree of the executive authority would be clearly contrary to the letter and the spirit of the Bill of Rights.

and the nature of the obligations of the administering States in relation to their colonial or mandated territories. The Slavery Convention of 1926 provided, in Article 5, that in territories in which compulsory or forced labour for other than public purposes still survives the parties shall endeavour "progressively and as soon as possible to put an end to this practice." The effect of the Bill of Rights would be to abolish altogether and immediately the practice of forced labour for purposes other than public works, notwithstanding any resulting economic inconvenience and disadvantages. Its maintenance for public purposes would be exceptional, temporary, and subject to international concern and supervision in accordance with Article 11 of the Bill of Rights. In fact, the exceptional and temporary character of forced labour in colonial and mandated territories was clearly recognized in connection with the Slavery Convention of 1926 and in the Resolution of the Assembly.[14] In the Convention of June 28, 1930, concerning forced or compulsory labour, the signatory States undertook "to suppress the use of forced or compulsory labour, in all its forms within the shortest possible period." [15]

FREEDOM OF RELIGION

Article 3
There shall be full freedom of religion.

The part which freedom of religion played in the development of the idea of inalienable human rights superior to the supremacy of any earthly power is well known. Those who in the sixteenth and seventeenth centuries raised the banner of freedom in matters of religion insisted that this was a province in which, both in the nature of things and by virtue of the innate right of man, the absolute autonomy of human will and conscience interpose an insurmountable barrier to interference by the State. Although security from the arbitrary interference of the executive with personal freedom, in the sense of freedom

[14] The Resolution was as follows: "The Assembly: While recognizing that forced labour for public purposes is sometimes necessary, is of the opinion that as a general rule it should not be resorted to unless it is impossible to obtain voluntary labour and should receive adequate remuneration."
[15] Hudson, *International Legislation*, V, 609. The Convention has been ratified by a large number of States, including Great Britain, Italy, and the Netherlands.

from physical restraint, was, historically, the first assertion of the rights of man against the State, the demand for religious freedom, by postulating an inviolate sphere of individual conscience, underlay more than anything else the doctrine of natural rights in the great American and French constitutional charters at the end of the eighteenth century. There is in this matter a revealing continuity of political thought from the Puritan movement in England, the Dutch practice of religious toleration and the first American immigrants and colonists to that remarkable proclamation of religious liberty embodied in the Virginia Bill of 1786 for Establishing Religious Freedom. Neither is it without significance that the first examples of the international protection of rights of minorities in the seventeenth and eighteenth centuries were concerned with securing religious freedom and equality of treatment irrespective of religion.[16] In the written constitutions of the nineteenth and twentieth centuries the guarantee of freedom of religion appears with impressive uniformity.

There are good reasons why freedom of religion should have played that prominent part in the development of the idea of the inalienable rights of man. In the first instance, while the securing of personal freedom from arbitrary arrest and otherwise was in the nature of a practical victory over the arbitrariness of the State, the assertion of the right to religious freedom was accompanied by—and drew its strength from—the vindication of an absolute right of the individual as against the State. Secondly, the recognition of freedom of religion on the part of the State was more than one aspect of the general admission of the right to freedom of opinion. For religion is apt to pervade with particular intensity the totality of the spiritual life of man. As such, it exhibits a

[16] See the treaties between France and Holland of 1678 and 1697; the treaties in connection with the partition of Poland in 1773 assuring freedom of religion to Roman Catholics; the Treaty of Kutchuk-Kainardji of 1774 between Russia and Turkey in which the latter undertook "constantly to protect the Christian Religion in all its churches"; the Treaty of 1814 in which the Powers guaranteed both religious toleration and equality of treatment for all religions in Holland (Article II of the treaty provided: "No innovation shall be made in the Articles of this Constitution, which assure equal protection and favour to every sect, and guarantee the admission of all citizens, whatever their religion may be, to public employment and offices"); the Protocol of 1830 guaranteeing the independence of Greece; the provisions of the Paris Protocol of 1856 relating to religious freedom in Moldavia and Wallachia; and the well-known provisions of the Treaty of Berlin of 1878 with regard to religious freedom in the Balkan States.

tendency to proselytism and intolerance on the part both of the domi-
nant majority and of the minority. In many cases religious organization, rigid, hierarchical, and combined with an allegiance transcending
the confines of the State, has seemed to threaten the power of established
authority. This explains to a large extent that strange turn of phrase in
Article 10 of the French Declaration of the Rights of Man: "Nul ne
doit être inquiété pour ses opinions, *même religieuses,* lorsque leur
manifestation ne trouble pas l'ordre public établi par la loi."

It would seem that with the spread of science and nationalism religious intolerance would tend to disappear and that the principle *cujus
regio ejus religio* would become obsolete. This is true to a large extent.
But, as a matter of more recent history, there has arisen a new danger to
religious freedom, not from religious exclusiveness on the part of the
State but from its opposition to religion in general. Thus, for a time
Soviet Russia seemed to have assimilated the view that religion has
proved in the course of history to be a menace to the welfare of man,
inasmuch as it diverted his energies from bettering his lot in this world
and caused him to acquiesce in the wretchedness of earthly existence
by compensated blessings in the world beyond. It is controversial
to what extent the government of Soviet Russia has in the past given
expression in practice to this anti-religious outlook. Even if no active
suppression of religion on the part of the State authorities has taken place
in Russia, it is probable that at some periods the authorities favoured
with some partiality the activities of individuals and organizations
waging active warfare against religion as such. In the Constitution of
Soviet Russia of 1936 the freedom of religious belief is fully safeguarded. On the other hand, in Germany under the National-Socialist
regime a brand of religion sponsored by the party in power received
encouragement which in practice often amounted to hostile interference with and suppression of the freedom of religion as generally
understood.

It would appear, therefore, that because of the part which claims of
religious freedom played in the development of the principle of the
innate rights of man and the ever-present potentialities for intolerance
coming both from religious and anti-religious zeal, the freedom of
religion must occupy a foremost place in the International Bill of the

Rights of Man. It will be noted that, subject to the operation of the principle of equality, freedom of religion is not incompatible with the declaration of a particular religion as the religion of the State.

FREEDOM OF SPEECH AND OF OPINION

Article 4

The freedom of speech and expression of opinion in writing and by other means shall not be denied or impaired.

It cannot be the object of the comment on this article of the draft to put the case for freedom of speech and opinion as a fundamental right of man and as a wise precept of government. Neither is it necessary to elaborate the point that that fundamental right, like any other similar claim, is limited by the legally recognized rights of others and by the requirements of the safety and the welfare of the State (as distinguished, it may be added, from the safety and the welfare of the government in power). With regard to the first, freedom of speech and of expression of opinion must, in particular, be limited by the law of libel. The extent of that limitation has varied—and must vary—in various countries. It has occasionally been suggested that in Great Britain and in the United States the law of libel has been allowed, especially of recent years, to impose an undue strain upon the crucial aspect of freedom of speech and opinion, namely, upon the freedom of the press. It would be outside the legitimate province of an International Bill of the Rights of Man to attempt to redress any such over-emphasis on what has been described in a leading treatise on natural law as the natural rights of man to veracity and reputation [17]—an attempt which French legislation and judicial practice have made, for a period of about a hundred years, by means of a minutely regulated *droit de réponse*, *i. e.*, the right of the individual, who deems himself aggrieved by a reference to his person in the press, to reply at a generously computed length.[18]

The same considerations apply to the question of the extent to which the restraints of the law of sedition can be allowed to limit the freedom

[17] Heinrich Ahrens, *Cours de droit naturel* (3d ed., Brussels, 1848), I, 193.
[18] See Article 13 of the Law of July 29, 1881, as amended by a Law of September 29, 1919.

of speech and opinion. The State must retain the right to suppress and to punish expressions of opinion in speech and in writing tending in their immediate effects to disturb the peace by advising illegal resistance to law, changes by illegal means of the existing form of government, or obstruction of the national effort in time of war. Undoubtedly the question of the extent to which the State exercises that right of self-protection is of the very essence of the matter. It may make all the difference between a tyrannical government and a government which, in deference to a tolerant and enlightened public opinion and a tradition of freedom, allows the law of sedition to remain dormant to the point of actual, though not legal, obsolescence. In England it is still the law that it is sedition to endeavour to degrade the King in the esteem of his subjects, or to create discontent or disaffection, or to incite the people to tumult, violence or disorder, or to bring the Government or Constitution into hatred or contempt, or to effect any change in the laws by the recommendation of physical force. But the extent to which that widely conceived law of seditious libel is allowed to limit the freedom of speech and of opinion is negligible. In the United States of America, where the Sedition Act of 1798 was, under the pressure of public opinion, allowed to expire in 1801, the predominant view is that, apart from the clear prohibition of previous censorship, the First Amendment did not take away from Congress the power to legislate against seditious libel and seditious conduct. But the exercise of that power has been the subject of jealous vigilance by courts in their determination to limit interference with freedom of speech and other expression of opinion to cases in which paramount social interest demands suppression and penalization of utterances and of conduct involving a clear and present danger to public peace and to the supreme interest of the State.

There is no doubt that—apart from the inconclusive intervals of the time of war—democratic countries have shown a pronounced tendency to keep the law of seditious libel in the background. In the United States the Supreme Court, by a widely approved act of judicial legislation, has extended the protection of the "due process" clause of the Constitution to cover also as against State legislation the protection of freedom of speech and opinion which the Constitution guarantees as against Congress and the Federal Government. Moreover, in these matters the Supreme Court has to a substantial degree abandoned the somewhat rigid presumption of reasonableness of State legislation on which it has acted in other matters, in particular in those of taxation.[19] This increased and emphatic protection of the rights of freedom at a time when it was being suppressed in many parts of the world was not accidental. It shows that once these fundamental rights have been recognized by the State, the courts may normally be trusted to preserve their effectiveness and vitality. At the same time there must always remain in the background that international reserve of power, which is of the essence of the International Bill of the Rights of Man, to act whenever interference with freedom of speech and opinion ceases to be a legitimate means of protecting public peace and the safety of the State, and threatens to become an instrument of tyranny in violation of the rights of man. That ultimate international guarantee of freedom of speech and opinion constitutes—as with regard to most of the other Articles of this Part of the Bill of Rights—the only novel feature in what is otherwise only a statement of a generally accepted principle.

It has been considered unnecessary to amplify this Article of the Bill of Rights by specifying the safeguards which modern constitutional practice has accepted as essential to that most important aspect of freedom of opinion, namely, the freedom of the press. These are the absence of censorship and the right of trial by jury in press offences. In England the main feature of the liberty of the press, conceived as absence of previous restraint upon publication, crystallized sufficiently during the eighteenth century for Blackstone to be able to say that it is essential to the nature of a free State (though it was probably not till the Fox's Libel Act of 1792 that the criminality of

[19] See *Whitney* v. *California* (1927) 274 U.S. 357; *Fiske* v. *Kansas* (1927) 274 U.S. 380, 387, where the Court reversed a conviction under a State statute against criminal syndicalism; *Stromberg* v. *California* (1931) 283 U.S. 359, where the Court held invalid a California statute penalizing the display of a "red flag . . . as a sign . . . of opposition to organized government." The Court said: "The maintenance of the opportunity for free political discussion to the end that government may be responsive to the will of the people and that changes may be obtained by lawful means, an opportunity essential to the security of the Republic, is a fundamental principle of our constitutional system"; *Schneider* v. *State* (1939) 308 U.S. 147, where the Court held invalid municipal ordinances the effect of which was, as a measure of preventing littering of the streets, to forbid distribution in streets of handbills discussing, *inter alia*, the Spanish Civil War and the administration of unemployment insurance; or *Bridges* v. *California* (1941) 314 U.S. 252, to the effect that the law of contempt of court must not be used as a means of preventing criticism of judicial decisions.

the matter published came clearly within the province of juries). In the United States the prohibition of censorship is universally regarded as implied in the First Amendment. Trial by jury of seditious libel and press offences generally is clearly within Article III of the Constitution which prescribes that "the trial of all crimes, except in cases of impeachment, shall be by jury." In France the prohibition of censorship foreshadowed in Article II of the Declaration of 1789 was given unqualified expression in the Constitution of 1791 (title 1, sec. 2): "The constitution guarantees as a natural and civil right: the right of every person to say, write, print and publish his thoughts without such writing being liable to any censorship or inspection before publication." Article 83 of the Constitution of 1848 laid down in clear terms that "the cognizance of all press offences belongs exclusively to the jury." Both principles—absence of censorship and trial by jury of press offences—have been adopted, with an impressive uniformity, in the written constitutions of modern States. But it must be borne in mind that while the prohibition of censorship is a substantive guarantee, trial by jury is, in essence, of a procedural nature. As Lord Kenyon said in *Rex* v. *Cuthill:* [20] The liberty of the press is neither more nor less than this, that a man may publish anything which twelve of his countrymen think is not blameable, but that he ought to be punished if he publishes that which is blameable." It is of importance that the procedural safeguard of trial by jury should not obscure the significance of the fundamental right of freedom of speech and opinion which must be binding alike upon juries, courts, and legislators.

FREEDOM OF ASSOCIATION AND OF ASSEMBLY

Article 5
There shall be full freedom of association and assembly.

The guarantee of freedom of association and assembly appears with regular uniformity in the constitutions of practically all countries. The

[20] 27 *St. Tr.* 674. For an interesting exaggeration of that statement see A. V. Dicey, *Introduction to the Study of the Law of the Constitution* (8th ed., London, 1915), p. 242: "Freedom of discussion is, then, in England little else than the right to say anything which a jury, consisting of twelve shopkeepers, think it expedient should be said or written."

general recognition of the right of peaceful assembly has suffered no reverse since it was adopted in the Bill of Rights of 1689 and copied from it in the American Bill of Rights and in the French Constitution of 1791.[21] It is, like any other fundamental right, subject to regulation in the interest of public peace, and the preventive and repressive functions entrusted in this connection to the police and other executive authorities have often prompted the assertion that the right of assembly is to a large extent nominal. Thus, in England the police have wide powers of regulating meetings in the street and public places and of ordering them to disperse on the ground that they are a public nuisance; meetings held in such a way as to alarm one person of reasonable firmness and courage are unlawful in themselves and may be dispersed; in strict law any meeting or procession on a public highway is an obstruction. In times of political strain—as, for instance, in the period 1930–1939, when there was a tendency in some countries to form private organizations of a semi-military character—such powers given to the police authorities have tended to increase.[22] However, in normal times these restrictions upon the right of assembly have been latent rather than actual. The possibility of an abuse of the powers of the Executive in this matter is no greater than with regard to other fundamental rights. Its continued validity and vitality needs no elaboration.

The right of association has had a more varied career. It was recognized early as an essential right of the individual, as one aspect

21 Which provided in title I, sec. 2: "The Constitution guarantees, as natural and civil rights . . . the right of citizens to assemble peacefully and without arms, in conformity with the laws of police." It was by reference to the latter qualification that, until the Law of June 6, 1868, public meetings required previous authorization on the part of the police. The Law of June 30, 1881, did away altogether with the requirement of previous authorization. However, such meetings must not take place on a public highway; they must not be prolonged beyond certain hours; and they must be notified to the police, who have the power to dissolve the meetings at the request of the organizers or where a breach of the peace is apprehended.
22 Under the Public Order Act, 1936, the police in England were authorized to prohibit processions for a period not exceeding three months and to regulate them. That Act also increased the punishment for using threatening, abusive, or insulting words or for behaviour with intent to provoke a breach of the peace. In *Duncan v. Jones*, (1936) 1 K.B. 218, a case decided under the Metropolitan Police Act, 1839, a speaker who refused to obey the order of the police not to hold a meeting in the vicinity of employment exchanges was convicted of obstructing the police in the execution of their duty to prevent breaches of the peace. For a comprehensive survey of legislative control of political extremism in European democracies in that period see Karl Loewenstein, "Legislative Control of Political Extremism in European Democracies," *Columbia Law Review*, XXXVIII (1938), 591–692, 725–774.

of that right of "free communication between citizen and citizen," which Jefferson claimed as an inalienable right of man.[23] But it was for a time opposed for the same reasons which limit natural rights in general: the security of the State and the legally recognized rights of others. In France it was not until 1848 that the Constitution recognized, in Article 8, "the right of citizens to form associations." It is probable that the authors of the Declaration of 1789 regarded freedom of association as a grave danger to the principle of individual freedom. Rousseau laid the doctrinal foundation of this attitude inimical to the freedom of association. He wrote in the *Contrat social:* "Il importe . . . pour avoir l'énoncé de la volonté générale qu'il n'y ait pas de sociétés particulières dans l'Etat et que chaque citoyen n'opine que par lui" (Book II, ch. iii). In this line of thought Article 1 of the well-known Loi Le Chapelier of 1791 prohibited in the following terms the creation of professional associations: "The abolition of all kinds of corporations of citizens of the same station and profession being one of the fundamental bases of the French constitution, it is forbidden to re-establish them in fact under whatsoever a pretext and in whatsoever a form." That fear of associations as a possible rival to the authority of the State characterized much of subsequent French legislation. And although the Law of July 1, 1901, recognized generally and generously the principle of freedom of associations, it curtailed much of their potential power by prohibiting them to acquire property by way of gift. The negative attitude of English law, until the Combination Acts of 1824 and 1825, to freedom of association with regard to trade unions illustrates the other reason for the traditional opposition to freedom of association, namely, the desire to protect the freedom of the individual. Richard Cobden believed that trade unions were based on tyranny and monopoly. And although Dicey did not apparently share the view of some English judges in the nineteenth century that the efforts of trade unions to raise the rate of wages was something like an attempt to defy a law of nature, he saw no error in their belief that trade unionism was opposed to individual freedom.[24]

[23] He said: "A right of free communication between citizen and citizen, on their joint interests, whether public or private, and under whatsoever laws these interests arise . . . is a natural right; it is not the gift of any municipal law, either of England, or Virginia, or of Congress": S. K. Padover, ed., *Democracy*, by Thomas Jefferson, p. 24.
[24] *Lectures on the Relation between Law and Opinion in England during the Nineteenth Century*, p. 196.

However, this opposition to the freedom of association as inimical to the authority of the State and to the freedom of the individual must now be regarded as no more than a passing phase in the history of the fundamental liberties of man. The State itself has come to be regarded as an association larger in scope and legal authority than other associations, but not entitled to a claim to exclusive allegiance. The economic and other complexities of modern life have tended to foster and finally to establish the conviction that there is no greater enemy of individual freedom than isolation, that association is the most potent instrument of the freedom of the person, and that richness of personality grows in proportion as it is woven into the structure of diverse associations. For these reasons freedom of association has become a uniform feature of the constitutional law of States and its affirmation must form an indispensable part of the International Bill of the Rights of Man. As in the matter of other rights, the degree and manner of its realization must be left to the municipal law of States. This must include, for instance, such questions as the right of association of persons in the service of the government.

SANCTITY OF THE HOME AND SECRECY OF CORRESPONDENCE

Article 6

The sanctity of the home and the secrecy of correspondence shall be respected.

Like the right of assembly and of association, the guarantee of the sanctity of the home and of secrecy of correspondence forms part of the practice and of the written constitutions of most modern States. It is a repudiation of one of the most reprehensible manifestations of tyrannical government over man. That double guarantee is emphatically formulated in the Fourth Amendment to the Constitution of the United States:

The right of the people to be secure in their persons, houses, papers, and effects, against unreasonable searches and seizures, shall not be violated, and no Warrants shall issue, but upon probable cause, supported by Oath or affirmation, and particularly describing the place to be searched, and the persons or things to be seized.

It gave expression to the condemnation, in the historic case of *Entick v. Carrington*,[25] of the practice of the general warrant under which the houses of Coke, Wilkes, and others were searched and papers of various descriptions seized. It denounced implicitly the practice of the writ of assistance, against which James Otis delivered his memorable address, authorizing general searches for goods on which duty had not been paid. The French Constitution of 1791 provided expressly that "no agent of a public authority may enter the house of a citizen except for the execution of the mandate of the police or of a court in cases formally prescribed by law." The Constitution of the Third Year laid down even more emphatically, in Article 359, that "the house of every citizen is an inviolable asylum. . . . No invasion of the domicile can take place except by virtue of a law or by a person or an object expressly designated in the warrant ordering the entry." Article 184 of the Criminal Code sanctioned the same principle.

Upon these general assurances of the sanctity of the home and of correspondence practice has engrafted interpretations and qualifications which have by no means impaired its vitality. Thus, the courts of the United States have in a number of decisions distinguished between reasonable and unreasonable searches and laid down in which cases search is permissible without a warrant. They have dealt with questions such as the opening of letters written in prison, the use of a searchlight, concealment in an open field, and tapping of telephone wires.[26] These decisions have been occasionally subject to criticism. So has been, in England, the practice, which is of controversial legality, of permitting the police to search the papers of a person who can reasonably be accused of an offence, or the practice, under an Act of 1819 (commonly called the Blasphemous and Seditious Libels Act, 1819), permitting the court in which a verdict for sedition or blasphemy has been given to order the seizure of all copies of the libel in the possession of the accused person or of any other person specifically named. So has been, in France, the lax interpretation of the statutory rule under

---

[25] (1765), 2 Wils. 275.
[26] In the well-known case of *Olmstead* v. *United States*, the Supreme Court held that there was no search within the meaning of the Fourth Amendment when officers obtained substantial evidence by tapping the telephone wires of the defendants and listening to their conversations, but without trespassing upon their property: (1928) 277 U.S. 438, 442.

which a public officer can always enter the home of a private person if the latter assents thereto—a practice which has taken advantage of the mere silence of persons intimidated or ignorant of the law. But the volume of criticism to which such practices have given rise, the projects of reform intended to remedy them, and the decisions of courts upholding the principle of the sanctity of the home and of secrecy of correspondence, even when its maintenance made the enforcement of other laws impossible or difficult,[27] testify to its ever-present urgency and importance.

EQUALITY BEFORE THE LAW

Article 7

All nationals of the State shall enjoy full equality before the law and equal treatment in all respects by the authorities of the State. In particular, there shall be no discrimination on account of religion, race, colour, language, or political creed.

Aliens shall not be denied the full and equal protection of the preceding articles of this Bill of Rights and of other rights granted to them by the law of the State in which they reside. No alien legally admitted may be expelled except in pursuance of a judicial decision or recommendation as a punishment for offences laid down by law as warranting expulsion.

The claim to equality before the law is in a substantial sense the most fundamental of the rights of man. It occupies the first place in most written constitutions. It is the starting point of all other liberties. The equality of man is the source of the claim to personal freedom, inasmuch as it rules out the arbitrary power of one person over another. Because men are equal, no person is entitled to exercise arbitrary physical restraint over another. The freedom of religion is based, in a sense, on the claim that one man's right to hold a particular religious belief

[27] Thus, for instance, the French Court of Cassation declared in 1911 that in the absence of an express statutory authorization government inspectors entrusted with the supervision of laws for the protection of women and children and those concerned with night work were not entitled to enter the premises of the factories and of the establishments concerned: Duguit, *op. cit.*, V, 71. And see *Ex parte Jackson*, where the Supreme Court held that although Congress had power to exclude lottery tickets from mails, its power to enforce that prohibition was rigidly circumscribed by the fact that "no law of Congress can place in the hands of officials connected with the postal service any authority to invade the secrecy of letters" and of sealed packages: 96 U.S. 727.

is not inferior to that of another. Freedom of opinion is due intrinsically to the fact that one man's right to hold or to express an opinion is as good as that of another. This is the reason why equality is historically the first fundamental right claimed for and by man. It was not freedom, but equality that underlay the philosophy of the Stoics. The equality of man is made real by the common possession of reason, which distinguishes man from other living beings and in comparison with which the physical and intellectual inequalities between man and man fade into insignificance. For equality does not mean that all men are equal in all respects. It means that they are equal in a most fundamental and decisive quality.

The principle of equality before the law is clearly an indispensable element of the very notion of the rule of law, inasmuch as generality of application is of the essence of the law. Yet it is not the purpose of equality before the law to establish material equality in other respects or to remove the effects of inequality in physical and intellectual powers or in economic wealth. It may be the business of the State to neutralize the effects of such inequalities in so far as the failure to do so is conducive to results which are inconsistent with the dignity of man and inimical to the social purpose of the State. But any claims which come under this head are not relevant to the principle of equality before the law with which alone this article of the draft is concerned. They may be relevant to the contention that one of the objects of the State is, in pursuance of a higher principle of justice, to remove or to modify some of the consequences of the natural inequalities between man and man.[28]

Secondly, it must be borne in mind that "equal treatment in all respects," as provided in the draft, does not imply identical treatment. It implies an equality relative to the situation. A purely mechanical absence of differentiation may result in inequality and injustice. There must,

---

[28] A comparison of the two successive French Declarations of Rights illustrates the difference to some extent. The Declaration of 1789 laid down that men are born and remain free and equal before the law. There is no express declaration of any natural equality of man. On the other hand the Declaration of 1793 provides expressly that "all men are equal by nature and before the law." According to some, this insistence of the second Declaration on the natural equality of man was in accordance with the absolutist tendencies of the regime for which mechanical equality was a convenient justification of a tyranny weighing equally upon all.

for instance, be inequality in taxation. The system of progressive taxation is not one of mechanical equality, but there are few who question it—although there are some who doubt the essential equality of the principle of total exemption from taxation of persons below a certain minimum of income. The individualization of punishment or the special protection afforded by the law to certain classes of persons, like women and children, are not contrary to the principle of equality. It must always remain a matter of controversy whether or not in any particular situation stereotyped equality amounts in fact to an inequality. Thus, it has been maintained that to impose the duty of military service in time of peace equally upon all classes of the population, irrespective of the situation and aptitudes of the persons concerned, is not to treat them on a footing of equality. And while it is generally agreed that some participation, through universal suffrage, of all persons in the exercise of political power is a necessary implication of equality, there are many who believe that the *equal* participation of all persons in universal suffrage, regardless of the service which they perform or are capable of performing, is a negation of the true principle of equality.

The numerous decisions in which the courts in the United States have interpreted Section 1 of the Fourteenth Amendment, providing that "no State shall . . . deny to any person within its jurisdiction the equal protection of the laws," show that the equal protection of the laws does not exclude distinctions between and classification of persons so long as these are based on reasonable grounds. When the Supreme Court in *Pembina Mining Co.* v. *Pennsylvania* laid down that "the inhibition of the amendment . . . was designed to prevent any person or class of persons from being singled out as a special subject for discriminatory and hostile legislation," [29] it gave expression to a general and inherent limitation of the right to equality of treatment. Wide discretion in establishing classifications by reference to various factors is essential to and not inconsistent with the principle of true equality so long as the basis of classification is reasonable. What is reasonable is a question which must, as a rule, be left for determination by national tribunals—even if such determination may on occasions puzzle the foreign observer unacquainted with the legal and social

[29] 125 U.S. 181, 188.

intricacies of the situation. Thus the Supreme Court of the United States has interpreted the Fourteenth Amendment as not forbidding segregation of Negroes in schools where the accommodation and the advantages are substantially equal to those given to other children. It has also held, for a similar reason and subject to similar conditions, that the segregation of Negroes on trains, in railway stations, and other public places is not contrary to the principle of equality. On the other hand, it has found that geographical segregation by legislation—but not that resulting from covenants in conveyances—is a violation of the equality clause.

Undoubtedly, in the decisions of the Supreme Court of the United States upholding as not inconsistent with the requirement of equality the segregation of Negroes in schools and public conveyances, the interpretation of equality conceived as a mechanical equality of opportunity and advantage was, especially in the eyes of foreign observers, stretched to breaking point. It implies the legalization of at least social discrimination, through legislation, against citizens on account of race and colour. It was not adopted without strong criticism within the Supreme Court itself.[30] And there are indications that it may be gradually abandoned by the Court as a whole.[31] Both these factors suggest that in these most intricate and delicate instances of the application of the principle of equality to situations of considerable historic and social complexity, reliance must first be placed on the national organs of the administration of the law and on the operation of public opinion. But such reliance is only possible on the assumption that there exists, as contemplated in the International Bill of the Rights of Man, an ultimate international power of supervision and rectification not only with re-

[30] See the strong dissenting opinion of Mr. Justice Harlan in *Plessy* v. *Ferguson* (163 U.S. 357), where the Supreme Court held that a State law requiring separate accommodation for white and coloured persons on the railroads was not contrary to the Thirteenth Amendment which prohibited slavery and involuntary servitude. He brushed aside the argument that the law in question did not discriminate between the two races: "Everyone knows that the statute in question had its origin in the purpose, not so much to exclude white persons from railroad cars occupied by blacks, as to exclude colored people from coaches occupied by or assigned to white persons. . . . If the Statute of Louisiana is consistent with the personal liberty of citizens, why may not the State require the separation in railroad coaches of native and naturalized citizens of the United States, or of Protestants and Roman Catholics?"
[31] See *Missouri ex rel. Gaines* v. *Canada* (1938) 305 U.S. 337; *Mitchell* v. *United States* (1941) 313 U.S. 580.

gard to any discriminatory legislation but also with regard to injurious discriminatory action of the executive and administrative organs of the State as, for instance, in the matter of admission to State offices and public employment.

For it is not only in the affirmation of the general principle of equality before the law that lies the practical purpose of this article of the draft but also in its object as an instrument for preventing discrimination against minorities. From this point of view this article is intended to perform the function for the fulfillment of which the Minorities Treaties were concluded after the first World War. But it would do so within the framework of a general principle equally applicable to all States and as part of an instrument of a universal character.

Equality of the sexes.—The present draft does not provide for the prohibition of discrimination on account of sex. Some will regard this aspect of the draft as a serious omission. But it is an omission which takes into account the fact that the full equality of women is a problem intimately connected with the legal tradition, the social conditions, and the state of public opinion on this subject in various countries. It is not a problem which can be solved within the framework of a general international instrument. The difficulties surrounding any such attempt may be gauged by the fact that the Seventh International Conference of American States declined in 1933 to act on a recommendation made by the Inter-American Commission of Women set up under a resolution of the Sixth Conference. Only the governments of Uruguay, Paraguay, Ecuador, and Cuba signed an Equal Rights Treaty which provided, in Article 1, that "the Contracting States agree that upon the ratification of this treaty men and women shall have equal rights throughout the territory subject to their respective jurisdictions." [32] It does not appear that the treaty has been ratified by any of these States. On the other hand, it may be possible to achieve a measure of equality by particular conventions providing for equality in a restricted sphere, especially in the matter of nationality. Thus the Seventh International Conference of American States adopted on December 26, 1933, the Convention on the Nationality of Women, which provided, in Article 1, that "there shall be no discrimination

[32] Hudson, *International Legislation*, VI (1937), 632.

based on sex as regards nationality, in their legislation or in their practice." [33] The Convention has been ratified, among others, by the United
States, and has entered into force. The Hague Convention of April 12,
1930, on certain questions relating to nationality laws, achieved substantial progress in this direction—although with regard to the principle
of complete equality of the sexes it was only able to agree on a recommendation to States to study the question whether it would not be
possible

  1. to introduce into their law the principle of equality of the sexes in
  the matter of nationality, taking particularly into consideration the interests of the children
  2. and especially to decide that in principle the nationality of the wife
  should henceforth not be affected without her consent either by the mere
  fact of marriage or by any change in the nationality of her husband.

A Resolution of the Thirteenth Assembly of the League of Nations in
1932 supporting these recommendations fell substantially short of
unanimity. Most Governments had previously expressed the opinion
that the provisions of the Hague Convention represented the "greatest
measure of agreement that is likely to be reached for the present in
regard to nationality of women"; the Swiss Government spoke of
them as representing "the maximum possible concessions."

In view of this conservative attitude of States in the matter of nationality, it would not be practicable to expect or to try to obtain the
necessary degree of agreement in regard to such matters as equal participation of women in suffrage or their admission to professions or
public offices. The attitude of American legislation and American
courts to the admission of women to juries illustrates the slowness of
the advance in this matter. Thus, while the courts held that the exclusion of Negroes from service on juries constituted a denial of the
equal protection of the laws, they have held that so far as women are
concerned the matter is one of legislative discretion. With regard to
the admission of women to professions, the following passage may be
quoted from the opinion of a number of justices of the Supreme Court
of the United States, in which they held that the refusal of the Supreme

[33] *Ibid.*, p. 590.

Court of Illinois to license a woman to practise law did not violate the Fourteenth Amendment:

In view of the peculiar characteristics, destiny and mission of women, it is within the province of the Legislature to ordain what offices, positions and callings shall be filled and discharged by men, and shall receive the benefit of those energies and responsibilities, and that decision and firmness which are presumed to predominate in the sterner sex.[34]

The recognition of equality of the sexes in the German Constitution of 1919 was doubly qualified. It recognized equality *in principle* with regard to rights and duties of *citizens*. In England the slow pace of the legislative and of the judicial process of freeing the woman—and especially the married woman—from the disabilities imposed upon her by the common law suggests that the full equality of women, if at all possible,[35] may have to be achieved by methods more evolutionary than an International Bill of the Rights of Man.[36] This attitude may appear to some unsatisfactory and savouring of compromise. So it is to some

[34] *Bradwell* v. *The State*, 16 Wall. 130.
[35] It is hardly possible, for instance, with regard to the obligations of military service.
[36] See Dr. C. K. Allen's pungent remark that prior to the legislative changes in 1882 "the rank and file of English wives remained under Common Law rules worthy only of an Oriental community" (*Law in the Making* [3d ed., Oxford, 1939], p. 295). See also the observations of Scott, L. J., in *Barber* v. *Pigden* [1937] 1 K.B. 664, at p. 678, on the "historical interferences by lawyers with the natural rights of woman." In 1936, acting upon a majority report of an Inter-Departmental Committee, the British Government announced that "the general interest of the State" would not be better served by the admission of women to the diplomatic and consular services. It is not without interest to note that while Godwin, for reasons of his own, began his *Political Justice* with a criticism of Paine's *Rights of Man*, Godwin's wife, Mary Wollstonecraft, published soon thereafter her *Vindication of the Rights of Woman* (1792). For an early claim to equality of the sexes see *Puritanism and Liberty; Being the Army Debates (1647-9), from the Clarke manuscripts with Supplementary Documents;* selected and edited by A. S. P. Woodhouse (London, 1938), p. 367, for an extract from a Petition of Women, Affecters and Approvers of the Petition of September 11, 1648: "Sheweth, that since we are assured of our creation in the image of God, and of an interest in Christ equal unto men, as also of a proportionable share in the freedoms of this commonwealth, we cannot but wonder and grieve that we should appear so despicable in your eyes as to be thought unworthy to petition or represent our grievances to this honourable House. Have we not an equal interest with the men of this nation in those liberties and securities contained in the *Petition of Right*, and other the good laws of the land? Are any of our lives, limbs, liberties, or goods to be taken from us more than from men, but by due process of law and conviction of twelve sworn men of the neighbourhood? And can you imagine us to be so sottish or stupid as not to perceive, or not to be sensible when daily those strong defences of our peace and welfare are broken down and trod underfoot by force and arbitrary power?" The learned editor suggests that this petition was probably drafted by men.

extent. A declaration of the rights of man is incomplete without an attempt to redress the legal inferiority of women. But account must be taken of the existing possibilities, as well as of the necessity of not impeding the acceptance of the Bill, whose principal provisions guarantee the fundamental rights both of men and women.

Position of aliens.—For the same reason, there is no provision in the present draft for full equality of treatment of aliens. Practically all States refuse to aliens some rights exercised or enjoyed by nationals. Aliens are generally excluded from the exercise of political rights proper; the reasons for that disability are obvious and unobjectionable. They are often excluded from engaging in certain professions and occupations or from acquiring all or certain categories of immovable property. In some matters, such as participation in the benefits of workmen's compensation, or depositing of security for costs, or benefiting from special legislative measures like rent-restriction acts, the exercise of the relevant rights on their part is conditioned by reciprocity. It would not be feasible to attempt to secure in the International Bill of the Rights of Man a provision of full equality of status for aliens, although some countries, notably Soviet Russia,[37] have gone a long way towards abolishing the disabilities of aliens. Neither is the need imperative. In many cases treaties provide for the removal, on the basis of reciprocity, of most of these disabilities.

Moreover, in practically all States the fundamental rights guaranteed by the constitution apply equally to aliens and to citizens. Thus, for instance, in the United States the Fourteenth Amendment lays down that no State shall "deprive any person of life, liberty, or property, without due process of law; nor deny to any person within its jurisdiction the equal protection of the laws." It has been held in a uniform series of decisions that the provision of Article 1, section 9, clause 2, of the Constitution guaranteeing the privilege of the writ of habeas

[37] According to Article 8 of the Preamble to the Civil Code of Soviet Russia, the legal capacity of foreigners is, on the whole, the same as that of Russian nationals. The same applies to protection of their labour and health and to social insurance. Subject to minor exceptions—like the right to act as captain or engineer of a ship or the right to be a member of the crew of a civil airship—they are not subject to any restrictions in regard to engaging in occupations or professions, including government service. See *The Legal Status of Aliens in Pacific Countries,* ed. N. A. M. McKenzie (London, 1937), pp. 302–316.

corpus is applicable to aliens; the same applies to the rights under the first nine amendments to the Constitution containing the Bill of Rights. These provisions do not refer to citizens; their wording is general; occasionally they refer to "the people." It has been held that the protection covers aliens who have entered the country illegally. Neither is it dependent upon reciprocity. The position in Great Britain is essentially the same. As recently as 1921 [38] it was held that the defence of Act of State is not available against the subject of a friendly State resident in British territory. The court was clearly of the opinion that as regards civil rights the status of an alien was assimilated, with minor exceptions, to that of a British subject. Even where in the constitutions of some countries—as in Article 109 of the Weimar Constitution, which provided that "all *Germans* are equal before the law" or in Article 4 of the Swiss Constitution of 1874, which laid down that "all Swiss are equal before the law"—the general consensus of opinion has been that notwithstanding the wording of the constitution the guarantees protect nationals and aliens alike.[39]

In principle there is no escape from these conclusions. The fundamental rights of the constitution are declaratory of the inherent rights of man as against the State; being the rights of man as such, they must be independent of nationality. But it is proper that the law should leave no doubts in this respect. This explains the wording of the draft. Aliens must be granted: (1) full and equal protection of the fundamental rights as guaranteed in Articles 1–6 of the Bill; (2) equal protection of such other rights as they enjoy by virtue of the law of the State. No distinction is made in the draft between resident aliens and others, though there has been a tendency in some countries, notably in the United States, to limit the protection of the constitution to resident aliens (this being the interpretation given to the phrase of the Fourteenth Amendment referring to aliens "within the jurisdiction" of the

[38] *Johnstone* v. *Pedlar* [1921] 2 A.C. 262.
[39] For an emphatic statement of this view see, with regard to the German Constitution of 1919, Gerhard Anschütz, *Die Verfassung des Deutschen Reichs* (11th ed., Berlin, 1930), pp. 449–452. He says: "Surely, it cannot be maintained that the German State is a State under the rule of law (*ein Rechtsstaat*) only in relation to nationals, but that as against aliens it is an arbitrary power, a 'police State.' "—*ibid.*, p. 450. As to France, see Duguit, *Traité de droit constitutionnel* (2d ed., 1925), V, 85, who is clearly of the view that the guarantee of personal liberty, "being a natural right of man," applies equally to Frenchmen and to aliens.

United States). "Resident aliens" are aliens residing in the country with the intention of establishing their permanent residence there. But an alien may reside in a foreign country for prolonged periods without having the intention of permanently establishing himself in it. Such persons must be protected by the fundamental guarantees open to other residents. Neither does there appear to be any cogent consideration of principle which excludes from such protection aliens residing in the country temporarily and for however short a period.

Expulsion of aliens.—It is a moot question whether the right, if any, to continued residence in the country—or, to put it negatively, freedom from expulsion—is included among the fundamental rights protecting the alien and the national alike. What is clear is that, subject, possibly, to the prohibition of an abuse of the right of expulsion,[40] international law permits States to expel aliens at their discretion. The purpose of the last paragraph of Article 7 of the present draft is to limit substantially this prerogative of States and to confer a corresponding right upon aliens. In the first instance, it is proposed that, regardless of the nature of the authority with which rests the final decision of expulsion, no expulsion shall take place except in pursuance of a judicial decision or recommendation. This was essentially the position in Great Britain in the period between the Aliens Act of 1905 [41] and the Aliens Order of 1920. According to the former, the court could, as part of the sentence, recommend deportation when an alien was convicted of a felony or misdemeanour or other offence for which the court had power to impose imprisonment without a fine. Expulsion was also permissible if a court of summary jurisdiction certified within twelve months from the date of the alien's entry into the country that in effect he was a pauper without ostensible means of support. The Aliens Order, without taking away from the courts the power to recommend deportation, conferred upon the Executive wide powers of expulsion.

In the United States the jurisdiction in matters of deportation, except in cases in which the person concerned claims to be an American citizen, lies with administrative boards. These can order expulsion only in cases

---

[40] See H. Lauterpacht, *The Function of Law in the International Community* (Oxford, 1933), p. 289; G. H. Hackworth, *Digest of International Law*, III (Washington, 1942), 690–705.

[41] Prior to that Act, the Executive had apparently no power to expel aliens.

specified by law, such as illegal entry (within three years), the existence of physical or mental defects such as warrant exclusion from admission, illiteracy, conviction of crime involving moral turpitude, liability to become a public charge (within three years of entry), holding of views advocating anarchy or overthrow of government by force (without time limit), and on some other grounds. Although the courts will not interfere with the discretion of the administrative boards in the matter, they regard themselves as bound and entitled to ensure that the administrative proceedings take place in accordance with the requirements of due process of law such as a fair hearing, however summary.

In France the power of expulsion conferred upon the Executive is practically without limits. It is a measure of police pure and simple. The Minister of the Interior in ordering the expulsion is not bound to adduce reasons for his decision, and it is even controversial whether the power of the *Conseil d'Etat*, which obtains with regard to administrative decisions in other fields, to enquire whether the discretion of the minister has not been abused, applies also to expulsion of aliens.[42]

The existing law of most States in the matter of expulsion is one of the manifestations of the inferiority of the status of the individual. The expulsion of a person, especially if he has established himself in the country and set up a family there, may entail for him consequences more grave and cruel than a long term of imprisonment. It is in many cases comparable to what is often referred to as civil death. Nothing short of most stringent judicial safeguards can in this matter reduce the possibility of State action violative of human dignity and utterly insensible to human sufferings. International tribunals, by stigmatizing such cases of inhuman and wanton expulsion as an abuse of the right of the State, have to some extent paved the way towards the recognition of a new principle in the matter of expulsion of aliens more consonant with the rule of law, with humanity, and with the dignity of man. That new rule ought to consist: (1) as a matter of substance, in limiting the right of expulsion to cases of previous conviction for expressly specified offences of the gravest character; (2) as a matter of procedure, in making expulsion depend, in addition, on a judicial decision or recommendation.

[42] Writers (see Duguit, *op. cit.*, V, 91) have urged the propriety of the *Conseil d'Etat* assuming such powers, but their suggestions for reform have not gone beyond that.

THE RIGHT TO NATIONALITY

Article 8

Every person shall be entitled to the nationality of the State where he is born unless and until on attaining majority he declares for the nationality open to him by virtue of descent.

No person shall be deprived of his nationality by way of punishment or deemed to have lost his nationality except concurrently with the acquisition of a new nationality.

This Article aims, positively, at securing to every individual the right to a nationality. Negatively, its purpose is the abolition of statelessness as a condition recognized both by international and municipal law. The subject is, in comparison with the other Articles of the Bill of Rights, of limited importance, and it concerns a limited category of individuals. At the same time it touches so significantly upon the question of the status of human personality in international and municipal law that an International Bill of the Rights of Man would be conspicuously incomplete without an attempt to do away with that offensive anomaly.

For the student of international law statelessness has presented an example of a baffling phenomenon in the international legal order. One of the assumptions of this order is that although the individual has no distinct status in international law, that disability is largely procedural. In his capacity as national of a State the individual benefits, through his State, from such rights and protection as international law, customary and conventional, lays down in his favour. To predicate nationality as a prerequisite of benefits and protection and to admit statelessness as a condition recognized and permitted by international law is a glaring inconsistency.

However, statelessness has constituted an anomaly transcending a mere inconsistency or inelegancy in the international legal system. It has been responsible for hardships hurtful to the dignity of man and his welfare. A stateless person does not enjoy the international protection of any State. He is a *caput lupinum*. He may be treated according to discretion by the State in which he resides. In cases in which aliens enjoy rights and advantages subject to reciprocity, the stateless person is excluded from such rights and advantages for the reason that he is not a national of any State offering reciprocity. He cannot, as a rule, possess a passport, and his freedom of movement is correspondingly impeded. There is no State to which he can be deported, and cases have frequently occurred in which stateless persons have been moved from one frontier to another and were subject to imprisonment by way of punishment for failing to comply with a deportation order. In countries in which nationality is based exclusively on descent, their children remain stateless.

The principal causes of statelessness are well known. They are due to the conflicting operation of *jus loci* and *jus sanguinis* in the matter of acquisition of nationality; to loss of nationality as the result of marriage; deprivation of nationality in consequence of prolonged residence abroad; cancellation of naturalization on account of fraud in obtaining it or of the subsequent ill conduct of the naturalized individual; and, above all, deprivation of nationality by way of punishment for disloyalty or other offences.

Before the end of the War of 1914–1918 statelessness was not, in practice, a frequent occurrence. The position has altered radically since 1918. What had hitherto been an occasional anomaly has become an international problem of wide dimensions and a source of distressing hardship for hundreds of thousands, if not millions, of persons. This is due only to an insignificant degree to the territorial changes resulting from the various peace treaties. The principal cause of the rapid growth of statelessness has been the denationalization policy of Soviet Russia, of Italy, of Turkey, and of Germany. That policy was adopted by Soviet Russia against the political refugees who refused to return to her territory. Italy, Turkey, and Germany, as well as some other States, have since resorted to denationalization on a wide scale for political and other reasons. It is this policy of collective and individual denationalization of a penal and political nature which has been responsible for the wide dimensions and the acute character of the problem of statelessness.

But whatever may be the causes of statelessness, its consequences, as outlined above, remain the same. It is unlikely that the problem of statelessness can be solved by the gradual removal of these causes. It cannot be solved except by the adoption and thorough-going application of the principle that statelessness in all its aspects is an anomaly which can and must be abolished. There is no major permanent interest of States which stands in the way of this much-needed reform. The work of the Hague Conference of 1930 on such questions as the nationality of married women showed that the removal of statelessness by way of international agreement is practicable. This view is fully confirmed by the manner in which an established rule of English law on this matter was changed without undue difficulty. Neither is there any compelling reason why States should continue to go outside the ordinary deterrents of criminal law and deprive persons of their nationality by way of punishment.[43] Such deprivation of nationality is often effected in disregard of the legitimate interests of other States. Like statelessness in general, it constitutes a denial of one of the basic assumptions of international organization by virtue of which the individual benefits from the protection of international law through the instrumentality of his State.

The harmony of international relations, the existing structure of international law, and, above all, the dignity of human personality— all point to the necessity of adopting a uniform rule as proposed in this article. The effect of the adoption of its first paragraph will be to eliminate statelessness in so far as it arises from the divergences of municipal law in the matter of acquisition of nationality by birth. The effect of the adoption of the second paragraph would be to make it legally impossible for a State to deprive a person of his or her nationality—whether by way of punishment, or as a consequence of marriage, or for any other reason—unless that person has validly acquired a new nationality. It would be a matter for a special international arrangement to define the status of persons already stateless at the time of the effective adoption of the International Bill of the Rights of Man and to prevent any enforced re-acquisition of their former nationality on the part of individuals who are unwilling to resume a connection associated with an experience of persecution and suffering.

---

[43] For the recent United States practice of denaturalization on the ground of disloyalty see Lawrence Preuss, "Denationalization on the Ground of Disloyalty," *American Political Science Review*, XXXVI (1942), 701–710; and see the same, "La dénationalisation imposée pour des motifs politiques," *Revue internationale française du droit des gens*, IV (1937), 1–24.

THE RIGHT OF EMIGRATION AND EXPATRIATION

˙Article 9

The right of emigration and expatriation shall not be denied.

What is generally referred to as the right of emigration involves, in effect, two questions. The first is the right of the individual to leave his country with the intention of permanently residing abroad. The second is his right, once he has emigrated and once he has acquired or is in a position to acquire a new nationality, to renounce effectively his nationality as against the State of his origin.

The fundamental character of the right of expatriation and its relation to human freedom were given eloquent expression by the chairman of the United States Delegation to the Hague Conference on Codification of International Law in a manner which merits quotation. He said:

For a century past it has been the policy of my country that the right of expatriation is an inherent and natural right of all persons. True it is that allegiance is a duty, but it is not a chain that holds one in bondage and that he carries with him to a new life in a new land. It is a duty and an obligation of a freeman that he casts off when he voluntarily assumes allegiance to the country of his new home and there takes over the duties and the rights of a national. When he takes over the new tie, the old one is loosed and gone. This principle is not a little thing. It is not a question of language, or of formulas, or of phrases. It is a principle of the rights of man and of the liberty of the human race.[44]

The same principle was expressed in 1868 in the Joint Resolution of Congress which began as follows: "Whereas the right of expatriation is a natural and inherent right of all people, indispensable to the enjoyment of the rights of life, liberty, and the pursuit of happiness . . ." It was foreshadowed with all requisite clarity, under the inspiration of Jefferson, in the Act of the Legislature of Virginia of 1779 "declaring who shall be deemed citizens of the Commonwealth" and basing one of its principal provisions on the "natural right which all men have of re-

[44] Mr. Hunter Miller, *Acts of the Conference for the Codification of International Law,* Meetings of the Committees, Vol. II. Nationality, p. 80. See also *ibid.,* p. 69 (Mr. Flournoy).

linquishing the country in which birth or other accident may have thrown them, and seeking subsistence and happiness wheresoever they may be able, or may hope to find them." The same Act spoke of any person relinquishing his citizenship as "having exercised his natural right of expatriating himself." [45]

It is clear that for a period of one hundred and fifty years the United States were enunciating in the form of a general principle of an inherent right of man a national policy dictated by the requirements of a country of immigration. But the intrinsic value and justification of that principle is not affected by the circumstance that it was propounded in conformity with or in pursuance of a national interest. Neither is it rendered purely nominal by the fact that the country which propounded it adopted in the twentieth century a rigid policy of limitation of immigration. It is true that without a corresponding right of immigration and naturalization the freedom of emigration tends to become theoretical. However, it is not altogether theoretical so long as immigration and naturalization take place, though on a reduced scale. Restrictions on immigration vary with changing economic and political conditions. It is possible that in a world in which the guiding policy of governments will be to stimulate production and employment by the direct action of the State the increased demand for labour may cause a reversal of the policy of drastic restrictions. However, this is a consideration of secondary importance compared with the major principle of freedom of emigration and expatriation. A State which denies to its citizens the right to emigrate reduces itself to the level of a prison. A State which, in so far as this lies within its power, refuses to its citizens in time of peace the right to renounce their allegiance, transforms into a relation of subjection what must be in essence a voluntary partnership. In both cases the law reduces its citizens to the status of persons *glebae adscripti*. In both cases there is an assertion of power violative of human freedom and dignity.

The refusal of the right of emigration and of expatriation has met with repeated condemnation. Cicero denounced it in his speech "Pro Balbo" when he relied on the old Roman rule "ne quis invitus civitate mutetur neve in civitate maneat invitus" (xiii. v. 31). When in the

---

[45] *Virginia Statutes at Large*, W. W. Henning's Collection, X (1822), 129.

Crito Socrates was adducing reasons for absolute obedience to laws, one of the reasons given was the right of emigration: "And if any one does not like the city and its constitution, there is no law to hinder or prevent him from going away whenever he likes, either to the colonies or to some foreign country and taking his property with him." Vattel, who showed conspicuous respect for the sovereignty of the State and its institutions, was emphatic as to the right both of emigration and expatriation.[46] In England there obtained for a long time the contrary doctrine "nemo potest exuere patriam." Coke gave it currency in his edition of Littleton's *Tenures* published in 1629: "Nemo patriam, in qua natus est, exuere, nec legiantiae debitum ejurare, possit." Blackstone extended to it full and emphatic approval in the *Commentaries*.[47] But the doctrine was unreservedly abandoned in England (except *pendente bello*) in the second half of the nineteenth century. The Royal Commission appointed in 1868 to consider the law of naturalization and allegiance gave it its *coup de grâce*. It came to the conclusion that everyone should be free, in time of peace, to expatriate and to denationalize himself and to transfer his allegiance to another State. The Naturalization Act, 1870, gave effect to its recommendations. The Nationality and Status of Aliens Act, 1914, provides in section 13 that "a British subject who, when in any foreign state and not under a disability by obtaining a certificate of naturalization or by any other voluntary and formal act, becomes naturalized therein, shall thenceforth be deemed to have ceased to be a British subject."

The adoption of Article 9 as proposed in the present draft would

[46] He said: "Every man is born free, and therefore the son of a citizen, when arrived at the age of reason, may consider whether it is well for him to join the society in which he happens to be by birth. If he does not find that it is to his advantage to remain in it, he has the right to leave it. . . . A citizen may therefore leave the State of which he is a member, provided it be not at a critical moment when his withdrawal might be greatly prejudicial to the State": *Du droit des gens; ou, Principes de la loi naturelle* (1758), Vol. I, Book II, sec. 220 ("The Classics of International Law," Fenwick's translation). He was of the opinion that in some cases the right of emigration and expatriation was absolute, in particular in cases in which the citizen can find no means of livelihood in his country or when the State seeks to impose upon him laws, in the matter of religion or otherwise, to which the compact of society cannot oblige him to submit and which are repugnant to him. These include cases in which a State decides to abandon the democratic form of government (*ibid.*, sec. 222).

[47] Book I, ch. x: "For it is a principle of universal law, that the natural-born subject of one prince cannot by any act of his own, no, not by swearing allegiance to another, put off or discharge his natural allegiance to the former: for this natural allegiance was intrinsic, and primitive, and antecedent to the other."

undoubtedly require a change in the legislation or in the practice of many countries. States, like Great Britain, whose law does not provide for the necessity of authorization as a condition of valid renunciation of nationality through naturalization in a foreign country, would have to abandon the practice of requiring release from the previous nationality as a condition of naturalization.[48] States which require an express authorization for release from their own nationality, would have to adopt the rule that acquisition of foreign nationality by naturalization automatically involves the loss of previous nationality for any person who has effectively taken up residence in the country of naturalization. States which require the fulfilment of certain conditions preliminary to conceding the right of emigration would have to change their legislation accordingly—subject, possibly, to the modification that in case of persons liable to military service the emigrant shall not be allowed to return to his country for a specified period of years.[49] This would exclude the fulfilment of the obligations of military service as a condition of permission to emigrate—a petty but persistent feature of modern practice. Neither would the adoption of this article be consistent with the refusal of the right of emigration on the ground of non-payment of debts or taxes—although this would not apply to the retention of the property of the emigrant sufficient to cover such obligations. A number of States provide expressly in their constitutions that the right of emigration must not be restricted, but that general provision is often vitiated by the qualification that it may be restricted by special laws.[50] States would not be giving up any major interest by agreeing to make that right as absolute as the prohibition of slavery. The sharp knife of fundamental policy as expressed in the International Bill of the Rights of Man must, in this matter, cut through the cob-

---

[48] The statutory basis of that requirement in Great Britain is not clear (see R. S. Fraser in *Transactions of the Grotius Society*, XVI [1931], 85). Many other States require similar authorization. For a survey of the law and practice of States on this and cognate matters see League of Nations, Conference for the Codification of International Law. *Bases of Discussion*, I (Nationality), 36–44.

[49] Swiss courts have expressly recognized that release from Swiss nationality cannot be made dependent upon previous compliance with the obligation either of actual military service or of payment of the tax of exemption.

[50] See Article 110 of the Czechoslovak Constitution of 1922 or Article 112 of the German Constitution of 1919 (with comment by Anschütz, *op. cit.*, p. 476).

web of restrictions offensive alike to the freedom of man and the dignity of the State.[51]

[51] The question of freedom of emigration must be distinguished from the restrictions which, by means of refusal of a passport or otherwise, a State may place in the way of its nationals wishing to leave the country temporarily. The right to issue a passport is usually conferred upon the foreign branch of the Executive which is in this matter endowed with discretionary powers. Such discretionary authority is, for instance, conferred upon the State Department in the United States by section 1 of the Act of July 3, 1926 (44 Stat. 887). In France the *Conseil d'Etat* has repeatedly affirmed the discretionary powers of the Executive in the matter (see *Recueil Sirey*, 1923, iii, 25, with a note by Hauriou). In strict law the passport is not a permission to leave the country, but a request for travel facilities addressed to a foreign State. In England, the right of emigration officers to prevent a British subject who is not in possession of a passport from leaving the country in time of peace has been questioned on occasions. For a clear affirmation of the view that the right of the Executive to refuse a passport is not absolute see Duguit, *op. cit.*, V, 56–60. The subject is, perhaps, not of sufficient general importance to be included in the Bill of Rights—although it has occasionally been included in national constitutions as a fundamental right. See for example, Article 67 of the Constitution of Peru of 1936.

CHAPTER X

THE SUBSTANCE OF PART TWO
OF THE BILL

THE RIGHTS OF MAN—his inherent and inalienable rights—are not absolute. They are and must be related to the rights of others and to the necessity of safeguarding the interests of the State upon the existence of which all rights depend. Subject to that overriding qualification, the rights guaranteed in Part I of the Bill are fully enforceable rights. According to Part III of the Bill of Rights, in addition to international powers of supervision and enforcement, they are contemplated as embodied in the constitutions of States, as enforced by municipal courts, and as protected against conflicting legislation. However, there exist claims of a cogency and justification not inferior in principle to those of the rights thus fully guaranteed but which, for reasons to be stated, cannot enjoy the same manner and the same degree of protection. They are the fundamental rights of freedom in relation to political independence, the right to the maintenance and development of cultural identity for persons belonging to a national minority, and the social rights to economic freedom, to a decent standard of work and life, and to educational opportunity. In relation to these rights—or claims—there exist imperative reasons why international society should prescribe standards and obligations of States. Without adequate protection of these rights, other fundamental rights tend to become purely theoretical. Yet, for reasons peculiar to each of these rights, their protection by the Bill of Rights must be different in form and less definite in degree than that of rights incorporated in Part I of the Bill. In particular, the rights of Part II, as proposed in this draft, are not normally enforced by municipal courts through an ordinary judicial procedure.

Article 10

No State shall deprive its citizens of the effective right to choose their governments and legislators on a footing of equality, in accordance with the law of the State, in free, secret, and periodic elections.

There are three reasons why the incorporation of the right to government by consent and the international guarantee thereof would appear to be an indispensable part of any International Bill of the Rights of Man: The first is that the right of self-government—which in developed society means government by persons freely chosen by and accountable to the electors—is in itself an expression and a condition of freedom. No individual at an adequate stage of development is free if he is governed against his will, that is, if the persons who exercise authority are not chosen by and accountable to the community at large. Wherever that happens, man wields uncontrolled dominion over man; the persons thus ruled are denied the right of freedom. They are also denied the right of equality. For the claim to be governed by consent is the direct corollary of the principle of equality. In this double sense the right of self-government is a natural right of man. It is in this sense that the words of Jefferson may be deemed to express an abiding truth: "Every man, and every body of men on earth, possess the right of self-government. They receive it with their being from the hand of nature." [1]

Secondly, under a tyrannical or despotic government there is no room for the other fundamental rights of man. Even if such government were minded to respect those rights and even if it actually respected them, they would still be precarious in so far as they would be dependent upon the uncontrollable will of a mere agency of force, however enlightened. An enlightened despotism which tramples upon the right of man to govern himself will soon find reasons to ride roughshod over other natural rights. Lord Acton's observation that power corrupts and that absolute power corrupts absolutely is more than a brilliant aphorism.

These latter considerations do away effectively with the idea that a despotic government may nevertheless be compatible with the maintenance of the personal rights of freedom if these rights are guaranteed by some such international obligation as an International Bill of the Rights of Man. If that obligation, it may be argued, were observed, the principal rights of man would seem to be secured irrespective of the form of government. A compromise of this nature might provide

[1] S. K. Padover, ed., *Democracy*, by Thomas Jefferson, p. 24.

a solution of the difficulty created by the existence of non-democratic States which might otherwise be thought fit to become part of the international system of which an International Bill of the Rights of Man would be one of the principal features. A compromise of that character might explain and render possible the—otherwise inconsistent—proclamation in the Atlantic Charter both of human freedoms and of the right of States to determine their form of government.

Abundant skepticism is justified with regard to any such arrangement. One of the main motives of the urge for an International Bill of the Rights of Man has been the conviction that despotic government is a *malum in se;* that it is an extreme glorification of the State inimical to the rights of man; that it is a denial of law; and that, whatever the motives or the programme of the despotic government may be, it is ultimately a mere assertion of force, a *magnum latrocinium,* with all the dangers of instability, arbitrariness, and corruption which absolute power is heir to. The removal of tyranny and of dangers of tyranny has been one of the principal motives of the idea of an international Bill of Rights. The intrinsic incongruity between the recognition of fundamental rights of man and a denial of his right of self-government is such as to preclude, to all appearance, the idea of any such accommodation.

Thirdly, the intimate connection between the right of government by consent and the maintenance of international peace—a connection which has been elaborated in the comment upon the Preamble to the Bill [2]—is a factor of vital importance.

The implications of any such proclamation of the right to self-government as part of the International Bill of the Rights of Man are, admittedly, formidable. They amount to an international guarantee of the democratic form of government of States. This does not necessarily connote an international guarantee of the stability of any particular democratic government or an outlawing of revolutions in the sense that any revolution against a democratic government would be a violation of the system established by the Bill of Rights. The system established by the Bill of Rights would not transform international society into a society for the mutual preservation of established gov-

[2] See above, p. 88.

ernments. There must always remain in the background that natural right of resistance, even against democratic governments, which no law can or ought to eliminate—although the régime established by the International Bill of the Rights of Man will tend to limit the contingency of abuse of power on the part of governments. What the international guarantee does mean is that any government which comes to power as the result of a revolution, must be a democratic government, namely, a government confirmed by free, secret, and periodical elections on a footing of equality.

The requirements under which, under a system of government by consent, the election of the supreme organs of legislation and government must take place are, it would appear, self-explanatory:

(1) The elections must be free in the letter and in the spirit. There must be no intimidation, victimization, or threat of victimization. There must be not only freedom of voting, but also freedom in the matter of nominating candidates. A system by which persons can choose or reject only one set of candidates imposed by the party in power is not a system of free elections.

(2) Elections must be secret in order to be free.

(3) Elections must be periodical. Except in time of war when elections are not feasible, the supreme representative organ must be chosen periodically. A Parliament which perpetuates itself in time of peace is only in degree different from a despotic body.

(4) The choice of the supreme representative body must be on a footing of equality—a requirement which, as will be seen, does not necessarily imply universal suffrage or absolute equality of suffrage. A legislature from the choice of which one part of the nationals is excluded for reasons which are not universally applicable or which are arbitrary is not a representative body.

Yet it is clear that this aspect of the right to self-government is fraught with formidable difficulties. It raises the question of disfranchisement of sections of the population on account of race, of sex, of tests of wealth or education, and for other reasons. Any rigid formulation of the Bill of Rights in this matter would probably reduce the chances of its acceptance to a negligible minimum. No Bill of Rights is likely to prove acceptable which in an inelastic or uncompromising

fashion makes the question of the franchise of the Negro population in
the United States or in South Africa a test of the democratic system of
those countries or a matter of direct and immediate international concern. The same applies to other tests of franchise or to differentiations
in voting power. For this reason, the present draft refers to the "effective right of citizens to choose their governments and legislators on a
footing of equality, *in accordance with the law of the State*, in free,
secret, and periodic elections."

The solution suggested may unquestionably create the appearance of
being subtle to the point of ingenuity and of a drastic emasculation of
the purpose of the Bill. That criticism is only partly justified. The requirement of equality is not rendered valueless by being qualified by
reference to the law of the State. For the wording and the spirit of the
draft are such as, in turn, to qualify the law of the State by reference to
the principle of equality. To say this is not to cover a half-hearted attempt at a compromise. For the fact is that the principle of absolute
equality in voting power has not invariably commended itself to all believers in government by consent. The test of literacy, for example, may
not, in certain circumstances, be altogether reprehensible so long as it is
not applied with partiality and for ulterior motives and so long as those
applying it are conscious that the very fact of illiteracy is a reflection
on the State. The justification of the property test has for centuries
been a matter of controversy. It was controversial when in the course
of the Cromwellian Revolution the participants in the debates at the
"General Council of the Officers" of the Army held in Putney in
October, 1647, were discussing the "Agreement of the People." [3] It

[3] The following extracts may be conveniently quoted:
"Mr. Petty: We judge that all inhabitants that have not lost their birthright should
have an equal voice in the elections.
"Colonel Rainborough: I think that the poorest he that is in England hath a life to
live as the greatest he; and therefore truly, Sir, I think it's clear, that every man that is
to live under a Government ought first by his own consent to put himself under that
Government; and I do think that the poorest man in England is not at all bound in a
strict sense to that Government that he hath nor had a voice to put himself under. . . .
"Commissary Ireton: For my part . . . I think that no person has a right to an
interest or share in the disposing of the affairs of the kingdom, and in choosing or
determining those that shall determine what laws we shall be ruled by here—no person
hath a right to this, that hath not a permanent fixed interest in this Kingdom. . . .
"Colonel Rainborough: Truly, Sir, I am of the same opinion as I was. . . . I do hear
nothing at all that can convince me why any man that is born in England ought not to
have his voice in election of burgesses. . . ." *Puritanism and Liberty; being the Army
Debates (1647-9) from the Clarke manuscripts*, edited by A. S. P. Woodhouse (1938),

was a subject of protracted debates at the time of the drafting of the American Constitution.[4] At the height of the Third French Republic the elimination of the property test was severely criticized by leading constitutional lawyers.[5] In the course of the controversy concerning the Indian franchise in Kenya, the Indians, speaking through a highly authoritative mouthpiece, the Secretary of State for India, demanded "a common electoral roll and a common franchise on a reasonable property basis *plus* an educational test without racial discrimination, for all British subjects." [6] It is clear, therefore, that it cannot be the purpose and that it is not within the power of the International Bill of the Rights of Man to lay down rigid tests for the principle of equality of suffrage.

But to what extent can the Bill of Rights be indifferent to the application of this vital aspect of the principle of government by consent? Can it, without rendering its provisions in this matter purely nominal, admit its inability to cope with situations such as the disfranchisement, partial or total, of large sections of the Negro population in the United States or in South Africa or of Indians in Kenya and South Africa? How far can the Bill of Rights leave full scope to "the law of the State" and permit disfranchisement on account of colour, race, and religion?

---

pp. 53–55. Cromwell was clearly on the side of the rights of property: "the consequence of this rule [as propounded by Ireton] tends to anarchy, must end in anarchy" (*ibid.*, p. 59). See also John Cartwright, *The Legislative Rights of the Commonalty Vindicated*, i. 35 (ed. 1777, pp. 28, 30): "Their poverty is surely the worst of all reasons for stripping them of their natural rights; let us rather reconcile to them the many hardships of their condition, by showing that it does not degrade them below the nature of man. If they have not wherewithall to gratify their pride, let them at least retain the dignity of human nature; by knowing they are free, and sharing in the privileges inseparable from liberty."

[4] Although John Adams was emphatically of the view that the only moral foundation of government is the consent of the people, he thought, in a letter written to Sullivan in 1776, that "such is the frailty of the human heart, that very few men who have no property, have any judgment of their own" (*Works*, ed. 1854, IX, 375, 376). In 1779, in his report on the constitution of Massachusetts, he proposed to limit the right of franchise to holders of freehold to the value of £3 or of personal estate to the value of £60. During the debates in the "Federal Convention" of 1787 Gouverneur Morris proposed, with regard to the Federal Constitution, that franchise to the Lower House should be limited to freeholders. This proposal was rejected. But opinion was divided, and the Constitution as finally adopted left the matter to the states. This inequality of representation was subsequently severely criticized by Jefferson as a "republican heresy in the first essay of our revolutionary patriots at framing a Constitution" (as quoted in A. J. Carlyle, *Political Liberty* [Oxford, 1941], p. 195).

[5] Duguit, *op. cit.*, III, 586.　　　[6] Dispatch of October 21, 1920; Cmd. 1311.

The answer to this question cannot be a simple one. It is probable that in this matter the Bill of Rights will have to adopt a solution which must leave room for future approximation to the fundamental principles of the Bill of Rights. These are the principle of equality, irrespective of race, colour, and religion, and the principle of government by consent, which is rendered nugatory by the disfranchisement of large sections of the population. In principle, no person ought to be excluded —except, possibly, by way of punishment—from a share, however small, in the formation of the collective will of the State. An individual who has no vote at all is not governed by consent; he is not free. Montesquieu gave clear expression to that principle when he laid down that in a free State every person who is considered to have a free spirit —a somewhat abstract qualification—should be governed by himself or his freely chosen representatives.[7] This is a consideration even more fundamental than the fact that the franchise is a condition of a just consideration of the claims of all subject to the rule of law.[8] In the meantime—the author of the present draft has adopted this solution with the greatest hesitation—it seems necessary to leave this question to developments more organic and more evolutionary than the International Bill of the Rights of Man. In the Union of South Africa the population of European descent numbers two millions; the native Bantu population numbers six and a half millions; that of coloured and Asiatic races one million. The implications, in this case, of an absolute equality of franchise need no elaboration. When the Government of South Africa explained at the Imperial Conference of 1923 why it deemed it impossible to grant the franchise to Indians, whose number did not exceed one quarter of a million, the principal reason was that once South Africa granted the suffrage to Indians, she would have to grant it to natives—a consummation which would signify the end of her Western civilization. The Prime Minister of South Africa said:

So far as South Africa is concerned, therefore, it is a question of impossibility. . . . For South Africa, for white South Africa, it is not a question of dignity, but a question of existence, and no government could for a

[7] *De l'esprit des lois,* XI, 6. Condorcet considered this to be the consequence of the natural and primitive equality of man.
[8] A consideration cogently put by Professor Laski in *Liberty in the Modern State* (1930), pp. 37-39.

moment either tamper with this position or do anything to meet the Indian point of view. . . . We are up against a stone wall, and we cannot get over it.[9]

The position in South Africa is *sui generis*, and it would be fatal to adapt fully the fundamental purpose of the Bill of Rights to exceptional situations of this nature. It is preferable to expect that States confronted with these situations should, consistently, with a far-sighted and enlightened conception of their vital interests, adapt their practices to the fundamental tendencies and needs of international society. An International Bill of the Rights of Man adapted to meet the lowest existing minimum standard would be a mockery of its purpose. It must implicitly reject certain conceptions as utterly inconsistent with its objects.[10] In refraining from adopting the principle of absolute equality of suffrage, the Bill of Rights renders possible the adoption of qualifications of property, of taxation, and of education as well as the setting up of separate electoral rolls. This is what is meant by equality of suffrage "in accordance with the law of the State." So long as there is no wholesale disfranchisement on account of race, colour, and religion, it is wise and proper that the Bill of Rights should depend upon the gradual operation of public opinion and the watchfulness of courts—both strengthened by the residuary powers of international concern in the matter—to bring about an approximation of national practice and legislation to the principles of the Bill of Rights.

It is in this manner that a solution can be found of the thorny problem of actual disfranchisement of large sections of the Negro population in some States of the United States without jeopardizing, on this account, the adherence of the United States to the Bill of Rights. That disfranchisement has not taken place through the exclusion of Negroes as such, but through the adoption of such tests and devices as property qualifica-

---

[9] *Proceedings of the Imperial Conference of 1923*, Cmd. 1988.
[10] Such as the reply given by President Kruger to a deputation of Indians who pleaded for just treatment of Indian traders. The President said: "You are the descendants of Ishmael and therefore from your very birth bound to slave for the descendants of Esau. As the descendants of Esau we cannot admit you to rights placing you on a footing of equality with ourselves. You must rest content with what rights we grant to you" (as cited by W. K. Hancock, *Survey of British Commonwealth Affairs, Problems of Nationality, 1918–1936* [New York, London, 1937–42], I, 189. In 1858 the Transvaal folk declared in their Grond-Wet: "The people desire to permit no equality between coloured people and the white inhabitants, either in Church or State" (*ibid.*).

tions, poll taxes, exclusion from voting as a consequence of commission of certain offences (these offences being those most commonly committed by the Negro population), tests of literacy and education, capacity to understand the duties and obligations of citizenship under a republican form of government, the notorious grandfather test, and, finally, the exclusion of negroes from membership of the principal political parties, with the result that they cannot take part in so-called "primary" elections. Some of these practices have been held by the courts to be in accordance with the Constitution; with regard to others, like the last-mentioned qualification, the tendency has been to hold the actual disfranchisement to be contrary to the "great restraints of the Constitution." [11]

The foregoing considerations explain why the guarantee of the right to self-government must be of the same character as the other political, social, and economic rights of Part II of the bill. These rights are not normally capable of enforcement by way of judicial process before national tribunals. Neither can they be sufficiently precise to call for adjudication by international courts. The general principle of Article 10 is clear; it constitutes an international obligation of States and a legitimate subject matter of international concern and enforcement. Because of the unavoidable elasticity of its clauses, that article must rely for its implementation in the international sphere on a machinery which, as will be seen, is administrative and political rather than judicial and legal. The supervision of the competent international organs, as outlined in Part III of the Bill of Rights, will in this matter look, not to the details, but to the general implementation of the Bill of Rights. Cases may, of course, arise which will leave no room for doubt. When a revolution, peaceful or violent, results in the establishment of a dictatorship which for a prolonged period denies to the people the right of self-government, the international guarantee will come fully into being. It will be in this prompt and unequivocal action of the international authority that the primary purpose of this aspect

[11] Mr. Justice Cardozo, in *Nixon v. Condon* (1932) 286 U.S. 73—on the ground that for the purposes of the election the political parties must be deemed to have become instrumentalities of the State. For a review of the legal decisions on the voting franchise of Negroes see C. S. Mangum, *The Legal Status of the Negro* (Chapel Hill, 1940), pp. 371-424.

of the Bill of Rights will assert itself. But apart from these obvious contingencies, the function of the international authority will have to be one of watchfulness, of publicity, of focussing the pressure of the public opinion of the world, of persuasion. It is in this way that it will deal with any particular infringement of the principle that elections must be free, secret, periodical, and on a footing of equality. However, a serious and cumulative violation of some or of all these requirements will provide ground for international action when it becomes clear that government by consent has ceased or is in danger of ceasing to exist.

The author of the present Draft is conscious of the fact that the proposed Article is likely to meet with more severe criticism than, perhaps, any other Article of the Draft. The notion of an international guarantee of government by consent must appear to many as wholly impracticable. Others will regard it as not even desirable. They will insist, with some impatience, that the rule of democracy cannot be artificially engrafted upon the body politic of any people and that it is the product of long experience, of painful growth, of an overriding sense of national unity, and of a certain minimum of culture and civilization. Some of these objections have been answered above by reference to the fundamental nature of the claim, upon which other freedoms ultimately depend, of the right to government by consent. To that extent its affirmation must be regarded as an indispensable part of the International Bill of the Rights of Man. However, it is arguable that legal and political institutions do not inevitably follow the path of logical necessity and that an International Bill of the Rights of Man may, even without an affirmation and a guarantee of the right to government by consent, constitute a significant, effective, and beneficent innovation. The eventual decision on the substance of the Bill of Rights as finally adopted must be the result of conscientious thought and discussion, for which the present Draft is intended as a starting point. In engaging in such discussion we must disdain any tendency, which is morally indefensible, to regard civilized human beings organized in independent States as fit to live under a system of government which, if applied to ourselves, we would consider as derogatory to the dignity of man and as inconsistent with essential human rights.

THE RIGHT TO POLITICAL INDEPENDENCE

Article 11

Whenever the political condition or the stage of development of a community which has not yet obtained full political independence or which constitutes a colony or a mandated territory require the continued application of the principle of trusteeship or of mandatory tutelage by another State, such modification of the right of self-government shall be subject to the supervision of and to ultimate control by international authority. There shall be formed for that purpose an International Statute of Peoples under Colonial and Mandatory Government.

Man's freedom is denied not only if he lives under a legal system which exposes him to arbitrary physical restraint and, generally, to arbitrary deprivation of personal liberty without due process of law. He is also deprived of his freedom if he is governed without his consent. Now man's freedom, thus conceived, can be denied in two ways. It may be refused to him by persons of his own race and nationality who within the borders of the national State establish a system of absolutism depriving the citizen of the right to choose his rulers and his lawmakers on the basis of free and periodic elections on a footing of general equality. The Bill of Rights is intended, in Article 10, to provide protection for this aspect of the right to freedom. However, there is no escape from the fact that the principle which denies the right of one man or group of men within the same people to rule others without their consent, applies also to the right of one people to rule another without its consent. The question thus put raises the entire problem of national self-determination in its double aspect.

It raises, in the first instance, the question of self-determination in its extreme form, namely, the right of any minority, political, national, linguistic, or other, to leave the State within which history and geography has placed it and to form a State of its own. The assertion of the right of self-determination in this form amounts to a negation of the State and of government in general. National self-determination is an enlightened and beneficent ideal to which the formation of States must conform if both justice and the peace of the world are to be secured. But it is not a principle which can always be consistently applied in defiance of facts of economics, geography, and history. Unless the international system is to be atomized to the point of anarchy, States must exist which comprise national minorities, even if these minorities, had the matter been left to their free will, would have decided to belong to another State or to form a State of their own. The principle of self-determination, if pushed to the extreme, results in a negation of the State. For there is no logical reason why political self-determination in the sense of the right to form a State should be a privilege of major groups only as distinguished from other minorities.

The existence of national minorities within the State cannot be avoided not only with regard to minorities either dispersed within the State or living in the midst of it in compact masses within closed geographical areas, but also with regard to minorities bordering on States of cognate race and language. Geographical, historical, political, and economic reasons may make self-determination, in the sense of incorporation within the parent State, impracticable or undesirable. It is possible that the delimitation of frontiers in a particular peace settlement may not stand the test of justice or wisdom, but the Bill of Rights is not the proper means of rectifying any such mistakes, except indirectly in that it protects minorities against discrimination and ensures their cultural needs as an ethnic entity with regard to the use of language, education, and otherwise. Moreover, it is reasonable to assume that the political claims for self-determination on the part of such minorities are likely to become less cogent in proportion as the State, true to the idea of equality, becomes a non-national State in the sense that members of the majority do not enjoy legal or factual privileges denied to the citizens of the national minority.

It would appear from the foregoing considerations that while national self-determination in the sense of the right to form or belong to political units of the same language is a rational and desirable principle, it is not so rigid or absolute as to bear a direct relation to the primary right of freedom.

The problem is radically different with regard to peoples who form a majority—if not practically the entire population—of colonies, of mandated territories, of protectorates, and of dependent territories at a more advanced stage of political development. The political questions raised by the position, the government, and future independence of these peoples are complex and delicate. So are many other problems raised by the Bill of Rights. The complexities of this problem, the impact of vested interests, considerations of sovereignty and of national dignity of the States in possession—all these would seem to suggest, for the sake of other interests protected by the Bill of Rights, that this particular problem should be left out of account. However, this is not a method which can be adopted consistently with the true significance and the purpose of the International Bill of the Rights of Man.

The Bill of Rights must face the problem of freedom in all its aspects and all its implications. It must give effect to the principle expressed in the Preamble that "the natural right of man to freedom comprises the right of self-government through rulers chosen by and accountable to him" and that "the equality of man regardless of nationality, race and colour demands an equal opportunity of self-government and cultural development." The application of that principle means that whenever one people exercises dominion over another to the extent of depriving the latter of the right of self-government, such dominion must have some justification and some limitation, however indefinite, in point of time.

The system of mandates gave expression to one aspect of that principle. Peoples which have not reached the requisite stage of development may, consistently with their own good and with the claim of ultimate self-determination, be governed by another people accountable to an international authority. The question whether colonial rule has, in general, been advantageous to peoples subject to foreign rule cannot be answered conclusively. The answer is different with relation to different colonizing powers. It may be a matter of dispute whether the evils of colonization—exploitation, vice, disease, forced labour, disruption of family ties, disintegration of native customs—have been sufficiently compensated by a higher standard of life. But these questions are not wholly relevant. What is relevant is that the acknowledgment of the equality of man and of his right to freedom is incompatible with man's rule over man unless it is for the benefit of the ruled. The acceptance of that principle involves the adoption of its corollary, namely, that the State entrusted with the rule of peoples which have not reached the requisite stage of maturity cannot remain the sole judge of the way in which it administers the trust; for this it must be accountable to a higher authority. From this point of view the question of the national or international character of the administration is of secondary importance. The balance of advantage is probably in favour of the retention of undivided administration by the States under whose sovereignty such territories are placed until the international authority may see fit to recommend the consideration of a change in their status. It can be assumed that such consideration will not be recommended lightly or hastily. Neither would the change take the form of a full transition to the status of full independence. It may, in the first instance, take the shape of a transformation into some kind of protectorate with varying degrees of internal independence. The next stage may be a large, if not complete, measure of international and external independence coupled with a close association, on the lines of Dominion status within the British Commonwealth of Nations, with the metropolitan territory. These various stages may succeed each other throughout many generations.

All this does not mean that in the meantime the adherence of the colonial powers to the principles of the International Bill of the Rights of Man in this matter, while leaving intact the administration and the sovereignty of those States, would be a mere gesture:

In the first instance, the colonial powers, by accepting the Bill of Rights, will expressly acknowledge the principle of trusteeship and disinterestedness as governing their administration of the colonies— a principle which, in turn, involves far-reaching consequences. Such acknowledgement of the principle of trusteeship would not in any sense be an innovation. Great Britain, the greatest colonizing Power, has given to it repeated and emphatic expression.[12]

Secondly, as one of the consequences of that principle, the colonial Powers would accept the obligation of rendering account of their

[12] See the White Paper of 1923 in connection with the Kenya controversy: "His Majesty's Government regard themselves as exercising a trust on behalf of the African population. . . . As in the Uganda Protectorate, so in the Kenya Colony, the principle of trusteeship for the natives, no less than in the mandated territory of Tanganyika, is unassailable": Cmd. 1922. And see White Paper of 1930 (Cmd. 3573; Cmd. 3574).

administration to an international supervisory body—the Colonial Commission—operating under an International Statute of Colonial and Mandated Territories and responsible to the supreme international authority. That commission would scrutinize the annual reports of the colonizing Powers from the point of view of the conformity of their administration with the welfare of the native population and its advancement to self-government. It is unecessary to discuss the question whether submission to such international supervision would amount to a partial surrender of sovereignty. Even if it did—although it is difficult to see how this would be the result—the concession would be small compared with the significance of the practical acknowledgment of the principle that no people, however advanced, is entitled to rule another, however backward, unless in pursuance of the duty of trusteeship. It is of the essence of that duty that account must be rendered and that there must be some measure of supervision by a disinterested agency. Such supervision need not interfere with the ordinary administration of the territory; far from detracting from the prestige of the sovereign power, it would add to it immeasurably. While, so far as the actual administration of the colonies is concerned, submission to international supervision would be to a large extent a gesture acknowledging the universality of the application of the fundamental ideas of the Bill of Rights, it would lift the entire problem of colonies to a higher plane of duty as distinguished from possession, conquest, and material interest. It would internationalize colonies, in a sense not purely nominal, without exposing them to the untried hazards of direct international administration.

A further consequence of the principle that the colonizing States are the trustees of international society for the welfare and the political development of the native populations would be the exclusion of any predominance of direct interest and profit for the colonizing Power. The interests of the native population must be paramount.[13] In par-

[13] This principle of paramountcy of the interests of the native population has been repeatedly given expression by the British Government. See the White Paper in connection with the Kenya Indian controversy: "Primarily, Kenya is an African territory, and His Majesty's Government think it necessary to record their considered opinion that the interests of the African natives must be paramount, and that if, and when, those interests and the interests of the immigrant races should conflict, the former should prevail" (Cmd. 1922, p. 9). And see the Report of the Joint Select

ticular, the colonizing Power could no longer reserve for itself and its nationals economic advantages in the matter of tariffs, access to raw materials, and otherwise, while withholding them from other States and their nationals. The making of profit may be consistent with the fulfilment of a duty, but it is a spurious combination which must be avoided in this case. It is possible that any such monopolistic and protectionist practices indicating a closer association with the metropolitan country may in a particular case confer a benefit upon the native population. But such advantage must be purely temporary and insignificant in comparison with the dangers of the abandonment of a vital aspect of the principle of trusteeship. There must, as in the case of mandated territories, obtain in the colonies the principle of equality of economic opportunity for the nationals of all States. Thus one of the indirect consequences of the adoption of the Bill of Rights in this matter will be a combination to the solution of the economic international problem with regard to access to raw materials, which has loomed large in public discussion and in declarations of governments.

Fourthly, the principles of trusteeship and of equality of opportunity may require, in addition to the task of international supervision and without interference with the unity of colonial government, international co-operation of States, both colonial and others, interested in the administration and development of colonial territories within defined regions of the world. It would be within the province of the Colonial Commission to formulate the principles of such co-operation. In 1943 the British Government expressed their concurrence in the principle of regional commissions for the purposes of such co-operation.[14]

Committee of 1931 on the same subject: "[Paramountcy] means no more than that the interests of the overwhelming majority of the indigenous population should not be subordinated to those of a minority belonging to another race, however important in itself" (H.C. Paper No. 156 of 1931, I, 31). See also M. R. Dilley, *British Policy in Kenya Colony* (New York, 1937), pp. 141–178.

[14] Speaking on July 13, 1943, in the House of Commons the Secretary of State for the Colonies said: "Those commissions would comprise not only the states with colonial territories in the region, but also other states which had in the region a major strategic or economic interest. While each state would remain responsible for the administration of its own territory, such a commission would provide effective and permanent machinery for consultation and callaboration so that the states concerned might work together to promote the well-being of the colonial territories. An important consideration in designing the machinery of each commission would be to give to the people

Finally, one of the consequences of the adoption of the principle of the Bill of Rights in the matter of colonies would be the obligation of the colonial Powers to co-operate loyally with the international authority with respect to any future proposals and recommendations for gradual changes in the status of the colonial territories.

Although the question of implementation and of machinery forms the subject matter of Part III of the Bill of Rights, it is in this case convenient to consider the international agencies appropriate to this article of the Bill. In the matter of the mandated territories no substantial changes would be necessary either with regard to the principles enunciated in Article 22 of the Covenant of the League of Nations or to the machinery created in pursuance of its provisions—subject to the important addition of the power to consider and to recommend changes in the political status of the territories on the way to self-government. But it would be desirable to incorporate the provisions as to mandated territories, which now form part of the Covenant, in a more comprehensive instrument—the International Statute of Peoples under Colonial and Mandatory Government—embodying the principles of Article 11 of the Bill of Rights and providing machinery for its implementation. Under that statute, a Colonial Commission would have to be constituted for colonial and other dependent territories.

The Colonial Commission would be constituted on lines corresponding to those of the Mandates Commission. It would receive general and periodic reports from the colonial Powers on the administration of the colonies. It would scrutinize them mainly by reference: (*a*) to the observance of the principles of the Statute, which in most respects would be analogous to those of Article 22 of the Covenant in the matter of colonial government (including, in particular, the policy of the colonial Powers in the direction of developing the institutions of self-government in the territories under their control and the observance of the obligations in the matter of equality of economic opportunity

---

of the colonial territories in the region an opportunity to be associated with its work. In this way it would be possible to have international co-operation which consisted of something more than theoretical discussion, but would be able to grapple with realities and get down to the solution of individual problems." In March, 1942, an Anglo-American Caribbean Commission was established within the province of which there entered some such co-operation in colonial matters.

for other States and their nationals); and (*b*) to the observance of the provisions of the Bill of Rights, both of Part I and of Part II. In this matter it would be more suitable if the supervision rested not with the High Commission, as provided in Article 19, but with the Colonial Commission proper. It would also be the duty of the Colonial Commission to consider and to recommend changes in the political status both of the colonial territories and of other dependent communities.

The activities of the Mandates Commission and the Colonial Commission would be concerned with the application of principles which are fundamentally identical. While the vastness of their task would necessitate the distribution of the work between these two agencies, they would operate under a single International Statute of Mandated and Colonial Territories.

The Statute might also include a provision for the constitution of regional colonial commissions for facilitating the co-operation of States interested directly or indirectly in the government of colonies in particular regions.

THE RIGHT TO PRESERVATION OF CULTURAL ENTITY

Article 12

In States inhabited by a substantial number of persons of a race, language or religion other than those of the majority of the population, persons belonging to such ethnic, linguistic or religious minorities shall have the right to establish and maintain, out of an equitable proportion of the available public funds, their schools and cultural and religious institutions and to use their own language before the courts and other authorities and organs of the State.

This article is concerned with what may be called the positive aspect of the question of national, religious and linguistic minorities, namely, their right to cultural development and to the assertion of their ethnic heritage on a footing of equality with other national, religious and linguistic groups within the State. The other aspect of the problem of minorities is covered by Article 7, in which the nationals and, with regard to fundamental rights, the residents of a State generally, are guaranteed equality of treatment regardless, *inter alia*, of nationality, race, religion and language. The combined effect of both these articles is an attempt to solve, within the framework of the International Bill of the Rights of Man, the question of the protection of minorities which formed the subject matter of the Minorities Treaties concluded in 1919 and in subsequent years.

The most difficult aspect of the question of minorities which the Treaties of 1919 intended to solve was that of discrimination against minorities because of their race, religion, or language. That feature of the problem of minorities is capable of solution, on a universal basis, within the framework of Article 7 of the Bill of Rights, in which the right to equality before the law and to equal treatment by the organs and authorities of the State is proclaimed as a legal right enforceable, like other clauses of Part I of the Bill, before the tribunals of the State and fully protected by the international machinery of the Bill of Rights. From this point of view the Bill of Rights eliminates one of the principal drawbacks of the system of protection of minorities as established by the treaties of 1919. It applies universally to all States and thus removes a frequently voiced objection by the States which were asked to subscribe to them. There is no doubt that it covers the most acute aspect of the question of protection of minorities.

However, the International Bill of the Rights of Man cannot ignore what may be called the cultural aspect of the problem of ethnic, religious and linguistic minorities. The Minorities Treaties, in addition to imposing upon the States in question the obligation to refrain from discrimination against the minorities, laid upon these States certain positive duties in the matter of the cultural needs of the minorities. Thus, in the Polish Minorities Treaty, Poland undertook, notwithstanding any recognition of an official language, to provide facilities for Polish nationals of non-Polish speech to use their language, both orally and in writing, before the courts. She agreed that Polish nationals who belong to racial, religious or linguistic minorities shall have an equal right to establish, manage, and control at their own expense charitable, religious, and social institutions, schools, and other educational establishments, with the right to use their own language. Poland agreed to provide, in towns and districts in which a considerable proportion of Polish nationals of other than Polish speech are resident, adequate facilities for ensuring that in the primary schools instruction shall be given to the children of such Polish nationals through the medium of their own language. In towns and districts where there is a considerable proportion of Polish nationals belonging to racial, religious, or linguistic minorities, these minorities were to be assured an equitable share of the sums provided out of public funds for educational, religious, or charitable purposes.

The claim of the individual to the preservation and development of his ethnic identity by at least some education in his native language and by being allowed to use it before the administrative and judicial authorities of the State and to maintain the cultural institutions of his ethnic group cannot be disregarded without doing violence to a principle of justice and stultifying human personality. Refusal of this demand has often resulted in conditions which are dangerous to international peace. This is why the Bill of Rights would be deficient if it failed effectively to acknowledge the right of the individual not to be thwarted in his development by a denial of his cultural rights. The recognition of those rights would undoubtedly impose a check upon any practice on the part of States calculated to force upon minorities a policy of assimilation. But it is the object of the Bill of Rights to check policies and practices inimical alike to the growth of human personality and to international peace.[15] In the present draft the cultural rights of minorities have been included—not without much hesitation—in Part II of the Bill of Rights, that is, among rights not capable of or suitable for enforcement by the ordinary legal process before the judicial authorities of the State. This is so not only because of the substantial administrative difficulties involved in the matter. In the first instance, while the position with regard to minorities which live in compact masses within definite geographical areas is comparatively simple, this is not so with regard to minorities dispersed among the population. Secondly, there must be considered the wishes of such minorities as desire cultural assimilation with the majority.[16] The decisive considera-

[15] Article 134 of the Czechoslovak Constitution of 1922 provided that "every manner whatsoever of forcible denationalization shall be forbidden" and that "violation of this principle may be declared by law to be a criminal offense."

[16] On the other hand, experience has shown that the requirements of uniform administration of the State, of a necessary degree of centralization and of a unity cemented by a common State language are not inconsistent with a broad-minded consideration for the cultural needs of minorities.

tion is that the respect for and active support of the cultural interests and values of minorities is not a result which can be secured by legal action before municipal courts. No measure of enforceability, however stringent, could bring about such a consistent and generous policy of respect for and active assistance in developing the cultural life of minorities as is shown by Soviet Russia,[17] Switzerland, and Great Britain.[18]

On the other hand, it cannot be denied that the right to use the minority language before courts and other authorities of the State can be enforced by legal processes. The same applies to the right to an equitable share in the public funds available for educational and similar purposes.[19] It would seem, therefore, that though the balance of advantage appears to indicate the inclusion of Article 12 in Part II of the Bill of Rights, cogent arguments might be addressed in favour of its inclusion in Part I.

While the right of national minorities to maintain and develop their cultural entity is not, according to the present draft, such as to be properly enforceable by legal process before municipal courts, it must, nevertheless, as has been shown, be recognized as an international obligation of States. To that obligation there must correspond the right of persons belonging to a minority to initiate, through petition and complaint, an international procedure of investigation, supervision, and enforcement. The High Commission of the Rights of Man, whose functions are set out in Part III of the Bill of Rights, would have for that purpose to be assisted by a Minorities Commission. The latter would receive and investigate petitions from interested individuals and

[17] A careful and scholarly observer has stated that "there seems no doubt that the Communists are genuinely trying to realize their own theories of the absolute equality of all nationalities . . . and the dissociation of nationality from questions of State:"— C. A. Macartney, *National States and National Minorities* (London, 1934), p. 462. In the autonomous republics there obtain two official languages: the local language and the Russian. In those dependent on another Union republic, there obtain three official languages: the language of that republic, the Russian, and the local language. There is general agreement that the aim of the central authorities of Soviet Russia has been not to establish the supremacy of Russian nationalism but to make of Russia a true unnational State.

[18] In Wales and in Scotland the principle that the use of Welsh and Gaelic in administration and before courts is regulated according to local demand, has become part of the established practice. See Llewellyn Jones in *Transactions of the Grotius Society*, XII (1920), 92–121.

[19] See Article 133 of the Czechoslovak Constitution of 1922 which provided for future legislation to define, in this connection, the expression "considerable proportion."

groups and representations from States. It would transmit to the High Commission for further action—the nature of which is indicated below in Part III—any cases of a general and persistent policy on the part of a State tending to disregard the obligations of the Bill of Rights in the matter of the cultural rights of minorities. At the same time it would act as an agency for collection and publication of information on the practice of States in the matter, on the various forms of cultural autonomy granted to minorities, and on arrangements between States such as the provision of facilities for education and training of minorities from other States.[20]

THE ECONOMIC AND SOCIAL RIGHTS

Article 13
States shall, within the limits of their economic capacity and development, make effective provision for securing the right to work, to education and to public assistance in case of unemployment, old age, sickness, disablement and other cases of undeserved want.

Article 14
States shall, in co-operation with other States and with the International Labour Organization, make provision for securing just and humane conditions of work.

Economic freedom in its wider sense includes the effective recognition of the right to work under proper conditions of pay and employment, the right to education and to an equal opportunity for education, and the right to economic security in case of unemployment, old age, sickness, disablement, and other cases of undeserved want. To say that the rights of political freedom are illusory without economic freedom is clearly an exaggeration. But it is true that the freedom of human personality taken in its totality is incomplete if the achievement of political freedom is not accompanied by a corresponding advance in the economic and social spheres. The political freedom and equality of the wage-earner are an asset of fundamental importance even if his economic liberty, expressed in the theoretical freedom to give or withhold

[20] Such as the arrangement between Germany and Denmark by which German teachers in Denmark were to undergo a year's training in Germany. Similar arrangements were made between Czechoslovakia and Rumania, and Rumania and Yugoslavia.

his services, is utterly meaningless because of the overwhelming impact of economic necessity and dependence. Yet it is true that the value of political freedom is impaired by the absence of substantive economic freedom, by economic insecurity, by undeserved want, and by absence of educational opportunity.

This economic freedom of the many, it will be noted, can in many respects be achieved only by putting economic restraints upon the few. In modern society economic freedom, conceived as the mere absence of restraints imposed by the State, results in economic anarchy, in exploitation of the weak and isolated individual by economically powerful and organized forces and in the denial of substantive freedom of contract.

It is significant that the close connection between political and economic freedom was clearly recognized at the end of the eighteenth century by Tom Paine, the author of *The Rights of Man*.[21] Neither was this connection unknown to the French Revolutionary Convention. In 1790 the Convention adopted a decree relating to mendicants in Paris which proclaimed that "society owes to all its members maintenance or work." In the Declaration of Rights of 1793 it was said: "Public assistance is a sacred duty. Society owes assistance to unfortunate citizens either by providing them with work or by assuring means of subsistence to those who are unable to work."[22] In

[21] In 1796 Paine published his *Agrarian Justice Opposed to Agrarian Law and Agrarian Monopoly*. This was a reply to Watson, Bishop of Llandaff, who had praised "the wisdom and goodness of God in having made both rich and poor." Paine denied that the distinction between rich and poor was of natural origin. While noting the spread of the idea of representative government, Paine insisted that the French Revolution would find an ally in the hearts of men only if that political system produced a social system under which all men and women could inherit the capital necessary to enable them to begin to earn their living and under which they would be able to escape the poverty of old age. He proposed a graduated tax on inheritances to form a national pool to allow the payment of a pension of £10 a year to every person over fifty and a sum of £15 to every person reaching the age of 21. Such persons "could buy a cow and implements to cultivate a few acres of land; and, instead of becoming burdens upon society, which is always the case, where children are produced faster than they can be fed, would be put in the way of becoming useful and profitable citizens." In his *Rights of Man* Paine attempted to determine the assistance of the State to men over fifty who "may feel it necessary or comfortable to be better supported than they can support themselves, and that not as a matter of grace and favour, but of right."
[22] Montesquieu had previously insisted (*Esprit des lois* [1794], Book V, ch. vi) that in a proper democracy every person ought to have the means of earning a livelihood. At the same time he pointed to the fact that Solon made idleness a crime.

England the social right to public assistance had for a long time been the subject of legislation, but it is significant that Blackstone in his *Commentaries* deals with it in the Chapter on "The Absolute Rights of Individuals."[23]

It is idle to speculate whether this claim to the assurance of a right to work and to other positive action on the part of the State is the consequence of any inherent natural right of man, or whether it is the result of an obligation of the State implied in the fact of social solidarity and independent of any individualistic doctrine of society.[24] The result is the same. Duguit, who rejects the individualist view that persons have a natural right against the State, is nevertheless emphatic in affirming that the State has an objective duty to provide work, to ensure proper conditions of employment, and to provide a minimum of free education. For, he says, the State is obliged not only to abstain from enacting laws which interfere with the free development of individual activity, but to assist it by positive measures.[25]

Modern constitutions of States have increasingly tended to recognize the right to work, to proper conditions of employment, to education, and to social security. In the Constitution of Soviet Russia of 1936 these rights are expressed in an emphatic manner; they are placed in the forefront of the list of the fundamental rights and duties of citizens.[26] The constitutions of some other States follow occasionally

[23] He says (Book I, ch. i): "The law not only regards life and member, and protects every man in the enjoyment of them, but also furnishes him with everything necessary for their support. For there is no man so indigent or wretched, but he may demand a supply sufficient for all the necessities of life from the more opulent part of the community, by means of the several statutes enacted for the supply of the poor. . . ." Already in the second half of the sixteenth century the law had recognized the right of the indigent, the infirm, the unemployed, and the labourers with inadequate wages, to assistance by the State. Legislation had been enacted on the subject in 1562, 1572, and 1601. Justices of the peace were empowered to levy for that purpose a poor rate on the inhabitants.
[24] In one of the best-known treatises on natural law in the nineteenth century, Ahrens's *Traité du droit naturel*, we find a clear statement that "the individual has no right to work as against the State" (II, 97).
[25] *Droit constitutionnel*, III (2d ed., 1923), 627–639.
[26] Article 118(1): Citizens of the U.S.S.R. have the right to work, i. e., the right to guaranteed employment and payment for their work in accordance with its quantity and quality.
   Article 119(1): Citizens of the U.S.S.R. have the right to rest and leisure.
   Article 120(1): Citizens of the U.S.S.R. have the right to maintenance in old age and also in case of sickness or loss of capacity to work.
   Article 121(1): Citizens of the U.S.S.R. have the right to education.

the same phraseology of fundamental and inherent rights.[27] As a rule, however, these rights are recognized by means of general clauses laying down social and educational principles and lines of policy for future legislation. Thus, for instance, the right to education is almost universally recognized in the form of the adoption of the principle that elementary education is both compulsory and free.[28] The right to work is recognized not only by a general guarantee thereof [29] but also by express clauses providing for a fair rate of pay,[30] for regulation of hours of work,[31] for weekly rest,[32] and for paid vacations. Finally, many modern constitutions recognize the right to social security by laying down the principle of insurance and of assistance by the State in cases of undeserved want.[33] The securing of the social and economic rights has loomed large in the proposals of private writers and or-

[27] Article 63 of the Constitution of Costa Rica of 1871 (as amended in 1942) declares social insurance "to be an absolute and inalienable right of all manual and intellectual workers"; Articles 60 and 277 of the Cuban Constitution of 1940 protects the inalienable right to work, while Article 65 establishes social security as an "irrenounceable and imprescriptible right of workers"; Article 42(1) of the Irish Constitution of 1937 "guarantees to respect the inalienable right and duty of parents to provide" for the education of their children.

[28] See Article 145 of the German Constitution of 1919; Article 118 of the Polish Constitution of 1921; Article 27 of the Swiss Constitution of 1874 (as amended in 1931); Article 130 of the Brazilian Constitution of 1937 (as amended in 1942); Article 72 of the Peruvian Constitution of 1933; Article 23 of the Greek Constitution of 1927; Article 50 of the Chinese Provisional Constitution of 1931; Article 25 of the Constitution of Hejaz of 1926. The constitutions of some States of the American Union, in providing for free and compulsory education, stress the close connection between the diffusion of knowledge through education and the preservation of the rights and of the liberties of the people; see Article 11(1) of the constitution of Missouri of 1875; Article 8(1) of the constitution of South Dakota of 1889; Article 7(1) of the constitution of Texas of 1876.

[29] See Article 163 of the German Constitution of 1919; Articles 60 and 277 of the Cuban Constitution of 1940; Article 136 of the Brazilian Constitution of 1937; Article 45(2) of the Irish Constitution of 1937. With this there may be compared sec. 15 of the English Poor Law Act, 1930, which re-enacts the Poor Law Act of 1601 and lays down that: "(1) It shall be the duty of the council of every county and county borough—(a) to set to work all such persons, whether married or unmarried, as have no means to maintain themselves, and use no ordinary and daily trade of life to get their living by."

[30] See Article 123(vi) of the Mexican constitutions of 1917 and 1942; Article 46 of the Peruvian Constitution of 1933.

[31] See Article 122 of the Bolivian Constitution of 1938 as well as the constitutions of most Latin-American States; Article 34 of the Swiss Constitution of 1874 (as modified in 1931).

[32] See Article 137 of the Brazilian Constitution of 1937; Article 32(8) of the Venezuelan Constitution of 1936.

[33] A provision to be found mostly in the constitutions of the Latin-American States.

ganizations concerned with an International Bill of the Rights of Man.[34] "Freedom from want" has repeatedly formed the subject matter of official declarations of "peace aims."

However, neither considerations of principle, which postulate that the claim to a decent standard of living, to social security, and to equality of education and opportunity is no less entitled to satisfaction than the rights of personal and political freedom, nor the instructive trend of constitutional provisions and of modern legislation on the subject, nor declarations of governments affirming freedom from want to be one of the major purposes of the War, nor corresponding expressions of opinion by private writers and organizations provide an answer to the question as to the nature and the purpose of the enunciation of these social rights in an international instrument. In so far as a solemn pronouncement by governments on this subject is no more than a declaration of intention on their part to follow the principles calculated to secure freedom from want, it may be of some effect in proportion as it becomes a guide for governmental action and for public opinion within the State. These principles may be made part of municipal law, in so far as they are not so already; they may be elevated to the rank of constitutional principles. But are they a proper subject

[34] See Articles 1 and 2 of Mr. H. G. Wells's Declaration of the Rights of Man in *The New World Order* (London, 1940), p. 139, and *Commission to Study the Organization of Peace, Third Report*, February, 1943, pp. 223–227. For a useful survey of the relevant constitutional provisions of various countries see *Constitutional Provisions concerning Social and Economic Policy*, Montreal, International Labour Office, 1944. In December, 1942, the United States National Resources Planning Board submitted to the President a report preceded by a New Bill of Rights in which the economic and social rights are placed in the forefront. The New Bill of Rights runs as follows:

1. The right to work, usefully and creatively, through the productive years;
2. The right to fair pay, adequate to command the necessities and amenities of life in exchange for work, ideas, thrift, and other socially valuable service;
3. The right to adequate food, clothing, shelter, and medical care;
4. The right to security, with freedom from fear of old age, want, dependency, sickness, unemployment and accident;
5. The right to live in a system of free enterprise, free from compulsory labor, irresponsible private power, arbitrary public authority, and unregulated monopolies;
6. The right to come and go, to speak or to be silent, free from the spyings of secret political police;
7. The right to equality before the law, with equal access to justice in fact;
8. The right to education, for work, for citizenship, and for personal growth and happiness; and
9. The right to rest, recreation, and adventure, the opportunity to enjoy life and take part in an advancing civilization.

matter of rules of international law whose validity and effectiveness is guaranteed by a measure of international co-operation, supervision, and, if need be, enforcement? Are they proper subjects for an International Bill of the Rights of Man conceived as part of the international legal order, and not as a mere declaration of principles?

There is one common element in the social rights of an economic character which, it would seem, renders them suitable and desirable objects of international obligation and regulation. Their effectiveness in one State is as a rule conditioned by their acceptance by other States. In a world of economic interdependence and free exchange of goods —a condition which must be assumed as part of an orderly and progressive development of international relations—improvements in social conditions cannot be fully achieved by the efforts of one State or group of States. This is the meaning of the fifth principle of the Atlantic Charter which contemplates "the fullest collaboration between all nations in the economic field with the object of securing for all improved labour standards, economic advancement, and social security."

Can the social and economic aspects of legislation properly form the subject matter of an international legal instrument and, generally, of the international legal order? They can be included if and when States agree that this part of the Bill of Rights is not only a declaration of common principles of policy but also a mutual legal promise to give effect to it; that all signatories to the Bill of Rights shall henceforth acquire a legal interest in the fulfilment of that promise by all other signatories; that the manner of its fulfilment is a legitimate subject matter of international concern and discussion; and that machinery must be set up for supervising and enforcing its clauses, if need be.

Subject to that general right of supervision and enforcement, the social and economic clauses of Articles 13 and 14 of the Bill of Rights must be in the nature of a somewhat indefinite declaration of principle. The Bill of Rights cannot prescribe the machinery by which States shall secure the right to work or to education; it cannot lay down a code for ensuring a minimum standard of wages or of holidays; it cannot determine the methods for securing humane conditions of work or of protection for women and minors; and it must abstain from prescribing the details of social insurance in its various aspects. National constitutions have not attempted a task of that immensity. Neither do they confer upon individuals any right of legal action to enforce the general principles of the constitution in this matter.

None of these limitations exclude the setting up of an effective international machinery of supervision and enforcement in accordance with the provisions of Part III of the Bill. This, as will be seen, centers round the High Commission set up under the International Bill of the Rights of Man and assisted in this matter, as well as in others, by a number of sections for the collection and publication of information and the preliminary examination of complaints of non-observance of the Bill of Rights. It would be the business of some of these sections to maintain close contact with the International Labour Organization in all matters coming within its purview and covered by the Bill of Rights. They would study the degree of participation of States in the conventions concluded under the auspices of the International Labour Organization. Machinery would have to be established by which the competent sections of the High Commission would receive, for further investigation and eventual action by the High Commission, any reports from the International Labour Organization pointing to the disregard by any State of its obligations under such conventions.

The sections would receive petitions from individuals and organizations and representations from States bearing on this and other aspects of the social and economic clauses of the Bill of Rights. The character of that supervisory function would be determined by the general nature of the function of the High Commission and of its sections in the matter of the observance of the Bill of Rights. They would not act upon, though they would investigate, every complaint alleging failure to supply an educational facility or a scheme of insurance. The sections would be concerned not so much with the disregard of individual provisions and laws as with conditions violative of the spirit and the purpose of the Bill of Rights. When, having regard to the economic capacity and the development of a State, the section should find a *prima facie* case of general disregard for the provisions of the Bill of Rights, it would draw the attention of the High Commission to the situation that had arisen. It would then be for the High Commission, bearing in mind the generality of the obligations of the Bill of Rights in the matter, to investigate the position from this point of view. The High Commission, whose function will be to investigate complaints not only with reference to the immediate facts of the situation but also to wider considerations, may find either that no action is required or that it will be sufficient to bring the matter to the knowledge of the State concerned. It may find, on the other hand, that formal representations are required with the view to persuading the State to take positive action; it may decide, eventually, that the matter must be brought before the Council of the supreme international authority. This would, as a rule, happen only in exceptional cases of cumulative, comprehensive, and obstructive disregard of the obligations of the Bill of Rights.

But such exceptional cases must be envisaged, and, with regard to them, the right and the duty of the Council to take the necessary coercive action must be recognized. For, ultimately, it is in that right, exceptional as it may be, that the legal nature of the obligation involved asserts itself in the international sphere. The effect of the social and economic clauses of the International Bill of the Rights of Man will to a large extent be in its moral authority and in its constant inspiration as a guide for domestic effort and legislation. That authority will be immeasurably strengthened by the fact that, in the long run, the judgment and the power of the international community will be brought to bear upon the wanton failure of any State to give effect to these obligations. The powers of the Council in this matter, after its persuasive influence has failed, must be determined by the character of its coercive function in the matter of violations of the Bill of Rights. This is set forth in Part III. It must include "such political, economic, or military action as may be deemed necesary to protect the rights of man." The nature of the action thus taken will vary with the circumstances and will of necessity be confined to political and economic action. It will be taken only in extreme cases. But it must remain in the background as the ultimate guarantee of the determination of the Society of States to maintain not only the personal and political rights of freedom but also the economic and social liberty of man.

SUBJECTS NOT INCLUDED IN THE BILL OF RIGHTS

It may be convenient to draw attention to four subjects which have not been included in this Draft of a Bill of Rights.

The right of property.—In the first article of the Declaration on the Rights of Man adopted by the Institute of International Law in 1929 it was laid down that "it is the duty of every State to grant to every person the equal right to life, liberty, and property." With regard to the latter, that article would appear unobjectionable so long as its intention is to declare it to be the duty of the State to respect on a footing of equality such rights of property as are enjoyed by virtue of the law of the land. To that extent the right of property is protected by the equality clause of Article 7 of the present draft. But in so far as the right of property is conceived as an absolute and inalienable right of man it finds no place in the draft. Deep social and economic changes have intervened since Locke considered property to be the most sacred right of all—so sacred that he explained the rights of personal freedom on the ground that man had a right of property in his person; since Blackstone, who alongside of personal security and personal liberty included the right of property among the three absolute rights "inherent in every Englishman"; since the first articles of the Virginia Bill of Rights of 1776, which pointed, as being the inherent rights of man, "to enjoyment of life and liberty, with the means of acquiring and possessing property"; and since the French Declaration of the Rights of Man of 1789 described property as "an inviolable and sacred right."

That character of sanctity and inviolability has now departed from the right of property. This is so not only because of the advent of States in which, not private property, but collective ownership of the principal means of production has become the pivot of the economic system. It is so for the reason that private property has tended increasingly to be regarded not only as a right but also as a social function and duty. In States in which private property is the basis of the economic structure, it has become the object of State interference through taxation, death duties, and regulation in pursuance of general welfare, on a scale so wide as to render its inclusion in a fundamental Bill of Rights somewhat artificial. Its protection, to the extent to which it is recognized, must, alongside of other rights, be achieved within the general requirement of equality of treatment.

Freedom of commerce.—The freedom "to buy and to sell," conceived as excluding the power of the State to regulate international commerce by tariffs, restrictions on imports and exports, and other means, has been suggested occasionally as one of the rights to be protected by an International Bill of the Rights of Man.[35] It is idle to speculate whether such freedom can be regarded as a "natural" right of man. It is certainly not part of the modern practice of States. The desirability and practicability of its general adoption are highly controversial. It is clear that its inclusion in the Bill of Rights would instil into it a distinct and contentious element of unreality prejudicial to the major purposes of the Bill of Rights, which cannot properly be regarded as an instrument for solving controversial and complex problems of economics in the national and international spheres.

Freedom of immigration —The same applies to the postulated right of immigration—a problem of the greatest complexity both from the economic and from the cultural point of view. Its rational solution can be achieved, if at all, by dint of world-wide planning for the development of vast and sparsely populated areas. It cannot be solved by a formula or by a theoretical recognition of an abstract right.

Right to acquisition of nationality after prolonged residence.—The Draft, while postulating, in Article 9, the right of emigration and expatriation, does not go to the length of adopting the principle that an individual shall be entitled to acquire the nationality of the State where he has resided for a considerable period of time. There is no necessary correlation, logical or otherwise, between any such right and the right of emigration and expatriation. In most countries, including Great Britain, the grant of naturalization, while regulated by statute, is in the discretion of the executive. In the United States the Constitution provides for no such right. Legislation has, in fact, conferred a right of naturalization in the United States upon "free white persons" who fulfil the requisite statutory conditions. The latter qualification excludes from the enjoyment of that right Chinese, Japanese, and Hindus,

[35] See Quincy Wright, "International Law and Commercial Relations," *Proceedings of the American Society of International Law*, 1941, pp. 30–40.

though by statute "aliens of African Nativity" and "persons of African Descent" have been made eligible for naturalization. The political and other difficulties in the way of conferring upon every person a legal right to naturalization would seem such as to make impracticable, in the present state of opinion, any attempt to incorporate it as part of the International Bill of the Rights of Man.

Part III

THE ENFORCEMENT OF THE
INTERNATIONAL BILL OF
THE RIGHTS OF MAN

CHAPTER XI

THE ENFORCEMENT OF THE BILL

THE PRESENT DRAFT of the International Bill of the Rights of Man is based on the assumption that it will be adopted, not as a mere declaration of international policy embodying a statement of principles, but as an instrument creating legal rights and obligations. These include the right and the duty of enforcement. Reasons have already been given why a Bill of Rights deprived of provisions for its enforcement would hardly merit description as part of the international legal order and why it would constitute a retrogressive event out of keeping both with the solemn pronouncements of the United Nations and with the requirements of international peace.[1]

Enforcement through individual intervention.—There are intermediate stages between a mere declaration of principle and a full legal international guarantee of enforcement. Thus the International Bill of the Rights of Man might contain a declaration, in the Preamble or in the body of the Bill, to the effect that observance of its principles by any of the signatory States is a matter of concern for all other signatory States on the ground that such observance is an essential condition of international peace. This method might be adopted by omitting altogether Part III of the present draft of the Bill of Rights and substituting for it one article on the following lines:

This International Bill of the Rights of Man is hereby declared to be an integral part of the Law of Nations. Its observance shall be deemed vital to the preservation of international peace and as such a matter of concern for all the signatories.

[1] Why, it may be asked, should enforceability be regarded as a condition of the legal character of the International Bill of the Rights of Man although not with regard to other international treaties? The answer is that all treaties are, like any other rule of international law, enforceable in the sense that a State injured by a violation of the treaty may have recourse to such unilateral means of redress as international law permits. That method of enforcement would be insufficient for and inconsistent with the purposes of an International Bill of the Rights of Man.

Such bare recognition of the legal interest of the signatories in the observance of the clauses of the Bill would probably [2] imply a right of individual intervention in order to make that legal interest effective. There ought to be little doubt that any such method of making the Bill of Rights effective would be rudimentary to the point of being academic. It would not impose upon the signatories of the Bill any duty to act on its behalf. Their right to act would not as a rule be prompted by an interest so direct as to outweigh the disadvantages of unilateral intervention. Moreover, the right of individual intervention would be open to all the dangers and temptations of misuse and abuse of which diplomatic history provides numerous examples. One of the objects of the Minorities Treaties concluded in and after 1919 was to prevent just this kind of intervention, which had often served as a cloak thinly disguising aggressive national interest.

Combination of individual and collective guarantee; the system of Minorities Treaties.—An alternative, and less rudimentary, method of securing the observance of the Bill of Rights would be to adopt, substantially, the procedure and the machinery of the Treaties for the Protection of Minorities. The failure of the system of protection of minorities, a failure which was essentially the consequence of the catastrophe which befell the system of collective security and, generally, of the rule of law established by the Covenant of the League, has to some extent obscured the far-reaching nature of the safeguards adopted by these treaties. They consisted: (*a*) in the express stipulation that the provisions for the protection of minorities shall constitute obligations of international concern; (*b*) in the provision that they shall be placed under the guarantee of the League of Nations; (*c*) in the undertaking that they shall be recognized as fundamental laws by the States accepting them and that they shall override any conflicting law,

---

[2] "Probably"—for account must be taken of the likely objection that the right to intervene cannot properly be deduced from the recognition of a legal interest. There may be force in the view that far-reaching changes in the international system cannot be achieved by dint of a controversial interpretation of a text which the signatories could have made unequivocal. Thus there were many who denied that the legal interest of the signatories of the General Treaty for the Renunciation of War in the observance of its clauses authorized neutral signatories to penalize the aggressor State by discriminating against it. It was only the magnitude of the violation of that treaty by Germany which properly swept aside any doubts hitherto entertained on the subject.

regulation, or official action; (*d*) in the conferment upon the members of the Council of the right to bring to the attention of the Council any infraction or danger of infraction of those provisions; (*e*) in the conferment upon the Council of the right to take such action and give such direction as it may deem proper and effective in the circumstances; (*f*) in the conferment upon the Permanent Court of International Justice of compulsory jurisdiction in any dispute between a member of the Council and any State bound by the Minorities Treaties in the matter of any question of law or fact concerning the provisions of these treaties. These safeguards and undertakings constituted both a drastic limitation of the sovereignty of States bound by these treaties and a significant, though not complete, transition from individual to collective enforcement. But that very incompleteness, which largely accounts for the failure of the system, has provided a valuable lesson for the future and a starting point for more general measures of the international protection of the rights of the individual. It would be a profound mistake if the framers of a more general instrument for the protection of the rights of man were not to avail themselves of the lessons and experience of the more limited attempt embodied in the Minorities Treaties.

In the first instance, the guarantee, such as it was, of the stipulations of the Minorities Treaties was only in part a collective guarantee. To a large extent, as interpreted in practice, it was an individual guarantee. For it was only as the result of the individual initiative and responsibility of members of the Council that cases of infraction of the treaties came before the Council. The so-called Committee of Three, which became the main instrument of the Council in this matter, was not a standing body distinct from the individual members of the Council and the States which they represented—although it occasionally served the purpose of enabling members of the Council to shift an odious responsibility upon the impersonal shoulders of a collective body. This fact was of more potent significance than the theory, seemingly underlying the Minorities Treaties and the procedure of the League, that the States bringing a complaint before the Council did so, not in their private capacity and in their private interest, but as defenders of the principles of the League and of the Minorities Treaties. These distinct survivals of individual intervention not only kept alive the admitted dangers and drawbacks of the old system of intervention, which it was the avowed purpose of the Minorities Treaties to abolish, but also imparted to the entire procedure a political character which was inimical to and largely destructive of their spirit and their object.

The second principal drawback of the Minorities Treaties, which by no means followed inevitably from the wording of the treaties, was that the practice of the League and of its Council interpreted the guarantee of the treaties, not as a guarantee of their general observance and effectiveness, but as a guarantee of the effectiveness of the decisions and directions of the Council and, possibly, of the Permanent Court of International Justice with regard to any specific cases brought before and decided by these bodies. The theory of a general guarantee, that is, the assumption of the duty of constant supervision through appropriate organs and with the co-operation of the States bound by the treaties, was expressly rejected by the Council. The activity of the Minorities Section of the Secretariat of the League was confined to receiving petitions which, without conferring upon the petitioners any procedural status of a legal character, were merely in the nature of information. A Permanent Minorities Commission composed of impartial experts and responsible, on its own initiative, for the working of the entire system never materialized—although it was not denied that a permanent commission, independent of active co-operation on the part of the States bound by the treaties, could be established as part of the procedure followed by the Council. There existed no organ competent to ascertain, as part of its normal activity, to what extent the Minorities States complied with the obligation to incorporate effectively the provisions of the treaties as part of their fundamental law and what legal and administrative machinery had been established to ensure the nullity of any "law, regulation, or official action" conflicting or interfering with the fundamental law of the constitution in the matter of minorities.

Any sound system of international protection must include an improvement in two directions upon the system established by the Minorities Treaties. In the first instance, it must be freed of any vestige of individual intervention; for only by becoming truly collective can intervention cease to be political. But if the initiative in setting in motion the machinery of protection is no longer to rest with individual States acting singly or as a committee, then it must be entrusted to an authoritative body which is neither purely administrative nor purely technical in character. Secondly, no system of protection of the rights of man can be satisfactory if the international machinery is called upon to act only after a violation of the law has occurred or is about to occur.

However, we are not likely to appreciate the difficulties in the way of enforcement of the International Bill of the Rights of Man unless we realize that there is a difference, which is fundamental in scope, between it and the system of protection of minorities. The latter is concerned only with one aspect of human rights related to a limited number of persons. The International Bill of the Rights of Man is concerned with the totality of human rights in relation to the entire human race. This means that, assuming that it is to become an effective part of the international legal order, the machinery for its enforcement must be correspondingly more comprehensive and intricate. But those who will frame it will derive much useful, though often negative, instruction from the two principal drawbacks of the system established under the Minorities Treaties.

Enforcement by way of international judicial review.—A method, which on the face of it would appear to be both logical and simple, of securing the observance of the International Bill of the Rights of Man would be to provide for the eventual jurisdiction of an international tribunal accessible to individuals who have been unable within their State to find a remedy against a violation of their rights under the Bill. This, to mention the most outstanding example, is the way in which the Supreme Court of the United States ensures the observance of the articles of the Constitution, of the Bill of Rights, and of other amendments of the Constitution in the matter of the fundamental rights of the individual. The International Bill of the Rights of Man may be violated by the enactment of laws contrary to its clauses; by judicial decisions interpreting it in a manner amounting to a denial of its benefits; or by executive or administrative action. The establishment of an international machinery of judicial review would mean that an international court would have jurisdiction to review and to nullify any of these acts as contrary to the International Bill of the Rights of Man.

This system of regular international review which would open to individuals the right to appeal against the laws, decisions and acts of the legislative, judicial, and administrative authorities of their State has been discarded from the present draft of an International Bill of the Rights of Man as unsound and impracticable. This is so not only because of the technical difficulties, which appear insurmountable. Of these the principal is that an international court acting in that capacity would draw upon itself an amount of litigation so vast that not one tribunal would be required, but many tribunals. This would be so even if its jurisdiction were conditioned by the previous exhaustion of the legal remedies available within the State. Even in that case the international court would be faced with a formidable volume of business from many parts of the world and touching upon all aspects of the Bill of Rights. Such volume of business, to be transacted with thoroughness and requisite authority, would require a great number of courts. Unless a still higher judicial international agency were to be superimposed upon a multiplicity of tribunals, this subdivision of the business of the court would be likely to result in a divergence of interpretation of the Bill of Rights and in an absence of an authoritative and continuous jurisprudence on its various aspects.

However, these technical difficulties are of minor importance when compared with the fact that international judicial review raises problems immeasurably more complex than does judicial review within the State. The latter has been subjected to widespread and emphatic criticism in the United States, the principal country which has adopted judicial review, and elsewhere as constituting a denial of the sovereignty of the legislature and of the people.[3] Can it be expected that countries in which opinion is sharply divided as to the merits of review of their legislation by their own tribunals will acquiesce in such review by an international tribunal in matters touching practically all manifestations of their national life? Can it be expected that countries which have no judicial review within their borders and in which legal opinion and legal tradition have resisted it vigorously and successfully, will entrust it to an international tribunal? This is not a matter of the de-

[3] See below, p. 189.

sirability or otherwise of surrender of sovereignty on a large and unprecedented scale. It is a question of the inherent merits of the system of judicial review both in the national and in the international sphere. This, one of the most baffling problems of law and government, cannot be solved by an International Bill of the Rights of Man.

The additional difficulties—other than those of the merits of judicial review in general and of the surrender of part of national legislative sovereignty to a foreign tribunal—of enforcement of the International Bill of the Rights of Man through international judicial review are obvious. The Bill of Rights is necessarily a document of great generality. Its details must be filled in by the mass of legislation and judicial precedent within the various States. Any Bill of Rights must be subject to two fundamental exceptions—the welfare of the State and the legally recognized rights of the members of the community. The way in which these exceptions operate in various States is the result of a variety of factors which must necessarily differ from State to State. The law of libel, which is a restriction upon the freedom of speech and opinion, differs in various countries; so does the law of sedition. The same applies to the safeguards which States have adopted for securing the liberty of the person as well as the procedural safeguards in the matter of criminal trials. What is regarded as a sufficient measure of protection in one State may be utterly inadequate in another. The fact is that within the orbit of fundamental rights there is room for a wide divergence of law and practice and, with regard to most of the rights guaranteed in the International Bill of the Rights of Man as here proposed, the law and the judicial practice of States have evolved their own solutions and their own procedures. It is possible—though highly improbable—that at some distant date the laws of States will merge into one world law in this and in other matters. The International Bill of the Rights of Man cannot attempt to introduce such a world law. On the contrary, it must be enforced through the law of States, suitably adapted, if need be, to the fundamental requirements of the Bill of Rights. That municipal law of States cannot be administered by international courts possessing no requisite knowledge of the law, of the legal tradition, and of the social and economic problems of the individual States.

The objections to regular international judicial appeal and review as a means of implementing an International Bill of the Rights of Man are so overwhelming that it may not be profitable to consider in detail suggestions for softening the radicalism of any such proposal. But they may be mentioned. One of them is that when the international tribunal or a subdivision thereof considers an appeal from the highest court of a State it should include a substantial number—possibly a majority—of judges who are nationals of the State concerned. A modification of that nature would to some extent meet the two principal objections outlined above. Alternatively, there might be set up in every State a division of the International Court composed of a majority of the nationals of that State. There might exist, in addition, a central division of the International Tribunal for resolving questions of particular difficulty and for introducing a measure of uniformity and continuity in the application of the more general provisions of the Bill of Rights. These modifications of the idea of international judicial review answer to some extent the objections arising on account of the great number of cases, of considerations of the sovereignty of States, and of the necessity of enforcing the Bill of Rights in the first instance as part of the municipal law of the States concerned. There is, indeed, some attraction in the idea that the international character of the Bill of Rights and the universal nature of the rights of man should be given expression by being applied and enforced by national tribunals including foreign judges. It is also arguable that some such modification of the idea of international judicial review might prove an acceptable transition to the idea of full international review. However, it is not believed that the time is ripe even for that transitory stage.

It must be noted that in any scheme providing for regular international judicial review there would still remain, as in other schemes, the question of measures for the enforcement of the findings of the international court—unless the view is adopted that the authority of the decision of the international tribunal will be such as to render unnecessary any machinery for enforcement. There is no such machinery with regard to the decisions of the Supreme Court of the United States, where, in fact, the theory has prevailed that the Federal Government will not lend its assistance for the enforcement of the decisions of the

Supreme Court against States of the Union either in disputes with other States or otherwise. There remains, of course, the question whether the forces operating within the United States in substitution for the physical power of the Federal Government are to be found in the less integrated community of nations.

Combination of national and international functions of supervision and enforcement.—The preceding review of the three principal possible methods of protecting the rights of individuals suggests the following guiding principles for giving effect to the International Bill of the Rights of Man:

a) The State must be the normal agency for implementing the Bill of Rights, which must, for that purpose, contain provisions enabling and obliging the States to act in that capacity. The Bill of Rights must, with regard to the personal rights of freedom formulated in Part I of the present draft, be made part of their municipal law and partake of the character of a constitutional enactment. States must confer upon their courts the power and impose upon them the duty to pass judgment or to express an opinion upon the conformity of the acts of the legislative, judicial, and administrative authorities with the clauses of the Bill of Rights.

b) The international guarantee of the Bill of Rights must be of a general character. This means that it must be concerned not only with persistent and grave violations of its clauses but also with the normal supervision of its observance. It follows that there must exist a permanent international authority, neither judicial nor political in character, charged with that task of general supervision, of investigation of complaints, and of initiation of intervention by the political international authority in case of disregard of the safeguards of the Bill of Rights on a scale warranting international action for their enforcement.

c) There must reside in the political international authority the ultimate and effective power to enforce the observance of the Bill of Rights.

This combination of the national and international method of enforcement applies, it must be noted once more, only to the rights of Part I of the Bill. While the political and social rights of Part II impose legal obligations upon States and are subject to international supervision and enforcement, they are not by nature such as to render possible their enforcement through the ordinary judicial organs within the State.[4]

[4] See above, pp. 135–136.

CHAPTER XII

ENFORCEMENT WITHIN THE STATE

Article 15

EVERY STATE shall, by appropriate constitutional means, adopt Part I of this International Bill of the Rights of Man as part of its domestic law and constitution. The effect of such adoption shall be to abrogate any existing statute or any other rule of law inconsistent with these articles of the International Bill of the Rights of Man. They shall not be abrogated or modified, by legislative action or otherwise, save in pursuance of international agreement or authorization.

This paragraph imposes upon States the duty to incorporate Part I of the Bill of Rights, by appropriate constitutional means, as part of their "domestic law and constitution." The distinction between "domestic law" and "constitution" is deliberate. As to the first, it is clear that in the absence of a special enactment or declaration by the national legislature, the Bill of Rights, even when ratified, would not, in most countries, necessarily become part of the municipal law of States ratifying it. In the United States Article VI(2) of the Constitution provides that

all treaties made, or which shall be made under the authority of the United States, shall be the supreme law of the land, and the judges in every State shall be bound thereby, anything in the Constitution or laws of any State to the contrary notwithstanding.

To that Article the courts of the United States have given a generous interpretation, amounting occasionally to an attribution to a treaty of an effect dangerously approaching that of a constitutional amendment.[1] But in other countries a duly ratified treaty is not part of municipal law until it has been made so by an express act of the national legislature. In Great Britain treaties affecting private rights—and these include practically all treaties—do not become the law of the land unless they have been made so by a special Act of Parliament. The

[1] *Missouri* v. *Holland* (1920) 252 U.S. 416.

Covenant of the League was only to a limited extent made part of English law, inasmuch as the Treaty of Peace Act, 1919, authorized the Government to pass Orders in Council under which the provisions of the Treaty could be carried out in Great Britain without further legislation.[2] The General Treaty for the Renunciation of War has never become part of the law of England.[3]

The effect of the express adoption of Part I of the International Bill of the Rights of Man as an integral part of municipal law will be to change as much of it as is inconsistent with the Bill of Rights. In order to remove any doubts in this respect, an express clause to that effect has been inserted in Article 15 of the present draft. In general, it will be found that no major changes will result. This is so for the reason that, with minor exceptions, Part I of the Bill of Rights is declaratory of the practice of civilized States.[4] But some changes there will be. This will be the case, for instance, with regard to the acquisition of nationality by birth or the recognition of the right to emigration. It might be a matter for consideration whether the Bill of Rights ought not to provide for an interim period to enable States to introduce the required legislative changes.

According to the present draft the signatories will undertake not only to adopt the Bill of Rights as part of their domestic law but also to elevate it to the higher rank of the fundamental law of their constitution. What is the reason for this clause, which introduces the seemingly insoluble difficulty arising out of the fact that in Great Britain there is no constitutional law distinct in authority and in the procedure of amendment from other parts of the law? The main purpose of a clause of this kind, in addition to the symbolic value of the recognition of the high rank of the Bill of Rights in the hierarchy of law, would be, in States with rigid constitutions, to prevent changes in the Bill of Rights by the national legislature except under special safeguards and

---

[2] Although for a time it was doubted in Great Britain whether the above-mentioned provision of the Treaty of Peace Act authorized measures for giving effect to sanctions under Article 16 of the Covenant, this was actually done in 1935 and 1936 in the course of the application of sanctions against Italy.

[3] In the United States, courts declined to interpret that treaty as having the incidental effect of changing some supposedly relevant parts of municipal law, namely, in the matter of the oath of allegiance as a condition of naturalization: see *In re Beale*, 2 F. Supp. 899; 71 F. (2d) 737.

[4] See above, pp. 79–80.

conditions such as are required for changing the constitution as distinguished from ordinary laws. This safeguard is not rendered unnecessary by the last sentence of Article 15 of the draft, which lays down that the clauses of Part I of the Bill of Rights shall not be "abrogated or modified, by legislative action or otherwise, save in pursuance of international agreement or authorization." For this prohibition is an international obligation of States; it is not one of which courts can, as a rule, take cognizance. The result of the adoption of the Bill of Rights as part of constitutional law would be, in States with rigid constitutions, that although courts would be bound to act upon any changes in the constitution in this matter brought about by the proper machinery of constitutional amendment, they would not, in countries which do not recognize the absolute supremacy of the legislature, be under any such compulsion with regard to ordinary legislation inconsistent with the Bill of Rights. Secondly, in Federal States in which, unlike the United States, treaties are not, in relation to the members of the Federation, placed on the same footing as the constitution, the adoption of the Bill of Rights as part of the national constitution would have the direct effect of bringing about the necessary changes in the law. Thirdly, in countries like the United States, where an act of the legislature can abrogate a treaty with an effect binding upon courts, that contingency would be avoided by making the Bill of Rights part of the constitution which could not be changed except by the exacting procedure of constitutional amendment. All these considerations apply also to States like Australia and Canada, in which the written constitutions have not yet embodied clauses for the protection of the fundamental rights of the individual.[5]

The position is altogether different with regard to States—notably Great Britain—which know of no written rigid constitution and in which the legislature is supreme not only in relation to courts but also

[5] In November, 1942, Dr. Evatt, the Australian Minister for Foreign Affairs, announced that direct constitutional guarantees of religious freedom and freedom of speech and expression, which would be binding on all States as well as on the Commonwealth, would shortly be incorporated in a bill amending the Commonwealth Constitution. Article 116 of the existing Constitution already contains some such provision, inasmuch as it forbids the Commonwealth to establish any religion or to prohibit the free exercise of religion, or from requiring a religious test as a qualification for any office under the Commonwealth.

against any law of the same or any previous legislature. There is in Great Britain no statutory or customary rule of law which Parliament cannot change overnight by a simple majority. It is this aspect of the British constitution, not the fact that it is not reduced to writing, that is of decisive importance for the subject under discussion. For actually substantial parts of what is generally regarded as constitutional law have been embodied in Great Britian in the form of a written enactment. It is sufficient to mention such questions as the succession to the throne, the duration of the House of Commons, its legislative prerogatives in relation to the House of Lords, or the powers of the Imperial Parliament in relation to the Dominions. The main difficulty is that Great Britain, a country with a flexible constitution, knows of no special machinery of amendment removing changes of any branch of the law from the operation of an ordinary parliamentary majority. No attempt to link up the acceptance of the Bill of Rights by Great Britain with the relinquishment of the principle of a flexible constitution would be acceptable, and none is made in the present draft. This explains the qualification inserted in the first paragraph of Article 15, which lays down that "every State shall, *by appropriate constitutional means*, adopt Part I of this International Bill of the Rights of Man as part of its domestic law and constitution." This means that the manner of the adoption of the Bill of Rights as part of the constitution must be in accordance with the constitutional principles and practice of the country concerned. This means that by declaring, by means of an ordinary Act of Parliament—the appropriate way of enacting constitutional laws in the United Kingdom—the Bill of Rights to be part of the fundamental law of Great Britain, that country would not be relinquishing the well-established principles of a flexible constitution.

The addition, thus incorporated, to the fundamental law of the Kingdom would be in the same category as any other part of the constitutional law of Great Britain. The checks upon its amendment by ordinary legislation would be political, not legal. That does not signify that they would not be potent in the highest degree. The authority and the permanency of the Statute of Westminster of 1931 is not affected by the circumstance that it can be changed overnight by a simple majority of the two Houses of Parliament. Neither is it advisable, in this connection, to attach exaggerated importance to the doctrine that Parliament cannot bind itself or its successors. Subject to any provisions as to denunciation, Parliament, by consenting to a treaty and by incorporating it as part of the municipal law, does bind itself and its successors. It can violate that obligation, and such violation, if unequivocal and intentional, will be given effect by the courts in a country in which the supremacy of Parliament is absolute. But these are theoretical contingencies. The legal possibility that Parliament may by a simple majority, as distinguished from the more exacting process of amending rigid constitutions, set aside the Bill of Rights, is of almost theoretical import when compared with the political implications of its solemn declaration as part of the fundamental law of the realm. On the face of it, the qualification that the Bill of Rights is to be adopted as part of the constitution of the State "by appropriate constitutional means" puts a country with a flexible constitution in a position which is more advantageous than that of countries with a rigid constitution. But it has been shown that such preferential treatment is of distinctly limited practical significance. It is, in any case, unavoidable. The International Bill of the Rights of Man cannot, if it is to become part of the international legal order, attempt the additional—and essentially unnecessary—task of changing the constitutional structure of States.

Article 16
The enforcement of any law safeguarding the legal rights of others or providing for the safety and the welfare of the community shall not be deemed to be inconsistent with the guarantee of the fundamental rights proclaimed in Part I of this International Bill of the Rights of Man.

The brevity of the comment to this Article is in no way indicative of its importance in the scheme of the present draft. The Article gives expression to the crucial problem of the Bill of Rights. Whatever designation of absoluteness we give to the rights of man—whether we call them fundamental, inherent, natural, or inalienable—they cannot be absolute. For they have a meaning only in relation to man living in society under the shelter of the political organization of the State. Even his fundamental rights must be exercised with due regard to the rights of others and to the safety and the welfare of the State. Freedom of speech and opinion can be recognized and protected only if it is made use of in a manner consistent with the law of libel and with public peace. Personal liberty cannot be absolute. It is subject to restraints and sanctions which the criminal law imposes for the protection of other members of the community and the common good. Even freedom of religion is conditioned by similar limitations.[6] There is no escape from the fact that the rights of man must be subject to social control by the State and that no definite limit can be set, in a legal instrument, to its regulative power. And yet it is of the essence of the rights of man that they are anterior and superior to the State and that they must be protected against its encroachments. Article 16 gives expression to that dilemma, which is of great antiquity, and attempts to solve it in so far as it is capable of solution. The rights of man are subject to the legislation of the State enacted for the protection of the rights of others and the welfare and the safety of the community at large. At the same time, the legislation of the State is made subject to the fundamental purpose and to the safeguards of the International Bill of the Rights of Man. It is the international legal order, of which the Bill of Rights would become an integral part, that may yet in this way solve the abiding legal and political problem of the relation of man and State.

Article 17

In every State the highest judicial tribunal of the State or a special Constitutional Court of Liberties shall have jurisdiction to pronounce judgment upon the conformity of legislative, judicial or executive action with the provisions of Part I of this International Bill of the Rights of Man.

The International Bill of the Rights of Man is intended as a legal enactment creating, in the first instance, rights of individuals against the State. Such rights have no reality unless there exist legal remedies for enforcing them. These remedies may be national and international. Reasons have been given why the enforcement of the Bill of Rights through an international machinery of judicial review or through exclusively political international action is not practicable. As the Bill

---

[6] Conscientious objection to bearing arms, polygamy, and denial of medical aid on the part of Christian Scientists are forms of religious belief which may fall within that category.

of Rights declares and creates primarily rights of the individual against the State, the judicial organs of the State must be the basic and normal means of its enforcement in respect of such rights—those of Part I of the Bill—which lend themselves to the machinery of judicial process. For this reason the Bill of Rights must lay down in clear terms the duty of States to possess or to institute tribunals for that purpose. It must be left to the States to determine whether that function shall be fulfilled by the existing tribunals or whether they will set up special judicial agencies such as a Supreme Court for Individual Guarantees or a Constitutional Court of Liberties. Whatever agencies they may establish, there must exist a judicial machinery, accessible to every individual, for testing the conformity of legislative, judicial, and executive action with the provisions of the Bill of Rights.

There ought to be no difficulty regarding the exercise of such jurisdiction with respect to decisions of lower courts and of administrative authorities. The recognition of the right of the individual to appeal to the highest tribunal in the State against decisions of lower courts is, of course, part of the normal administration of justice. The same applies to the acts of the executive authorities. Even when by virtue of the existing law these authorities are entrusted with the power to decide according to discretion, in most countries courts are competent to examine whether such discretion has been exercised properly, not arbitrarily. Whatever the present position may be, one of the results of the adoption of the Bill of Rights—a result which is expressly stated in Article 17—must be that courts, in particular the highest court, would be competent to review the conformity of executive and administrative action with the Bill of Rights irrespective of any wide degree of discretion which the law of the State may have hitherto left to executive and administrative authorities. In this respect the adoption of the Bill of Rights must in some countries result in a change of practice. The function of courts as trustees of the observance of the Bill of Rights must be unhampered by *droit administratif*. In fact, from this point of view the Bill of Rights may beneficently fulfil the part of checking any tendencies of administrative law to develop in directions inimical to freedom.

If international judicial review is excluded, it follows that the decisions of the highest municipal tribunals must be final and that there cannot normally lie an appeal by individuals to an international judicial authority. However, as is shown later, the enforcement of the Bill of Rights by the national judicial authorities must remain a matter of effective international interest operating through the instrumentality of other than judicial agencies. There must exist an international reserve of power to remedy violations of the guarantees of the Bill of Rights by municipal courts as the result either of deliberate miscarriage of justice on their part or of their having to comply with national legislation violative of the Bill of Rights in States in which courts have no authority to refuse to give effect to legislation even if inconsistent with the provisions of the constitution. For it is here that there reveals itself the real and, at first sight, almost insurmountable obstacle to the enforcement of the Bill of Rights by national courts. The difficulty arises in connection with the legislation of the State inconsistent with the clauses of the Bill of Rights. Statutes may be enacted which in fact, although not by design, are in violation of the Bill of Rights. Moreover, the legislature may deliberately disregard the obligations of the Bill. What shall be the function of courts in the face of such statutory enactments?

Assuming that the Bill has been adopted as part of the constitution of the State, the position would be relatively simple in countries in which courts have the power to review the constitutionality of the acts of the legislature and to declare invalid or inoperative legislative acts inconsistent with the constitution. There are very few countries which have fully adopted the system of judicial review enabling courts to act in that capacity in the matter of the fundamental rights of the individual guaranteed by the constitution. In the United States, by long-established practice—though not in pursuance of any express provision of the Constitution—the Supreme Court has exercised that power since its decision in the historic case of *Marbury* v. *Madison.*[7] This is also the position, by virtue of an express constitutional provision, in Brazil,[8] Venezuela,[9] and some other Latin-American countries,

[7] 1803, 1 Cranch 137.

[8] Articles 59 and 60 of the constitutions of 1891 and 1926. In Argentina Article 100 of the Constitution of 1860 has often been interpreted as conferring such powers upon the Supreme Court, but in practice they are said to have been exercised only twice in the period between 1863 and 1930 (see C. G. Haines, *The American Doctrine of Judicial Supremacy* [2d ed., Berkeley, Calif., 1932], p. 578. Professor Haines's work

in Czechoslovakia,[10] Rumania,[11] and the Irish Free State.[12] In a number of countries—such as Australia, Canada, and Germany (in the Constitution of 1919) [13]—judicial review is limited largely to questions relating to the respective legislative competence of the Federation and of the member States.

On the other hand, in many States the constitution specifically excludes the interpretation of laws—and a fortiori any declaration of their invalidity—from the purview of the judiciary.[14] Judicial review

may be regarded as the standard work on the subject. Appendix II, pp. 573–662, contains a useful review of the constitutional provisions in various States on this subject.)

[9] Article 129 (9a) of the Constitution of 1928; Article 83 of the Cuban Constitution of 1901; Article 99 of the Constitution of Haiti of 1918; Article 135 of the Constitution of Honduras of 1925; Article 122 of the Constitution of Nicaragua of 1911.

[10] Articles 1 and 2 of the Constitution of 1920. In the Austrian Constitution of October 1, 1920, Article 89 provided generally that the courts may not enquire into the validity of any duly promulgated law. But Article 140 of the Constitution gave that power to the Constitutional Court of the Republic. It provided that the Constitutional Court shall give judgment in all questions as to the unconstitutionality of laws.

The Spanish Constitution of 1932 established, in Article 121, a Court of Constitutional Guarantees which had jurisdiction, *inter alia*, to hear appeals on the ground of unconstitutionality of laws and for the protection of individual guarantees. The appeal was open, among others, to every individual or collective person, even if not directly affected. See also R. J. Bonner, *Aspects of Athenian Democracy* (Berkeley, Calif., 1933), for the Athenian procedure for protecting the people from the unconstitutionality of laws by means of an action brought by any citizen against the enforcement of an unconstitutional law.

[11] Article 103 of the Constitution of 1923.

[12] Article 34 of the Constitution of 1937 confers upon the High Court, which is a court of first instance, jurisdiction as to questions involving the validity of any law having regard to the provisions of the Constitution. It provides expressly that no law shall be enacted excepting such cases from the appellate jurisdiction of the Supreme Court.

[13] Probably such judicial review as existed in Germany under the Weimar Constitution was confined to the question of the conformity of the legislation of the States with that of the Reich. Article 13 of the Constitution provided that in case of doubt or difference of opinion as to whether a law of a State is compatible with the law of the Reich, the competent authority of the Reich or of the State may appeal to the Supreme Court. See Johannes Mattern, *Principles of the Constitutional Jurisprudence of the German National Republic* (Baltimore, London, 1928), pp. 575 ff., and C. J. Friedrich, "The Issue of Judicial Review in Germany," *Political Science Quarterly*, XLIII (1928), 188 ff.

[14] See Title III, Article 28, of the Belgian Constitution of 1921; Article 28 of the Greek Constitution of 1927 (which, apparently, did away with the former practice of Greek courts in the matter); Article 73 of the Italian Constitution of 1848; Article 81 of the Polish Constitution of 1921. This, by implication, seems to be the position also in Peru (Articles 16 and 98 of the Constitution of 1920), and in Guatemala (Article 54 of the Constitution of 1879), in Paraguay (Article 103 of the Constitution of 1870), and in Ecuador (Article 6 of the Constitution of 1906). Article 113 of the Swiss Constitution indirectly denies the power of judicial review of the laws passed by the General Assembly. But the Federal Court is competent to review the constitutionality of cantonal legislation.

of legislation is contrary to the constitutional doctrine of France and, above all, of Great Britain, where the supremacy of Parliament is absolute. Although the Constitution of Soviet Russia of 1923 gave (in Article VII, sec. 43) the Supreme Court of the Union the power to render decisions, at the request of the Central Executive Committee of the Union, on the constitutionality of any regulations made by the Republics of the Union, no such powers have been conferred upon it by the Constitution of 1936.

In those States in which the constitution or constitutional practice allow judicial review of laws concerning their conformity with the constitution, so long as the Bill of Rights remains part of the constitution the position would be comparatively simple. The tribunal would be in a position either to declare such laws to be unconstitutional and invalid or, without any such declaration, to grant relief either by setting aside the decision of the lower court based on the offending statute or by any other form of specific relief. This, for instance, is the position with regard to the writ of *amparo*—a combination of the writs of habeas corpus, certiorari, and mandamus—as provided in Article 107 of the Mexican Constitution. The principle of the writ is that the court grants specific relief without making any general pronouncement on the validity or constitutionality of the law in question.

The real and serious obstacles to enforcement arise in States, like Great Britain and France, in which the legislature is supreme and courts are under the clear duty to apply laws enacted by the legislature. The regular enforcement of the International Bill of the Rights of Man in these countries cannot be made dependent upon the abandonment on their part of what they regard as a fundamental constitutional doctrine. It is true that the International Bill of the Rights of Man is not an instrument which States can adopt without changes in their substantive law. But the experience of countries in which judicial review has been in operation has been sufficiently controversial to warrant the utmost caution in urging the substitution, as inherent in the acceptance of the Bill of Rights, of the full system of judicial review for the existing constitutional practice. The doctrine of judicial review has been defended with fervent approval by great lawyers in the United States and elsewhere. Daniel Webster and Francis Lieber praised it as a bulwark of liberty. Lord Bryce was of the view that "there is no part of the American system which reflects more credit on its authors or has worked better in practice." [15] Dicey was a strong believer in the doctrine of the supremacy of Parliament in England. But he was emphatic that it was "the glory of the founders of the United States" [16] —in fact the doctrine of judicial review was adopted a quarter of a century after the foundation of the Republic—to have established a system of protection of the Constitution essential to a federal system (actually, the exercise of the power of judicial review by the Supreme Court has borne little relation to the fact of the federal structure of the United States). Tocqueville praised it as most favourable to liberty and to public order. After one hundred and forty years of operation it has the unqualified support of a large—perhaps predominant—section of American legal opinion as a bulwark of liberty of the people against the rashness and the tyranny of short-lived legislative majorities.[17]

On the other hand, the doctrine of judicial review has found from its very inception violent opponents and detractors in the country of its origin. Jefferson and Madison denounced it. Great teachers of constitutional law, such as J. B. Thayer, have drawn attention to the dangers of attempting to find in the Supreme Court—instead of in the lessons of experience—a safeguard against the mistakes of the representatives of the people.[18] That criticism has grown in the last fifty years to the point of bitter denunciation as the result of the exercise of the power of judicial review in a manner which, in the view of many, has made the Supreme Court a defender of vested rights and social statics.[19] Some French jurists, who were attempting to find a remedy for the absence of an effective guarantee of fundamental rights in their own constitution have come to regard the experience of judicial review in the United States as a sufficient deterrent against introducing judicial review in

[15] *The American Commonwealth* (New York, 1912), I, 256.
[16] *Introduction to the Study of the Law of the Constitution* (8th ed., 1927), p. 154.
[17] See, for example, Charles Warren, *The Supreme Court in United States History,* II (rev. ed., Boston, 1937), 751–756, for an impressive survey of opinion to that effect.
[18] *Legal Essays* (Boston, 1908), pp. 39–41.
[19] See Haines, *op. cit.;* E. S. Corwin, *The Twilight of the Supreme Court* (New Haven, London, 1934).

France.[20] In countries other than the United States, in which judicial review of legislation is recognized, it has been exercised only in rare cases for the protection of the rights of the individual. This being so, there is no justification for urging the general adoption of the principle of judicial review as part of the machinery of enforcement of the International Bill of the Rights of Man.

Yet the fact remains that since international judicial review must be left out of account as a method of enforcing the Bill of Rights and since municipal courts must needs fulfill that function, some more elastic solution must be sought for the purpose. How can this be accomplished by a method short of full judicial review conceived as an express declaration of unconstitutionality and invalidity of the offend-

[20] See Edouard Lambert, *Le Gouvernement des juges et la lutte contre la législation sociale aux Etats-Unis* (Paris, 1921). In France, the attempts to provide machinery for the review of the constitutionality of laws are as old as the Revolutionary Convention. As early as 1793 Robespierre and others urged the necessity of protecting the rights of man against the legislature. In 1795 Abbé Siéyès, who took a leading part in the drafting of the Declaration of 1789, proposed for that purpose the creation of a constitutional jury, composed of three-twentieths of the legislature. The proposal was rejected, but in the period of the Consulate, at the suggestion of Siéyès, a "*sénat conservateur*" was set up "for maintaining or annulling acts referred to it as unconstitutional by the tribunate or the government" (a function analogous to that which the Momophylakes discharged at Athens). In the course of time the "*sénat conservateur*" became a pliable instrument of the First Consul and of the Emperor. In the Constitution of 1852 a Senate was set up "as the guardian of the fundamental compact and of public liberties" with the right to oppose the promulgation of laws "contrary or derogatory to the Constitution, religion, morals, freedom of religion, individual liberty, equality of citizens before the law, inviolability of property or the principle of the immovability of the magistrature." In 1870 the Senate was divested of these functions and became the Second Chamber of the legislature. For a survey of the French literature on the subject of judicial review see George Jaffin, "New World Constitutional Harmony: a Pan-Americanadian Panorama," *Columbia Law Review*, LXII (1942), 557. See also Théry, *Les Attributions du Sénat du premier Empire concernant la justice et les droits individuels* (1922); Trouillard, *Le Sénat conservateur du Consulat et du premier Empire* (1912).

In the United States, the Constitution of Pennsylvania of 1776 provided for the creation of a Council of Censors for enquiring "whether the constitution has been preserved inviolate in every part and whether the legislative and executive branches of government have performed their duty as guardians of the people or assumed to themselves, or exercised other or greater powers than they are entitled under the Constitution." The Council was given the power to recommend to the legislature the repeal of laws deemed to be contrary to the constitution. The Council came to an end in 1798. For a survey of its "inglorious career" see Haines, *op. cit.*, pp. 73–78. And see *ibid.*, pp. 78–87, for an account of the equally ineffectual Vermont Council of Censors set up in 1777 and of the New York Council of Revision established in the same year and empowered to veto "laws inconsistent with the spirit of the Constitution or with the public good." However, the veto could be overridden by a vote of two-thirds of each house of the Assembly.

ing statute? One method would be for the courts to refuse to apply the statute while refraining from making a general pronouncement as to its validity. The highest court would merely grant relief from the effects of the decision of a lower court. This in fact is the position, in some cases, in countries such as Mexico [21] and in some other American States.[22] It is this method which some French writers have suggested as likely to overcome the deadlock resulting from the absence of full judicial review and the necessity of safeguarding, as against the omnipotence of the legislature, the fundamental rights of the individual. They have pointed out that in declaring a law to be unconstitutional and in refusing to apply it to the case before them, the tribunals do not annul the law. It remains on the statute book. Another tribunal —or even the same tribunal in another case—may arrive at a different conclusion. There is no encroachment by the tribunal upon the sphere of the legislature. What the tribunal does, when confronted with a conflict between a rule of the constitution and a specific law, is to give effect to the former.[23]

However, even that attenuated right of judicial review may prove unacceptable to some countries, for example, to Great Britain, where the doctrine of the supremacy of the King in Parliament forms an integral part of the law and of legal tradition. As stated, it will not be practicable to urge the relinquishment of that doctrine as part of the acceptance by Great Britain of the International Bill of the Rights of Man. How, then, shall we meet the difficulty? In the first instance, it must be remembered that the Bill will form part both of the domestic law of Great Britain and of her international obligations. In theory,

---

[21] See above, p. 188. .

[22] See, for example, Article 86 of the Constitution of Chile of 1925: "The Supreme Court, in private cases under its cognizance, or which may have been submitted to it on appeal brought in a cause pending before the tribunal, may declare ineffective for that case, any legal ruling as contrary to the Constitution."

[23] See Duguit, *Droit constitutionnel*, III (2d ed., 1923), 672. (In the first edition [I, 159] of the same work Duguit denied that the courts have any power whatsoever to appreciate the constitutionality of laws).—There are many who believe that this is exactly what the Supreme Court of the United States does in such cases. Thus, in Dicey's view (*op. cit.*, p. 153) the Supreme Court does not pronounce an opinion upon an Act of Congress; it merely refuses to take it into account since it goes beyond the constitutional powers of Congress. Probably this is a case of a distinction without a difference—in the same line as the opinion of Francis Lieber (*On Civil Liberty and Self-government* [Philadelphia, 1859], p. 164) that the Court, far from invalidating a statute, merely pronounces it void.

being part of her domestic law, it may be modified or abrogated by subsequent statute with an effect absolutely binding upon the courts. But it is important to keep in mind that as the Bill of Rights will at the same time be a fundamental international instrument to which Great Britain is a party, nothing short of an express enactment deliberately designed to abrogate the Bill of Rights or part thereof will be interpreted to that effect by English courts. Failing any such express and undoubted intention to violate the international obligation of Great Britain, the courts, following an accepted canon of interpretation, will construe the statute so as to negative the intention to depart from a binding treaty which has been adopted, in significant circumstances of solemnity, as part of the law of the land. The rule of interpretation according to which courts, if only possible, will not impute to the legislature an intention to violate a treaty or any other rule of international law is a consistent feature of English judicial practice. Neither is the fundamental character of the particular enactment without importance. The Statute of Westminster of 1931 is an enactment of this character. It is, in constitutional theory, an Act of the same rank as any other Act of Parliament. But it is clear that a statute enacted with the avowed intention of abrogating the inter-imperial agreement which underlay the Statute of Westminster would be in the nature of a revolution, and that there would be the greatest reluctance on the part of courts to interpret it in this way. Similar considerations would probably apply to the International Bill of the Rights of Man.

Yet, situations must be taken into account in which no interpretation will be able to deprive of its obvious meaning an Act of Parliament clearly designed to change or to abrogate an obligation of the Bill of Rights. In that case the question must be squarely faced as to the part which courts will play in the enforcement of the Bill of Rights in countries in which the supremacy of the legislature is the paramount rule with the result that courts can neither declare the enactment to be unconstitutional and invalid nor, without any declaration of unconstitutionality, grant relief in individual cases. In such cases, it is believed, the courts, while giving effect to the statute, must be given the right—and must be under a duty—to declare that the statute is not in conformity with the Bill of Rights. No immediate *legal* result would attach to any such declaration. But apart from its potential effect in bringing the violation of that fundamental instrument definitely and authoritatively to the mind of the legislature, it would be the starting point for bringing into operation the international machinery of investigation and enforcement as provided in other Articles of the Bill of Rights. In particular, any such declaration will open the way, not, indeed, to an appeal before a higher international judicial authority, but to a petition by the individual concerned or to a representation by a State to the international agency set up in conformity with Article 19 of the Bill of Rights. This is the meaning and the object of the phraseology used in the present draft to the effect that the highest municipal court "shall have jurisdiction to pronounce judgment upon the conformity of legislative, judicial, or executive action with the provisions of Articles 1–11 of this International Bill of the Rights of Man." The court does not pass the judgment upon the validity of the statute in municipal law. Neither does it decline to apply the statute. But as no law can deprive the courts of the right to express an opinion upon the adequacy, the reasonableness, or the justice of any particular enactment, so no law can divest it of the right to make a declaration as to its conformity with the international obligations of the State. Moreover, the words "shall have jurisdiction" are—and they are intended to be—wide enough not only to confer upon the court the right but also to impose upon it the duty to make a declaration of this nature.

It would thus seem that the manner in which the municipal courts would be called upon to enforce the International Bill of the Rights of Man would vary from State to State. In some countries the courts will have the power to declare unconstitutional and, as a result, invalid any legislation held to be inconsistent with the Bill of Rights; in others the courts, without making any such general declaration binding in future cases, will have the power either to decline to enforce the statute or to give affirmative relief; in others, still, while enforcing the offending statute, they will have the right and the duty to make a formal pronouncement declaring it inconsistent with the Bill of Rights. It has already been stated that in the last case the degree of enforcement, although substantially reduced, is by no means nominal. It is of significant political potency in the domestic sphere; it constitutes a starting point for the international procedure of protection and enforcement.

CHAPTER XIII

INTERNATIONAL ENFORCEMENT

Article 18

THIS INTERNATIONAL BILL OF THE RIGHTS OF MAN is hereby declared to be an integral part of the Law of Nations. It is placed under the guarantee of the United Nations of the World. Its observance shall be a matter of concern to all the United Nations.

The present draft is based on the view that the machinery of the State must be the normal instrument for implementing the Bill of Rights. States will incorporate it as part of their fundamental law; their tribunals will watch over its enforcement. Reasons have been given why the manner and method of implementing the Bill of Rights must be left primarily to the signatory States, even if the result must be attendant with some risks of divergency and elasticity. At the same time, it is of the essence of the Bill of Rights that it shall transcend the interests and the competence of any single State and that its ultimate safeguard shall lie in international supervision and, eventually, international enforcement.

In declaring the International Bill of the Rights of Man to be an integral part of the Law of Nations, the Bill of Rights goes beyond the registration of the fact that having been incorporated in a treaty it has become part of conventional international law. The intention is to express, in so far as this can be accomplished by means of a treaty, a change in the attitude of international law toward the position of the individual within the State. Article 18 constitutes a solemn affirmation of the claim of international society to a normal and permanent interest in the welfare of the individual. What has been called humanitarian intervention and has hitherto remained within the orbit of a practice which has been controversial, sporadic, hesitating, and infrequent is now transformed into a normal rule of international law and practice in a comprehensive sphere covering a wide range of human activity and human relations. In that sense the International Bill of the Rights of Man signifies a revolutionary change in the status of the individual. It is, from this point of view, of minor importance whether and to what extent the Bill will effect a procedural change in the position of the individual in international law. There is no provision in the Bill for direct access of individuals to an international judicial authority by way of appeal from a final decision of national courts—though there is a clear and emphatic provision safeguarding the procedural right of petition.[1] That latter right is conceived as a legal right to set in motion an international procedure of investigation by the international agency charged with the supervision of the observance of the Bill of Rights. The radical character of the innovation would lie in the fact that the protection of the rights of the individual is declared to be the task of the Law of Nations. That declaration, it is true, would be expressed in what would be no more than a treaty, but it would be a treaty of a constitutional and potentially universal character. It would be part of the constitution of international society. Although its clauses might be changed by a subsequent international agreement, there would be no provision for its termination. The constitution of international society and any drastic changes in its structure must necessarily be based on a treaty. But it would be a treaty concluded with the intention of effecting fundamental changes, and that circumstance, coupled with the absence of provisions for termination, would impart to the Bill of Rights a character of finality affecting the nature of the international legal system as a whole. This, in relation to the position of the individual in the international society, would be the effect of the declaration of the International Bill of the Rights of Man as an integral part of the Law of Nations.

In placing the Bill of Rights under the guarantee of the International Organization of the United Nations—a term provisionally describing the future political organization of the society of States—and in laying down that its observance *shall* be a matter of concern for all the United Nations, the draft postulates more than a collective right of the international society for the purpose of securing the observance of its provisions. By agreeing that the observance of the Bill of Rights *shall* be a matter of concern for all the United Nations, they would concede that such concern is not only a right but also a duty. It would be an

[1] See below, p. 201.

imperfect obligation, inasmuch as it, in turn, could not be enforced. But of the legal nature of that duty there would be no doubt.

Article 19

There shall be established within the framework of the political organization of the United Nations of the World a High Commission for the supervision of the observance of the International Bill of the Rights of Man.

The Commission shall consist of independent persons of the highest distinction appointed by the Council of the United Nations. The Commission shall be assisted by a Secretariat appointed by the President of the Commission.

The Commission shall collect information and receive petitions and representations bearing on the observance of the International Bill of the Rights of Man. The Commission shall, in the matter of such petitions and otherwise, communicate with and receive observations from the States concerned. The Commission shall submit annual reports to the Council of the United Nations and, whenever necessary, draw the attention of the Council to such infractions of the Bill of Rights as may call for action by the Council of the United Nations.

The right of individuals and organizations to petition the High Commission in the matter of the observance of this Bill of Rights shall not be denied or impaired.

The international machinery for securing the observance of the International Bill of the Rights of Man must be of two kinds—of supervision, in its widest sense, and of enforcement. Article 19 is concerned with the first. By "supervision in its widest sense" is meant all activity calculated to ensure the observance of the Bill of Rights short of actual enforcement by political or physical means of compulsion. It includes the collection and publication of information, the receipt of petitions from private sources and representations from States, the communication with governments concerning such petitions and representations, the submission to the highest international political authority of periodical reports on the operation and observance of the Bill of Rights, and, finally, the transmission to that authority of cases of infraction of the Bill sufficiently serious to call for further investigation, for negotiation by the political authority, and, if necessary, for collective enforcement. For the fulfilment of all these functions it is proposed that there shall be established a special agency which may be provisionally described as the High Commission of the Rights of Man.

It is assumed that the future political organization of nations—and it is clear that an effective International Bill of the Rights of Man cannot be conceived except within the framework of some such organization—will set up a number of agencies of a technical and administrative character for the purpose of fulfilling various functions in the domain of economics, finance, health, transport and transit, intellectual cooperation, reduction of armaments, and the like. The High Commission of the Rights of Man will be one of these agencies. But its functions will be wider, its responsibilities more intricate, and its task more delicate than in the case of the other agencies. In view of this, the name "High Commission" may not be inappropriate.

The intricacy and the delicacy of the task of the High Commission will arise from the fact that the observance of the Bill of Rights is not a matter which can be ascertained by rule of thumb. Most of its provisions are limited—and unavoidably limited—by the general exception of Article 16 which qualifies the Bill of Rights by reference to the necessity of safeguarding the legal rights of other members of the community and the welfare and the safety of the State and which qualifies the latter by reference to the fundamental purpose and the international safeguards of the Bill of Rights. The International Bill of the Rights of Man cannot concern itself in detail with questions such as when a national emergency calling for a proclamation of martial law requires the temporary suspension of civil liberties, to what extent the law of libel or of sedition must modify the right of freedom of speech and opinion, or the limits within which freedom of assembly can be exercised with due regard to public peace. These are matters which must be determined in the first instance by the law and the administration of each State. Yet, unless the Bill of Rights is to be reduced to a nominal declaration of principle, the manner in which States adapt its observance to that comprehensive exception of legally recognized rights of others and of the requirements of the safety and welfare of the State, must be a matter of international interest and supervision. Failing that, the exception may become an instrument for obliterating the very purpose of the Bill.

The same considerations apply in relation to the fact that because of the necessarily general nature of the principles of the International Bill of the Rights of Man its clauses must be implemented in conformity with the legal forms and tradition and the general standard of civilization and development of any particular State. Here, again, unless the necessarily elastic application of the Bill is to render its purpose nugatory, there must exist a measure of international supervision to hold the balance at the requisite level. This is even more so with regard to that category of rights which the Bill regards as fundamental, but for the protection of which no procedure of legal action and judicial safeguards, even within the State, is appropriate. These are the rights under Part III of the Bill—the right to government by consent, the right to political independence, the cultural rights of minorities, and the so-called "social rights" in the field of economic welfare and security. With regard to these rights, the obligations of States, however far-reaching, are not ordinarily such as to make them capable of a breach of duty cognizable by judicial tribunals. Yet they may be flagrantly violated by the action or inaction of States. In all these matters the method of international control cannot be that of an international court. Neither can it be that of a purely political body likely to sacrifice a vital principle to political exigency or expediency. The supreme agency of normal international supervision of the International Bill of the Rights of Man must be that of impartial and expert statesmanship combining political, legal and administrative qualities of the highest order. These requirements explain the elaborate care that will be needed in determining the composition of the High Commission and of the Secretariat created for the purpose of assisting it.

THE FUNCTIONS OF THE HIGH COMMISSION

Collection of information.—One of the important functions of the High Commission must be, through a suitable machinery, to keep itself informed as well as to supply to the Council and to everyone interested information on all matters relevant to the observance and the enforcement of the Bill of Rights within the various States. Such information must include not only relevant legislation and judicial decisions but also such material as private writings and articles in the press on the subject, records of parliamentary debates and reports of activities of organizations interested in the observance of the Bill of Rights. The periodical publication of that information would, in addition, constitute a valuable contribution to comparative legal study.

Above all, such independent collection of information would enable the High Commission to act irrespective of petitions from individuals and representations from States. For it is an essential feature of the High Commission, as here contemplated, that it would be charged with the constant and independent supervision of the working of the regime established under the Bill of Rights. Thus, for instance, it would be its duty to act *proprio motu* if a State were to change its constitution in a way clearly restrictive of the liberty of the citizen. In 1938 Rumania altered its Constitution in that direction. It laid down, in Article 7, that "no Rumanian is allowed to advocate, by speech or writing, any change in the form of government of the State, the division or distribution of the property of others, exemption from taxes or class warfare." In 1935 Poland, under the impact of similar tendencies, enacted a Constitution in which the chapter on "General Duties and Civic Rights" of the previous Constitution was suppressed and replaced by generalities emphasizing the absolute submission of the individual to the State and laying down, in Article 6, that "a citizen's right to influence public affairs shall be measured by his merits and by his efforts for the common good." In such cases it would be the right and duty of the High Commission to initiate the requisite action. The guarantee of the Bill of Rights, unlike that of the Minorities Treaties, must be general. Petititons by individuals and representations by States will be one of the means, but not the only means, at the instance of which the comprehensive responsibility of the High Commission will be discharged.

Receiving of petitions and representations.—The supervisory function of the High Commission would not be limited to the passive collection of information. Primarily it would consist of active participation in implementing the objects of the Bill of Rights. The High Commission would have to act both as an agency for removing, through negotiation and by the authority of its findings, any violations of the Bill of Rights and transmitting to the highest international authority reports of those cases of violation of the Bill of Rights which it is unable to remove by its own exertions. In addition to acting on its own information, the High Commission would receive petitions from private individuals and organizations and representations from States.

a) PETITIONS. IN GENERAL. Petitions would not be in the nature of an appeal from the final judicial finding of the highest municipal court. Reasons have been given showing why the regular enforcement of the Bill of Rights through international judicial review is unsound and impracticable. On the other hand, any international guarantee of the Bill of Rights must recognize the necessity for an international machinery, other than judicial review, to ensure the observance of the Bill of Rights within the territory of each State. The highest municipal tribunal may be compelled to give effect to laws contrary to the Bill of Rights, even if it may be allowed to append to its decisions a declaration that the law which it is under a duty to administer is inconsistent with the Bill of Rights. Or the State may have failed to set up a "highest jurisdiction" competent effectively to enforce the Bill of Rights. Or the highest tribunal may have circumscribed its functions in the matter by procedural or substantive conditions which render redress impossible or nominal. Or it may, under political pressure or in pursuance of a philosophy of its own, have adopted an interpretation of the Bill of Rights which is destructive of its purpose. In all these cases there would be room for investigation by the organs of the High Commission. As a rule it will not be within the province of the High Commission to attempt to substitute its own view of the law for that of the highest municipal tribunal. But it will be competent and bound to act upon any petition if on the face of it the judicial decision of which the petition complains bears marks of a clear denial of justice or of an interpretation of the law which, to all appearances, makes a travesty of the Bill of Rights. These cases will probably be exceptional, and it must be insisted that the High Commission will not be a regular court of appeal from judgments of the highest municipal tribunal. But although such decisions must be the last word within the State concerned, they cannot, in relation to the international supervision of the enforcement of the Bill of Rights, be endowed with absolute finality.

The detailed treatment in this Chapter of the question of the finality of the decisions of the highest national tribunals in the matter of the Bill of Rights is no indication of the probable frequency with which the High Commission would have to concern itself with petitions arising out of such decisions. These are likely to be exceptional. They are more likely to take place in connection with legislative measures infringing the Bill of Rights or with the failure of national legislation to provide remedies against executive violations of the Bill of Rights. Above all, the bulk of the petitions received by the High Commission would be concerned, not with the observance of those articles of the Bill of Rights which will be made part of the constitutional law of States and which will be normally enforced by courts (Articles 1–9 of the Bill), but with the political, cultural, and social rights of Part II of the Bill of Rights. It is with regard to these rights that the greatest calls will be made upon that combination of statesmanship and judicial approach which must characterize the work of the High Commission.

b) THE RIGHT OF PETITION. The last paragraph of Article 19 of the Bill of Rights provides that the right of individuals and organizations to petition the High Commission in the matter of the observance of the Bill of Rights shall not be denied or impaired. This is, in the first instance, an obligation imposed upon States. It would not be lawful for States to restrict by legislation or administrative action the right of individuals or organizations to petition the High Commission. Such attempts were occasionally made in connection with the working of the system of protection of minorities. Secondly, the Bill of Rights must establish the right of petition as a legal right of the individual in the international sphere. This would be in sharp contrast with the position which obtained under the system of protection of minorities where petitions were merely in the nature of information supplied to the Minorities Section of the Secretariat of the League.

c) REPRESENTATIONS FROM STATES. Circumstances must be foreseen in which individuals may not be in a position—or may be unwilling—to avail themselves of the right of petition and when the general interest of States in the implementation of the Bill of Rights is neverthe-less affected. For this reason every State signatory to the Bill must possess the right—and, indeed, in view of Article 18, the duty—to bring to the notice of the High Commission any infraction of the Bill of Rights. This right and duty are independent of the rights and duties under Article 20, according to which any State can bring before the Council or the General Assembly any infraction of the Bill of Rights. It must be assumed that the latter would be confined to cases of ex-ceptional gravity, obviousness, and urgency. As a rule the High Com-mission must be the normal channel for setting the international ma-chinery in motion, and its action must constitute the first stage in the proceedings.

THE PROCEDURE OF THE HIGH COMMISSION

It must be assumed that there will be a considerable number of peti-tions. The procedure of the High Commission would have to provide for preliminary examination of the petitions by its Secretariat and for the elimination of those which are clearly unfounded, frivolous, or insignificant. It would be essential that such preliminary examination should be entrusted, not to a single member of the Secretariat, but to boards—of which there may have to be several—consisting of at least three members and including one or more who have had judicial ex-perience. The Commission ought never to incur the reproach or the sus-picion that a petition, from whatsoever a quarter, has not received due attention. Petitions or representations which have stood the test of the preliminary examination will be handed over, for detailed investiga-tion, to a committee—or committees—composed of the higher mem-bers of the Secretariat. The committee will prepare a report and submit recommendations for the decision of the High Commission. It may conclude that no action is called for; or it may find that a *prima facie* case has been established such as to warrant a request to the govern-ment concerned for information and comments. In acting upon that report and after obtaining the observations of the government in ques-tion, the High Commission would approach the most difficult and most delicate aspect of its task. It is important to dwell in some detail upon the *modus procedendi* of the High Commission as here contemplated, for it throws light upon both the nature and the significance of its work as an agency, which is neither political nor judicial and in which lies the centre of gravity of the entire system of the protection of the Rights of Man. The High Commission may come to the conclusion that the petition or representation was well founded and that a violation of the Bill of Rights has taken place. Yet, if confronted with a case of minor importance, it would be free to decide that no action, save of giving publicity to its findings, need be taken. For it would be of the essence of the system that the political machinery of enforcement by the executive international authority would be called into action only as a last resort in matters of grave and persistent violation of the Bill. Whenever there is room for a legitimate difference of opinion as to the meaning of the Bill of Rights, the High Commission would properly give preference to the interpretation adopted by the legislature, the judiciary, or the government of the State concerned. In cases in which it decides to act on the maxim *de minimis non curat praetor,* the Commission might communicate with the Government concerned and express its apprehension as to the situation that has arisen.

With regard to the provisions of Articles 9–14 of the Bill of Rights, the task of the High Commission would be especially responsible and delicate. These rights are not contemplated as enforceable by municipal courts. The nature of the difficulties likely to confront the High Commission with regard to what may be called political rights of government by consent and of independence (Articles 10 and 11) have already been indicated. The same applies to the cultural rights of minorities under Article 12. In so far as these rights are not enforceable by municipal courts, the obligation undertaken by States will be necessarily inferior to that under the other articles of the Bill of Rights. This will be so particularly with regard to the rights of economic freedom, equality of educational opportunity, and social security under Articles 13 and 14. These obligations in question are necessarily elastic and circumscribed by the internal conditions and the general economic development of the State. Yet they are intended to be substantial obligations. They will be violated by the maintenance and the perpetuation of conditions which are in flagrant disregard of the objects of the Bill of Rights and by an obstructive refusal to co-operate with other States in matters in which such co-operation is essential to general and parallel improvement. Specialized sections of the Secretariat of the High Commission will have to be formed for the constant study and investigation of the progress in the implementation of these clauses of the Bill of Rights. It will be desirable to maintain for that purpose machinery for information and consultation with the International Labour Organization or a department thereof specially set up for the purpose. But the final responsibility for initiating any action of an international character with regard to States which have failed in their obligations concerning social rights will rest with the High Commission as such. It will not, in this matter, be confronted with any clear and easily ascertainable breach of an international duty. It will have to act on a cumulative experience of indifference, laxity, or ill-will of the State concerned. With regard to any specific breaches of existing international labour conventions, the means of enforcement will as a rule be found in these instruments. It is clear that with regard to both categories of rights entrusted to its responsibility—the rights of Part I and of Part II of the Bill—the task of the High Commission will require the highest qualities of competence and statesmanship. It will have to exercise its supervisory function with a latitude and an elasticity unhampered by the necessity of applying the full measure of the law. But this will be not a discretion based on mere expediency typical of a political body, but a statesmanlike supervision of the working of some of the most intricate aspects of the government of men.

THE ORGANIZATION OF THE HIGH COMMISSION

The importance and the nature of the task of the High Commission must be decisive in determining its organization and composition. The draft provides that it "shall consist of independent persons of the highest distinction appointed by the Council of the United Nations." It will be necessary, either as part of the Bill of Rights or independently of it, to frame a Statute of the High Commission, defining in more detail its functions, its procedure, and its composition. As to the Commission, its members will have to be placed, with regard to their status, their emoluments, and their duties (including the relinquishment of any other occupation or profession) on the same footing as the judges of the Permanent Court of International Justice. It will be useful for some of its members to have had judicial experience, but no legal qualification ought to be required for appointment to a task, in which the highest qualities of statesmanship, as distinguished from purely legal qualifications, are of the essence.

THE SECRETARIAT OF THE HIGH COMMISSION

The Secretariat of the High Commission must, numerically and otherwise, be adequate to its task as outlined above. This includes the fullest degree of competence and impartiality such as is required of the other branches of the international civil service. For this reason it will be essential that its composition should be determined by the High Commission itself, to the exclusion of any political factors.

The detailed manner in which this draft and the comment elaborate the composition and the functions of the High Commission may seem to some excessive. But it must be borne in mind that the High Commission is contemplated as the normal and pivotal part of the structure of the international supervision and enforcement of the Bill of Rights. This is so, although the supreme political agency of the International Authority will be the final agency of enforcement and will bear the final responsibility for the implementation of the Bill of Rights.[2]

Article 20

PARAGRAPH 1

The Council of the United Nations shall be the supreme agency for securing the observance of the International Bill of the Rights of Man.

The essential feature of the International Bill of the Rights of Man as proposed in this draft is that it is considered to be an enforceable part of the international legal system. It is not merely a declaration of principle, or a general guide for legislation, or even an expression of international concern accompanied by an indefinite right of intervention. For this reason the question of the implementation and en-

[2] The Commission to Study the Organization of Peace published in 1944 a valuable statement on "International Safeguard of Human Rights" in which a proposal is made for a United Nations Commission of Human Rights and for a United Nations Conference on Human Rights. See *International Conciliation*, September, 1944, Pamphlet No. 403.

forcement of the International Bill of the Rights of Man occupies a prominent place in this draft.

The implementation of the Bill of Rights is primarily a matter for the States and their courts enforcing their municipal law of which the Bill of Rights has become a part. The High Commission, a body neither political nor judicial in character, is the normal and the principal international agency for supervising and ensuring the observance of the Bill of Rights. But the final guarantee of the Bill of Rights must rest with the supreme political authority of the international community.

PARAGRAPH 2

It shall be the right of any of the United Nations to call the attention of the Council to any infraction of the Bill of Rights.

In the present draft the term "Council of the United Nations" is used to denote the principal executive authority of the future organization of international society.

The Council will be apprised of any violation of the Bill of Rights, either by the High Commission or by any State member of the organization of the United Nations. The more normal course for the latter will be to bring the matter before the High Commission in the first instance. But it will be necessary to provide for the independent right of States to seize the Council in matters of grave urgency and importance as well as in case of an adverse decision of the High Commission with regard to a representation made by a State.

PARAGRAPH 3

The Council shall frame such Rules of Procedure as will best enable it to fulfil its duties as the supreme agency for the enforcement of the International Bill of the Rights of Man.

There are cogent grounds for postulating the necessity of safeguarding, through the adoption of binding rules of procedure, the efficiency and the impartiality of the Council as the principal political agency for enforcing the Bill of Rights. While reasons of some persuasiveness may be adduced for permitting the procedure of the Council in the matter to develop by the evolutionary method of trial and error, the balance of utility and of experience counsels the adoption in advance of a well-defined procedure. The Council must be able to fulfil its function as the protector of the Bill of Rights unhampered by temporary considerations of expediency. It must avoid that kind of elasticity which is a cloak for evasion. It must be enabled to prevent, in so far as this is possible through written rules, the enforcement of the Bill of Rights from becoming a function of politics pure and simple.

PARAGRAPH 4

The Permanent Court of International Justice shall at the request of the Council give an Advisory Opinion on any question of law relating to the observance of the International Bill of the Rights of Man.

The fact that a petition or representation has been brought before the Council will often be an indication of its complexity not only from the political but also from the legal point of view. In such cases it may be necessary to obtain an opinion of the most authoritative judicial body, namely, the Permanent Court of International Justice. This will be so particularly when the State against which the complaint is directed maintains that its action is in accordance with the Bill of Rights.

The objections to any normal procedure of international judicial review of the Bill of Rights have been stated elsewhere. They do not apply to situations in which a case has been brought before the Council by a State or by the High Commission.

PARAGRAPH 5

If the Council finds by a majority of three-fourths of its members that there has taken place an infraction of the International Bill of the Rights of Man such as to warrant action by the United Nations, the Council shall make a pronouncement to this effect. If the State in question persists in its refusal to remedy the situation violative of this Bill of Rights, the Council shall take or order such political, economic, or military action as may be deemed necessary to protect the Rights of Man.

This paragraph constitutes an essential feature of the Bill of Rights. Its provisions are based on the view that the Bill of Rights is not only a declaration of principle but also an enforceable part of the international legal order. The enforcement of international law against sovereign States is appropriate not only with regard to the duties of pacific settlement but also in respect of other matters upon which peace vitally depends. It is a basic assumption of the Bill of Rights, expressed in its Preamble, that respect for and security of the rights of man are conditions of international peace and of the healthy functioning of international society. Once these premises are accepted, the enforcement of the Bill of Rights by the supreme executive authority of the organization of States follows naturally and inevitably.

At the same time, some important considerations must be borne in mind in this connection. As in the case of the High Commission, so also with regard to the action of the Council, the enforcement of the Bill of Rights must be of considerable elasticity. This applies both to Part I and to Part II of the Bill of Rights. Cases will, of course, occur in which the violation of its principles will be so obvious or on a scale so large as to render the pronouncement of the Council almost automatic. But this will not invariably be so. A case may come before the Council in which it will be necessary for it to determine the border line between the implementation of the Bill of Rights and the safeguarding of legal rights of other members of the community or of the welfare and security of the State—although the fact that the matter has been brought before the Council by the High Commission will be a prima-facie indication that the border line has been overstepped. Similarly, it may be assumed that the High Commission will not bring before the Council cases of infraction which, though obvious or undisputed, are of minor import. Yet the Council must retain the supreme political power of decision—a power which may amount to a dispensation from or modification of individual clauses of the Bill of Rights. This is the meaning of the first sentence of paragraph 4, which requires the Council to make a formal pronouncement, as a starting point for further action, only if "there has taken place an infraction of the International Bill of the Rights of Man such as to warrant action by the United Nations." But the Council may find that there has taken place an infraction of the Bill of Rights which does not justify international action. There is nothing in the draft which prevents the Council from reaching and publishing a decision of this nature—a decision which, though not accompanied by an intimation of any coercive action, might be not without influence.

Similarly, the persuasive rather than the coercive powers of the Council will be important in connection with the rights incorporated in Part III of the Bill of Rights. Thus, with regard to the claims of "a community which has not yet obtained full political independence or which constitutes a colony or a mandated territory" the matter will normally come before the Council from the agency set up under the International Statute of Peoples under Colonial and Mandatory Government, before which such claims must come in the first instance. However, except in extreme cases, the action of the Council may have to remain in the domain of indirect pressure in the form of appeal to the public opinion of the State concerned and of the world at large.

This will also be the position in the matter of the social and economic rights under Articles 13 and 14 of the Bill of Rights. These, like other rights in Part II of the Bill, will not normally come within the sphere of municipal courts. They are an acknowledgement of the general duty of States in relation both to persons under their jurisdiction and to other States. The implementation of their purpose must be left, as a rule, to the States concerned. On the other hand, elastic as that obligation is, it constitutes an international duty which will be violated by a palpably backward policy of a State or by an obstructive policy which hampers improvement through general and parallel international action. In such cases the Council, apprised by the High Commission or by any State, will find, after further investigation, that the situation violates the Bill of Rights. But even in that case it may, and normally will, refrain from finding that the violation calls for international action.

However, in the last resort, whether the matter arises under Part I or Part II of the Bill of Rights, there must remain with the highest political authority of the Organization of States the legal power to give effect to the Bill of Rights by means of coercive action. Such action will be exceptional, but it is that ultimate power which will give to the Bill of Rights the impress of an organic part of the international legal order. It is that ultimate power which will lift the Bill of Rights from the inconclusive and ineffectual sphere of a mere declaration of principle and will constitute the Bill of Rights a revolutionary departure, commensurate with its intended and proclaimed object, in the protection by the society of States of the welfare and the sanctity of human personality. This draft and comment are not the proper occasion for answering the general objection to the coercion of sovereign States. For those who accept the International Bill of the Rights of Man as an essential condition of the progress of human society and of international peace, its ultimate enforcement by the collective effort of the Society of States is an inescapable conclusion.

It is proposed in the present draft that before resorting to positive action the Council shall give the offending State the opportunity to remedy the situation violative of the Bill of Rights. It is only after that opportunity has been disregarded that there will be room for recourse to coercive action. The draft lays down that the Council "*shall* take or *order* such political, economic, or military action as may be necessary to protect the Rights of Man." Whatever discretion the Council may use in finding whether there has taken place a violation of the Bill of Rights calling for international action, once such finding has been arrived at, the only discretion left to the Council is to choose means for giving effect to the Bill of Rights. Its decision in the matter is not contemplated as being in the nature of advice given to the members of the Organization of States. The duty to enforce the Bill of Rights is theirs as well as the Council's. It will probably be found advisable to incorporate in the Rules of Procedure governing the action of the Council under the Bill of Rights some provisions relating to the machinery of enforcement. That machinery and the obligations of the members of the Organization of the United Nations in this matter ought to be governed by the principles applicable to the enforcement of the obligations of pacific settlement of disputes. But the implementation of the Bill of Rights may call for additional political means appropriate to the occasion.

The final supervision and enforcement of the Bill of Rights by the supreme executive organ of the international authority is an essential feature of the Bill of Rights. Once it is assumed that the international recognition and protection of the rights of man is an essential feature of the future international order and an indispensable condition of peace, membership of the future international organization of States must involve adherence to the Bill of Rights. The latter cannot be a refinement to which enlightened States, if they so wish, may pay homage. It must be an absolute condition of participation in the benefits of the organized society of States.

The elaboration of the details of the machinery for supervising and enforcing the International Bill of the Rights of Man is open to the kind of criticism to which most proposals in the sphere of international organization are exposed. To reduce a weighty theme to controversial and rigid aspects of procedure is almost in the nature of an anticlimax. The answer to this criticism is, in the first instance, that the machinery here proposed is elastic in so far as elasticity is consistent with the effectiveness and the legal nature of the Bill of Rights. Machinery, like any other matter of procedure, may be a tedious topic. In fact, it is only another word for legal remedies without which substantive rights, however wide and generous, are worthless.

Moreover, the consideration of machinery brings to light the measure of the limitation of the sovereignty of States implied in the proposal for an International Bill of the Rights of Man. That measure is, in a sense, substantial. States would not only agree to the incorporation of certain principles as part of their domestic law but also renounce the right to abrogate them without international authority. They would consent to international supervision, discussion, interference, and, if need be, enforcement. It is easy to say that the incipient practice of humanitarian intervention and of treaties for the protection of the rights of the individual in various spheres deprives this proposed International Bill of Rights of the character of an absolute innovation. To say this would be to disregard the fact that humanitarian intervention has been infrequent, often abused, and controversial. On numerous occasions the legal reason given for intervention was merely that the effects of the inhuman action were prejudicial to the interests of the State making the representation. The various treaties for the protection of the individual have touched only the fringe of the matters covered by the Bill of Rights. Moreover, the provisions for their enforcement have been rudimentary in the highest degree. With insignificant exceptions they do not confer upon individuals any measure of procedural capacity. There ought to be no doubt that in all these matters the Bill of Rights would constitute a radical innovation in derogation of the external aspects of the sovereignty of States.

At the same time it must be borne in mind that the substantive innovation of the Bill of Rights in the sphere of domestic law would in many cases be distinctly limited. Subject to minor exceptions—for instance, in the matter of statelessness—the substantive provisions of Part I of the Bill of Rights could be adopted by most States without essential alterations in their municipal law. This is so for the simple reason that, in the main, the proposed Bill of Rights is a codification of what may be called the general principles of constitutional law of civilized States in the matter of the fundamental rights of man. Its innovation lies in the international guarantee of these rights and in the consequent elimination of the contradiction which underlay the conception of fundamental rights of man recognized as against the omnipotence of the State and protected by the omnipotent State alone. There are many States in which these rights have prospered in security under the shelter of national tradition and of the supremacy of the law wielded with restraint, with reasonableness, and with a wise consideration, grounded in a community of citizenship more powerful than the law, for the interests of the minority. In such States the attempt to introduce an outward element of supervision and interference into the most intimate recesses of national life might be regarded as unnecessary and almost sacrilegious. This, it is believed, would be a complacent and shortsighted view.

Neither would the acceptance of the International Bill of the Rights of Man be tantamount to a radical change in the structure of international law or in the international relations of States. It would not in itself subject States to any process of affirmative international legislation. The enhanced procedural capacity of the individual would not result in conferring direct access, under the provisions of the Bill of Rights, to international tribunals. Yet its acceptance would go a long way toward assisting the political integration of international society. It would foster the sense of international loyalty and solidarity consequent upon the realization that the rights of man everywhere are grounded ultimately and effectively in the organized Society of States.

It would be one of the factors working toward the accomplishment of the final political aim of organized society, namely, the establishment of a Federation of the World as an essential prerequisite of the development of the capacities of the human race through progress and peace. It is unlikely, as it is probably undesirable, that that end can be achieved at once—vertically, as it were—by any radical and rigid scheme of World Federation. It is more probably capable of achievement by the gradual evolution of institutions, arrangements, and effective obligations which in the fullness of time—horizontally, as it were—will lead the looser association of States as expressed in the existing or any future League of Nations, to a more integrated Federation of States. An International Bill of the Rights of Man, conceived as an effective part of the international legal system, would clearly be a paramount factor in that process. In that perspective the consideration of the minutiae of the supervision and enforcement of the Bill of Rights appears in its rightful and proper significance.

Note on the Dumbarton Oaks Proposals in Relation to the International Protection of Human Rights

The manuscript of this book was completed in the autumn of 1943 and the draft, here put forward, of an International Bill of the Rights of Man does not therefore take into account the scheme for an International Organization put forward in the Dumbarton Oaks Proposals. Chapter IX, entitled "International Economic and Social Co-operation," of the Proposals provides as follows:

With a view to the creation of conditions of stability and well-being which are necessary for peaceful and friendly relations among nations, the organization should facilitate solutions of international economic, social, and other humanitarian problems, and promote respect for human rights and fundamental freedoms. Responsibility for the discharge of this function should be vested in the General Assembly and under the authority of the General Assembly in an Economic and Social Council.

The British official commentary on the Dumbarton Oaks Proposals draws attention to that provision. It says: "It will be noted that there is special mention of 'human rights and fundamental freedoms,' respect for which the Organization should promote" (Cmd. 6571, p. 10). The Commentary adds: "The methods by which these ends shall be obtained would be left to the Organization itself to determine" (*ibid.*). It would be in keeping both with the prominence which the protection of fundamental human rights has acquired in the official declarations of the United Nations and with the intrinsic significance of the matter if the Charter of the United Nations, as finally adopted, were to contain a specific reference to an International Bill of the Rights of Man as the basis and the framework of the activities of the International Organization in this direction. It must be a matter for consideration whether the High Commission of the Rights of Man, as suggested in this book, should form a subdivision of a Social and Economic Council or whether its significance is such that it must be accorded a separate and independent position in the general scheme of the Organization.

The scheme here put forward for an International Bill of the Rights of Man is based on the assumption that it will become an effective and enforceable part of International Law and of the Organization of the United Nations. The direct consequence of that assumption is that the highest executive organ of the Organization, namely, the Council, must assume responsibility for its ultimate enforcement. In the Dumbarton Oaks Proposals no executive powers of enforcement are conferred upon the Assembly which is to bear the general responsibility for the protection of human rights and fundamental freedoms.

CHAPTER XIV

MINORITIES TREATIES IN RELATION
TO THE BILL

THE MINORITIES TREATIES were an integral part of the system of
collective security and of preservation of peace established under the
aegis of the Covenant of the League. They were accepted by—or imposed upon—the States concerned for the reason, among others, that
they were an essential condition of peace [1] and, as some of them perceived it, of the guarantees of their security and their territorial
integrity.[2] The moral, as distinguished from the legal, authority of
those Treaties derived, not from any spontaneous acceptance on the
part of the States in question, but from that association with a comprehensive system of international justice and security. That system
came to grief almost from the very inception, owing both to the shortcomings of its constitution and, even more, to the unwillingness of its
members to implement it. A far-sighted determination to make it effective would have atoned for its weaknesses. For though the Covenant, in some of its crucial aspects, did not impose clear and automatic
legal obligations, it contained a far-reaching authorization of individual
and collective action. Under suitable conditions and in the hands of
governments with a statesmanlike conception of realism it would have

[1] In his speech of May 31, 1919, largely calculated to answer the objections to the imposition of the Minorities Treaties, President Wilson said: "We are trying to make
a peaceful settlement, that is to say, to eliminate those elements of disturbance, so far
as possible, which may interfere with the peace of the world. . . . It is unreasonable
and unjust that not as dictators, but as friends the Great Powers should say to their
associates: 'We cannot afford to guarantee territorial settlements which we do not
believe to be right, and we cannot agree to leave elements of disturbance unremoved,
which we believe will disturb the peace of the world.' Take the rights of minorities.
Nothing, I venture to say, is more likely to disturb the peace of the world than the
treatment which might, in certain cases, be meted out to minorities. And therefore,
if the Great Powers are to guarantee the peace of the world in any sense is it unjust
that they should be satisfied that the proper and necessary guarantees have been
given?"
[2] In 1929 Poland, Greece, Rumania, Yugoslavia and Czechoslovakia submitted to a
Committee of the Council identical memoranda in which they pointed to this connection between the promised guarantee of their territorial integrity, which had not in
fact materialized, and their assumption of the obligations under the Minorities Treaties
(League Doc. C.8. M.5., 1931., I, p. 193).

become a powerful instrument for peace and security. As it happened, most members of the League availed themselves of the elasticity of the Covenant in order to emphasize their freedom of action rather than their duty to make its objects effective.

The same phenomenon was repeated in the matter of the regime of minorities which formed part of that general system of security. The legal potentialities of the system of minorities were tremendous. It was placed under the guarantee of the League, in particular of the members of its Council. That guarantee did not amount to a mere right of intervention; it was a legal duty of the members of the Council. It was, in French legal terminology, a *compétence liée*. It signified a right to act. But it was a right which the members of the Council were under a duty to exercise. To that duty the members of the Council did not measure up. Their individual obligation was merged in the anonymity of a Committee of Three which decided on the receivability of the petitions. Almost from the very outset they adopted an interpretation of the Treaties which took into account the susceptibilities of the States bound by them rather than the rights of the minorities. There was nothing in the terms of the Minorities Treaties which prevented a liberal interpretation of the guarantee contained therein in terms of a general guarantee implying permanent organs charged with the constant duty of supervision. In the first paragraph of Article 12 of the Treaty with Poland—and in the corresponding articles of other treaties and declarations—the stipulations of the treaties were, in general terms, placed under the guarantee of the League. The second paragraph provided specifically for the right of members of the Council to bring before it any cases of infraction, or of danger of infraction, of the Treaty and for the duty of the Council to take necessary action. It is not inconsistent with a sound rule of interpretation of the Treaty to maintain that the second paragraph provided for one, but not all the means for giving effect to the general guarantee. But the Council adopted the conclusions of a strong committee of its members [3] which held that

the Treaties contain no provisions permitting the Council to exercise constant supervision with regard to the situation of minorities, i. e., a

[3] M. Adatci, Sir Austen Chamberlain, and Señor Quiñones de Leon.

supervision capable of being exercised apart from cases in which a member of the Council has drawn the latter's attention to an infraction or danger of infraction of the Treaties.

That interpretation determined the practice of the Council, but it was not an inevitable construction of the terms of the Treaty. It contrasts significantly with the interpretation given in similar cases by the Permanent Court of International Justice.[4] There was consequently nothing in these treaties which would have given the Minorities States the right to refuse co-operation with any organs set up in conformity with the theory of a general guarantee. But such was the restraint with which the members of the Council interpreted their rights and obligations that they denied themselves the right to establish a Permanent Minorities Commission—a right which they possessed irrespective of any doctrine of a general guarantee.

Neither did it necessarily follow from the terms of the Treaties that the petitions of minorities or of signatories acting on their behalf were merely in the nature of information; that the petitioners were to be deprived of any legal *locus standi* in the matter; and that they were not even entitled to know the grounds of a negative decision reached without their co-operation. The authors of the Treaties had rejected the proposal to endow minorities with the right to appeal directly to the Permanent Court of International Justice, but it did not follow that otherwise they intended to reduce the role of minorities in the international procedure to a mere source of information. Similarly, there was no warrant in the terms of the treaties for the view, on which the Council acted, that its part was one of mediation and persuasion

[4] While the second paragraph of Article 12 provided in general terms that in cases brought before it the Council may take such action as it may deem necessary, the third paragraph laid down that in the case of a difference of opinion as to questions of law in the matter of the interpretation or application of the treaty any member of the Council may refer the dispute to the Permanent Court of International Justice. Poland contended that in view of the latter provision the Council as a whole was prevented from bringing the matter before the Court. The Court rejected that contention. It said: "The fact that a question brought before the Court by the Council under Paragraph 2 might conceivably be brought before the Court by a single Power as an international difference under Paragraph 3, cannot be accepted as a reason for preventing the Council from discharging its duties under Paragraph 2" (Permanent Court of International Justice, Series B, No. 6, p. 23). There is a suggestive similarity between the question settled in this Opinion of the Court and the problem of the general guarantee.

as distinguished from insistence on the fulfilment of its clear stipulations. The fact is that, as in the matter of the provisions of the Covenant relating to the obligations of pacific settlement,[5] the interpretation and the observance of the treaties became a function of the general political conditions of the world. It was not by accident that Poland denounced the Minorities Treaty, in so far as it involved international supervision, at the time of the Italian defiance of the principles of the Covenant or that at the time of the successful challenge of these principles by Japan the number of petitions received dropped from 204, in the year 1930–1931, to 101 in the year 1931–1932, and to 57 in the year 1932–1933. The failure of the system of protection of minorities —and it was to a large extent a failure in the actual operation of the protection afforded to minorities—was not inherent in the treaties as adopted in 1919. It was a concomitant of the fate which befell the more comprehensive system of which it was a part.

Secondly, it must not be forgotten that in spite of the shortcomings and the relative ineffectiveness of the operation of the Minorities Treaties, noteworthy improvements did take place. The Minorities Department of the Secretariat of the League was after a time, in pursuance of Resolutions adopted in 1922,[6] considerably enlarged. It provided itself with a—somewhat rudimentary—source of information through a newspaper-clipping service. Its members occasionally visited the Minorities States. While previously the Committee of Three seldom communicated to the Council the results of their deliberations in cases in which they decided not to proceed with the petition, from 1929 onwards the practice of regular communication to the Council was

[5] Thus, for example, the interpretation given by the Council to Article 11 of the Covenant in the course of the invasion of Manchuria in the sense that its decision thereunder required the absolute unanimity of all its members—including the vote of the State charged with a violation of the Covenant. On the other hand, the Permanent Court of International Justice found in its 12th Advisory Opinion in connection with the dispute between Turkey and Great Britain concerning the Mosul boundary that the general requirement of unanimity under the Covenant is subject to the overriding principle that no one can be judge in his own cause and that while all members of the Council are entitled to vote, the votes of the parties to the dispute were not to be taken into account for the purpose of ascertaining unanimity.

[6] One of these Resolutions referred to the Secretariat as having "the duty to collect information concerning the manner in which the Minorities Treaties are being carried out."

adopted. Moreover, the Committee were instructed to "consider carefully the possibility of publishing, with the consent of the Government concerned," the results of their investigations.

Finally, although the system of Minorities Treaties failed to afford protection in many cases of flagrant violation and although it acquired a reputation for impotence, with the result that after a time the minorities often refrained from resorting to petitions in cases where a stronger faith in the effectiveness of that system would have prompted them to seek a remedy, the protection of the League was frequently successfully invoked on important occasions—as, for instance, in the case of German Settlers in Poland, a case of both grave political implications and legal difficulties. The frequent violation of the Minorities Treaties must not be allowed to obscure the advantages of their normal operation. In assessing their effectiveness we must consider the situations that might have arisen but for their existence. The prophylactic effect of legal rules and prohibitions cannot be easily estimated, but it is nevertheless real. History, especially recent history, has shown the potentialities of discrimination against and oppression of minorities. Some of it cannot be avoided by any system of legal protection. Social prejudice and a spirit of intolerance will always find avenues for circumventing the safeguards of the law. For this reason legal provisions can only incompletely prevent a subtle and ingenious policy of economic oppression, for instance, through the refusal to give the minorities their due share in contracts awarded by the State or by autonomous territorial bodies like county and municipal councils or through measures apparently aiming at the general welfare, but in fact directed against minorities. The same applies to cultural discrimination and persecution, as may be seen in the manner in which Hungary contrived to carry through her intention of introducing the *numerus clausus* in her universities.[7] However, there are obvious forms of discrimination of direct character which no ingenuity can conceal; they can be prevented by clear obligations and prohibitions in a treaty. There is no doubt that

---

[7] After it had become clear that the League would not countenance restrictions on admission to universities based on quotas for each nationality, the Hungarian Government introduced a new law in which the quotas were based on the profession of the father of the applicant. The results of either test were substantially identical.

the Minorities Treaties, however emaciated by the manner in which they were applied, afforded a substantial degree of protection.[8]

It is clear from what has been said that the abandonment of the present system of protection of minorities without an alternative and compensating international arrangement would mean a disservice to the minorities, to the cause of the international protection of human rights, and to international peace and progress. By a "compensating international arrangement" is meant, not a vague declaration, however lofty in expression, but an international legal instrument comprising specific and enforceable obligations on the lines of the International Bill of the Rights of Man as here proposed. Various States hitherto bound by the Minorities Treaties have advocated replacing them by an international charter of the rights of man or some such innovation. It must be axiomatic that upon such States there rests the onus of disproving the charge that they are using a great and weighty idea of law and government as a convenient means for obtaining relief from what they consider to be an odious obligation. That duty can be discharged only by the propounding of or association with schemes of universal protection of the rights of man which in the scope of its obligations and safeguards is not inferior to those of the Minorities Treaties.

It will not be sufficient to rely on the revival of the customary criticism of the Minorities Treaties, namely that they apply only to a limited number of States. The view that the absence of universality in the protection of minorities constitutes a standing reflection upon the States bound by the Minorities Treaties is of little persuasive value. In retrospect, the argument by which the Principal Allied Powers justified, in 1919, the unilateral imposition of these Treaties seems less devoid of foundation than appears to some critics. The appeal to the precedent of the last hundred years in the course of which the creation of new States or large accessions to the territories of existing States were accompanied by the imposition of obligations for the protection of minorities was not a purely historical argument. It showed the necessity of eliminating, at the very inception of statehood or when ter-

---

[8] See the authoritative study by Jacob Robinson and others, *Were the Minorities Treaties a Failure?* (New York, 1943).

ritorial responsibilities were considerably increased, the disintegrating elements of intolerance and persecution. Moreover, in most, if not in all, of the States bound by the Minorities Treaties the existence of large minorities—in many cases coupled with a disquieting experience of the treatment of these minorities in the past—warranted the imposition of the special regime. In turn, the operation of the system after 1919 provided ample *post factum* justification for its continuance. It is true that occasionally minorities looked for protection to the States of the same race and language and that in that sense these treaties perpetuated a spirit of irredentism. But this was so largely because the minorities were not always in a position to be confident that the machinery of the League would operate justly and, what is equally important, with all the appearance of justice, on its own initiative and responsibility.

For these reasons there would seem to be little merit and little persuasive power in the proposals to extend the existing system of protection of minorities to States which either do not include minorities in the accepted sense or whose history and tradition testify to the absence of any necessity for that particular regime. No treaty can provide better safeguards for the protection of national minorities than those already found in Soviet Russia, in Great Britain, and in Switzerland. There is no prospect that these and similarly situated States will feel inclined or consider themselves under a moral duty to accept an international regime of supervision out of consideration for the susceptibilities of the States bound by the Minorities Treaties. The inducement must be grounded in considerations of wider import and deeper significance—such as may prompt a willing submission to an international charter of human rights. An effective International Bill of the Rights of Man—which attempts to solve an abiding problem of human freedom in the relation of man to State in a manner transcending the protection of national and linguistic minorities—would be a proper and desirable substitute for the system of protection of minorities by treaties binding upon a limited number of States and safeguarding a limited area of rights of limited numbers of the population. There is in the Minorities Treaties no substantive right and no procedural safeguard which is not to be found in the Bill of Rights as here proposed. At the same time the latter is free from the drawback associated with the system of Minorities Treaties such as the objection felt by some members of minorities and by the States concerned that a distinctive status might be created that would be prejudicial both to the unity of the State and to the minorities.

At the same time, it is necessary to face the question of the prospects of the adoption of the Bill of Rights as an effective instrument of the Society of States. The cogent reasons of overwhelming advantage and principle in favour of the Bill of Rights have been repeatedly stressed in this book; so has the fact that its adoption would be in accordance with a solemnly proclaimed object of the second World War. But improvements in human society, especially in international society, do not always follow the interests of reason and advantage. History has known lofty pronouncements of belligerents to be treated as aspirations of the future rather than as binding factors in the peace settlement.

There are two main obstacles in the way of an International Bill of the Rights of Man. The first is the probable disinclination of governments to submit to the restrictions of sovereignty implied in the Bill of Rights. These restrictions, it has been shown, are not, in fact, far-reaching. In the main, they do not imply any radical changes in the substantive law of most States. In matters such as the right to government by consent and the respect of the cultural needs of minorities, the practice and the tendencies of enlightened States have not been inconsistent with the clauses of the Bill of Rights. But the latter makes vast phases of national life—including questions of colonial policy—a subject of international concern, discussion, and, if need be, interference. Probably what would be affected is, not so much the substance of national sovereignty, as its appearance and its susceptibilities. Yet this is a factor of considerable, if not decisive, importance. The same applies to the opposition, which is likely to come from many quarters, to attempts to contain the most intimate manifestations of national life within the narrow compass of a legal instrument.

The second reason for caution in assessing the prospects of the International Bill of the Rights of Man is the fact that as here formulated it can function only within the framework of an effective international organization of law and power set up on a universal basis. The certainty of the establishment of such an organization cannot be assumed.

For these reasons, should the acceptance of an effective International Bill of the Rights of Man prove impossible, then the continuation of the system—strengthened in the light of past experience—of protection of minorities must be aimed at as a duty owed both to the minorities and ·to the idea of protection of human rights within such sphere as is practicable. As pointed out above, undue importance need not be attached to the doubtful moral merits of any claim to generalize the system as a condition of its continuance. Circumstances may prove favourable to extending it to some countries—such as Germany—having regard to their past conduct. For the fact is that whatever may have been the legal arguments adduced by the Principal Allied Powers in 1919 in support of their insistence on the acceptance of the Minorities Treaties by some States, the presence in these States of large minorities averse or unsuited to assimilation and anxious in the light of their past experience to obtain international protection, constituted the decisive feature of the situation. The working of the Minorities Treaties between the first and the second World Wars affords no warrant whatsoever for the view that these treaties were unnecessary. A peace settlement which, while containing no provision for an International Bill of the Rights of Man, failed to continue the regime of protection of minorities as established in 1919 would be deficient in a vital respect. The interconnection between the protection of some European minorities and the maintenance of European peace is as obvious now as it was when it was stressed in 1919 by President Wilson and other Allied statesmen. At the same time, should the adoption of an effective international charter of human rights on the lines of the proposed International Bill of the Rights of Man prove impracticable, there would still be some advantage, subject to the continuation of the Minorities Treaties, in the adoption of a general declaration of the rights of man unsupported by international safeguards, but of considerable potency in its solemn appeal to public opinion and to the conscience of governments. Moreover, cogent reasons may be adduced in favour of the view that, in its initial stages, a regime of an International Bill of the Rights of Man will be, in any case, experimental and that it may constitute in practice a retrogressive step unless it is accompanied, in respect of certain countries and certain regions, by an improved system of protection of minorities on the lines of the Minorities Treaties of 1919. It would be of the essence of any such improved system that it should contain provisions for the direct access of the minorities to the competent international organs, judicial and others.

INDEX

League of Nations (*Continued*)
on arbitration, 77; and Minorities Treaties, 170-72, 215-19, 221
—— Secretariat of, Minorities Department, 218, 219
Levellers, and freedom of conscience, 21; and natural law, 30; and natural rights of man, 59
Libel, law of, 107, 114, 175
Lieber, Francis, 188, 191*n*
Literacy test, for voting, 138, 142
Locke, John, 11, 22, 34, 45, 54, 58, 59, 62-63, 64, 163
Louis X, 29
Louis XIII, 43

Macaulay, T. B., 58
Machiavelli, Niccolo, 21
Mackintosh, Sir James, 51
Madison, James, 189
Magna Charta, 21, 55, 56-57, 58, 93
Maitland, F. W., 56*n*
Manchuria, invasion of, 218*n*
Mandatory governments, 11, 48, 82, 145-51
Mandelstam, André, 9
Marcus Aurelius, 28
Marsilius of Padua, 20
Miller, D. H., 7*n*
Milton, John, 23, 30, 54, 59, 64
Minorities, 9, 11, 48, 82; and self-determination, 144-45; and preservation of culture, 151-55
Minorities treaties, 7, 9, 47; procedure and machinery of, for enforcement of International Bill of the Rights of Man, 170-73; under Covenant of League of Nations, 215-19, 221; in relation to International Bill of the Rights of Man, 221-24
Montesquieu, Baron de, 140, 156*n*
Morris, Gouverneur, 139*n*
Mosul boundary, 218*n*

Nationality, right to, 126-28
Nationality and Status of Aliens Act, of 1914, 131
Naturalization, 164-65
Naturalization Act, of 1870, 131
Natural law, and rights of man, 3 ff., 16, 23, 26, 27-31, 39-40; Greek idea of, 17; and Roman idea of slavery, 20; in Middle Ages, 20-21; and sovereignty of State, 24, 30; and international law, 26, 28-29, 41-53; and positive law, 27-30, 34 f.; and law of God, 29-30, 38; and slavery, 29, 35-36, 39; effect of, on American and French revolutions, 31;

Aristotle's and Stoics' conceptions of, 32; Epicureans' conception of, 32-33; Cicero's conception of, 33; conceptions of, in Middle Ages and after, 33-40; and poverty, 36; and vested economic interests, 36-37; and freedom of contract, 37; misuse of, 38-39; and rights of man, 49-53; and supremacy of Parliament, 61
Natural rights of man, 3 ff.; idea of, 16-25; and State, 16 ff.; in Greek and Roman political philosophy, 17-20; in Middle Ages, 20-21; affected by Reformation, 21-22; and theory of social contract, 22; in constitutional law, 23-25; as affected by positive law of State, 26-28; and law of nature, 27-31, 39-40, 49-53; and international law, 28-29, 42-53; and interpretation of Fourteenth Amendment, U.S. Constitution, 37; and sovereignty, 45 f.; British attitude toward, 54-65; as declared in International Bill of the Rights of Man, 86-88
Negroes, 11, 37; segregation of, and U.S. Supreme Courts interpretation of Fourteenth Amendment, 118; disfranchisement of, 138 f., 140-42
Ning Yi-Ching and Others, 14

Otis, James, 31, 114
Overton, Richard, 56*n*

Paine, Thomas, 63-64, 156
Parliament, absolute supremacy of, 19, 23, 54, 58, 60-62, 182-83, 191; attempted limitation of, 21; qualifications of, 60 f.; and rights of man, 62-65
Parson, Theophilus, 24
Party membership test, for voting, 142
Passports, 133*n*
Peace, international, 85, 88-89, 136
Peonage, 103
Pericles, 18
Permanent Court of International Justice, 8-9, 9*n*, 13, 24, 42, 48; compulsory jurisdiction of, 77; advisory opinion of, concerning retroactive legislation, 99*n*; jurisdiction of, in minorities cases, 171 f.; and Minorities Treaty, 217; advisory opinion of, on Mosul boundary, 218*n*
Petition of Right, 55, 58
Philip the Fair, 29
Plato, 18
Plessy v. *Ferguson*, 118*n*
Poland, treatment of minorities in, 152-53

Streit, C. K., 6n
Suffrage, see Elections
Supreme Court, U.S., 12, 14, 37; and natural rights of man, 87n; its exercise of
power of judicial review, 186, 188-89,
191n

Thayer, J. B., 189
Tocqueville, Alexis de, 189
Toleration, religious, 21, 105
Totalitarianism, political philosophy of,
4n, 24
Townsend, John, 36
Trade, freedom of, 77
Treaties, and domestic law, 179-80; see also
Minorities Treaties
Trials, see Criminal trials; Habeas corpus;
Jury, trial by
Trusteeship, 89-90; and colonies, 147-51

Ulpian, 19-20, 29
United Nations, 6; declarations of, 84-86;
International Organization of, 195-213;
see also Colonial Commission; Council
of United Nations; High Commission
United States Federal Constitution, see
Federal Constitution
United States state constitutions, see State
constitutions, U.S.

United States Supreme Court, see Supreme
Court, U.S.
Upper Silesian Convention of 1922, 48

Vattel, Emmerich de, 42, 45, 131
Vico, G. B., 16n
Victoria, Franciscus de, 42
Virginia Bill of 1786 for Establishing Reli-
gious Freedom, 105
Virginia Bill of Rights of 1776, 163
Virginia Statute for Religious Freedom,

Wallace, William, 4n
Walwyn, William, 56n
Watson, Bishop of Llandaff, 156n
Webster, Daniel, 188
Weimar Constitution, 27n
Wellington, Lord, 102n
Wells, H. G., 6n
Williams, Roger, 21, 57n
Wilson, Woodrow, 6, 7n, 88, 215n, 223
Wollstonecraft, Mary, 121n
Working conditions, proper, 157-62
Work, right to, 156-62; guarantee of,
Constitution of Soviet Russia, 151
World Jewish Congress, 86
World peace, see Peace, international
Wright, Quincy, 6n

Zimmern, A. E., 17n

CPSIA information can be obtained
at www.ICGtesting.com
Printed in the USA
BVHW031312140821
614448BV00001B/10